WOUNDED HEALERS

Freud was addicted to cocaine and nicotine, Jung was psychotic for several years, and Margaret Mead remained closeted throughout her lifetime. Yet, adversities notwithstanding, they all made monumental contributions that still shape our views on ourselves and the world. This book includes biographies of fifteen modern explorers of the mind who altered the course of history. All of them were wounded healers who made great discoveries while struggling with traumatic life crises and emotional problems in their personal lives. Full of unexpected twists and turns, their life stories alone are worthy of our attention. In linking their maladies with their creativity, showing the vulnerable and human side of these giants, this book makes the greats approachable and illuminates their scientific findings through narrating their life stories.

Keh-Ming Lin is Professor Emeritus at UCLA, USA, and Distinguished Life Fellow of the American Psychiatric Association. He has published 250 papers and 11 books, including translations of books by Sigmund Freud, and is co-editor of *Ethno-psychopharmacology* (Cambridge University Press).

Advance Praise for *Wounded Healers*

This book is a tour de force. With the skills of an esteemed neuroscientist and clinician, Keh-Ming Lin presents a scholarly examination of fifteen extraordinary, but wounded, psychotherapists. He suggests that a wounded healer exists within all of us and, if properly contained, might contain the seeds for a talented psychotherapist.

Warren R. Procci, Clinical Professor of Psychiatry, UCLA School of Medicine, USA, and the 64th President of the American Psychoanalytic Association

This volume integrates and balances the important areas of relational and mediated communication. It reflects a growing aspect of communication scholarship and the way many relational partners interact today. The writing style is informative for scholars and approachable for those new to the topic, which is no small feat.

Jennifer L. Bevan, Professor of Communication, Chapman University, USA

This is a wonderfully readable testimony to some of the most important pioneers in psychotherapy. Keh-Ming Lin makes each of these individuals come alive as vivid and complex human beings, while making their ideas accessible and linking them to the far older tradition of the wounded healer.

John Launer, Honorary Lifetime Consultant, Tavistock Clinic, UK

After reading Keh-Ming Lin's excellent book, I am happy to report that I enjoyed and appreciated this important work very much. It presents a scholarly study and thoughtful meditation on the personal coping methods and seminal theory of giants in psychology. It is both inspiring and compassionate – perfect for clinicians and patients alike.

Mitchell Weiss, Professor Emeritus of Epidemiology and Public Health, Swiss Tropical and Public Health Institute, Switzerland

Weaving together Eastern and Western culture within a study of famous psychotherapists, this book has it all. For therapists, aspiring therapists, and healers in general, Keh-Ming Lin reinforces the idea that greatness can spring from adversity and may even be a prerequisite for such innovation.

Ira Lesser, Vice Chair and Professor of Psychiatry and Biobehavioral Sciences, UCLA, USA

Thich Nhat Hanh reminds us, "No Mud, No Lotus." Suffering is fuel for enlightenment. Without the wound, there is no need for the journey. Keh-Ming Lin shows us how the greats looked inwards and developed understanding, empathy, and medicine. May we do so as well!

Ravi Chandra, psychiatrist and author of Facebuddha: Transcendence in the Age of Social Networks

In this beautiful book, an esteemed professor of psychiatry describes how fifteen mental health luminaries wrestled with their own inner adversities to open new therapeutic pathways. As all "healers" have mental obstacles to overcome, these stories will inform and inspire a wide range of mental health devotees.

Joel Yager, Professor of Psychiatry, University of Colorado School of Medicine, USA

Wounded Healers is an account of how emotional experiences and interpersonal difficulties influenced leaders in the mental health field and suggests possible origins for the creative genius of those leaders. It is powerful, touching, engaging, and insightful – a major contribution to the mental health field.

Stanley Sue, Emeritus Distinguished Professor of Psychology,
Palo Alto University and University of California, Davis, USA

Originally appearing as essays in Chinese, published in Taiwan, this book illustrates how a Chinese-American psychiatrist came to understand ideas about mental illness and psychiatric treatment that are European and American in origin, but have now been globalized.

Arthur Kleinman, Professor of Anthropology and Psychiatry,
Harvard University, USA

Keh-Ming Lin breaks down the stigma of emotional and mental suffering as the plight of "others" who are cared for by "the healthy." This absorbing work shows how emotional health is a process, earned by sustained effort, rather than the passive state it appears to be from the outside.

Roberto Lewis-Fernández, Professor of Clinical Psychiatry,
Columbia Vagelos College of Physicians and Surgeons, USA,
and President of the World Association of Cultural Psychiatry

Fascinating and perceptive . . . Keh-Ming Lin brings to life the early suffering and struggles that shaped the theories and teachings of fifteen founders of contemporary psychology. Practitioners of mental health must read this, as well as anyone interested in the triumph of the human spirit.

Albert C. Gaw, Clinical Professor of Psychiatry,
University of California, San Francisco, USA

An eloquent testimony of resiliency and personal struggles, *Wounded Healers* offers an original historical analysis of the lives of fifteen psychiatry and psychotherapy heroes. The reader will share their frailties, triumphs, doubts, and challenges, as the book puts forward a vibrant message of courage and hope.

Renato D. Alarcón, Emeritus Professor of Psychiatry,
Mayo Clinic School of Medicine, USA

In this engaging book, Keh-Ming Lin – international leader in culture and psychopharmacology – examines psychiatry's early masters coping with themselves amidst sociocultural vicissitudes. Ultimately, "woundedness" suffused their work, helping patients find meaning and self-acceptance. Clinician-readers, who may recognize similar hurdles in their ongoing development, will most certainly want this volume in their libraries.

Joe Westermeyer, Professor of Psychiatry and
Adjunct Professor of Anthropology, University of Minnesota, USA

Wounded Healers

Tribulations and Triumphs of Pioneering Psychotherapists

Keh-Ming Lin

University of California, Los Angeles

For Huei-Ling & Rayton

Thanks for enriching our lives.

Keh-Ming

3/14/2021

CAMBRIDGE
UNIVERSITY PRESS

CAMBRIDGE
UNIVERSITY PRESS

University Printing House, Cambridge CB2 8BS, United Kingdom

One Liberty Plaza, 20th Floor, New York, NY 10006, USA

477 Williamstown Road, Port Melbourne, VIC 3207, Australia

314–321, 3rd Floor, Plot 3, Splendor Forum, Jasola District Centre, New Delhi – 110025, India

79 Anson Road, #06–04/06, Singapore 079906

Cambridge University Press is part of the University of Cambridge.

It furthers the University's mission by disseminating knowledge in the pursuit of education, learning, and research at the highest international levels of excellence.

www.cambridge.org
Information on this title: www.cambridge.org/9781108479912
DOI: 10.1017/9781108801164

© Keh-Ming Lin 2021

Originally published in Chinese by Psygarden Publishing Company (2014) in Taiwan, and China Legal Publishing House (2016) in China.

First published in English by Cambridge University Press in 2021.

A catalogue record for this publication is available from the British Library.

Library of Congress Cataloging-in-Publication Data
NAMES: Lin, Keh-Ming, 1946– author.
TITLE: Wounded healers : tribulations and triumphs of pioneering psychotherapists / Keh-Ming Lin, University of California, Los Angeles.
DESCRIPTION: Cambridge, United Kingdom ; New York, NY : Cambridge University Press, 2021. | Includes bibliographical references and index.
IDENTIFIERS: LCCN 2020022962 (print) | LCCN 2020022963 (ebook) | ISBN 9781108479912 (hardback) | ISBN 9781108801164 (ebook)
SUBJECTS: LCSH: Psychotherapists – Biography. | Psychiatrists – Biography.
CLASSIFICATION: LCC RC438.5 .L46 2021 (print) | LCC RC438.5 (ebook) | DDC 616.89/140922–dc23
LC record available at https://lccn.loc.gov/2020022962
LC ebook record available at https://lccn.loc.gov/2020022963

ISBN 978-1-108-47991-2 Hardback
ISBN 978-1-108-79096-3 Paperback

CONTENTS

ACKNOWLEDGMENTS

You may have guessed that I see myself as a wounded healer. By this I don't mean to be conceited. I do not compare myself with the luminaries included in this book, either in terms of their achievements or the difficulties encountered in their lives. However, I do have my share of tribulations and *angst*, making life difficult for myself and for those around me. Living with a wounded healer is no piece of cake; yet through all these years, with all its ups and downs and twists and turns, my wife, Wen-Ling, has stood by my side, accepting my weaknesses, appreciating (at times) my idiosyncrasies, sharing our life journeys together. For all this, I'm truly grateful. This book is, first and foremost, dedicated to you, Wen.

So many people have made my life meaningful and possible. First on the list is our daughter, Jessica. Jess, you never complained about having an absent-minded father, and you are always patient listening to my endless ramblings. And now that you have recruited Andrew into our family, I'm so pleased to have one more person to share our tastes for exotic food and esoteric ideas.

Expressions of gratitude are long overdue to my parents, who provided unyielding support even though (I suspect) most of the time they were unsure what I was doing or why I was so discontent and difficult. An ancient Chinese tale described someone lamenting, "The tree wants to stand still, but the wind keeps on blowing; Now I want to get close to you, you are nowhere to be found." Likewise, I'm grateful to my parents-in-law for accepting me as I am, even though they may have wished that I were less wounded.

Sisters Linda and Ching have indulged and tolerated my egocentrism all my life. Brother Shyng has enriched our lives with his energy and audacity. It's wonderful sharing so many indelible memories with all of you, in Taiwan and in this promised land of ours called the United States of America.

In my long quest of becoming myself, I have been blessed with a great many remarkable mentors who pointed the ways to distant mountains and reminded me to appreciate the flowers blossoming along our shared path. In

Taiwan, while Wen-Shing Tseng showed me the richness of the unconscious world, Chu-Chang Chen persuaded me that psychiatry is a worthy profession. In Seattle, Arthur Kleinman taught me the power of culture and healing, and Minoru Masuda made me believe that it is possible to live a good life in a world of diversity, conflict, and uncertainty. In Los Angeles, Milton Miller convinced me that existentialism is not just Sisyphus and his boulder, but an essential tool enabling clinicians to help their patients, as well as negotiating with the powers that be for better care of populations. He also gave me the support and freedom to venture into uncharted territories, be they the mental health care of Americans of Asian and Pacific descent, the influences of genetics and culture on drug response, or, even more importantly, how to become a "good enough" healer in this puzzling modern world.

In Los Angeles I also found my blood brothers in Ira Lesser, Russell Poland, and Stanley Sue, who assured me that an academic career isn't just a rat race but is about doing it together to make things happen. It's also about asking questions and finding answers, in clinics, in laboratories, in the classrooms and in communities.

And how wonderful it is to have colleagues like Warren Procci and Charles Grob to bounce crazy ideas off of, drawing parallels between the twentieth-century psychoanalysts and the ninth-century Zen Buddhist Masters, and marveling at the mystery of ayahuasca and the ingenuity of native Amazonians in inventing such a powerful brew.

The idea of this book geminated during my year at the Center for Advanced Study in the Behavioral Sciences at Stanford (CASBS), where the theme of "wounded healers" first coame to mind. However, the actual writing of these biographies would not have happened without the encouragement of many of my "comrades" from our medical school days, who provided space in *Medicine Today*, giving me the much-needed structure to come up with one chapter each month. Friends including Yun-fang Liaw, Chi-Wan Lai, Sunhoo Foo, and Hai-Gwo Hwu, and many others, combed through these pieces sentence by sentence, paragraph by paragraph, to make sure they are coherent and relevant. Hao-Wei Wang and Doris Wang, founder and editor-in-chief of Psygarden Publishing Co. in Taiwan, helped me to package these pieces into a book. It was through their labor of love that the Chinese version of the book has been issued in Taiwan and, separately, in China as well.

The English version of the book has benefited tremendously from editorial input from Marciana Poland and Jack Adler, as well as comments from two groups of friends we made since moving to San Francisco. One of them is an informal group of seasoned mental health professionals including Albert and Tina Gaw, George and Gail Hamilton, Robert and Anita Mixon, and Stanley and Sophia Sue. The other is the biweekly writer's group sponsored by the Mechanics' Institute, whose members include June Johnson, Harlan Lewin, Barbara Michelman, Stephen Sagar, and Rolene Walker. Other friends and colleagues who have supported and encouraged me to complete the project include Renato Alarcon, Ravi Chandra, Susannah Frearson, Laurence Kirmayer, John Launer, Roberto Lewis-Fernandez, Francis Lu, William Todd Schultz, Mitchell Weiss, Brant Wenegrat, Joe Westermeyer, and Joel Yager.

Last but not least, it was my great fortune to work with Janka Romero, commissioning editor at Cambridge University Press. Janka patiently guided me through the long process of reviewing and revising the manuscript and passionately advocated for the book, leading to its acceptance by the venerable Press, for which I am immensely grateful. As well, I am grateful to Adam Hooper, Mathivathini Mareesan, Joshua Penney, Gary Smith, Ilaria Tassistro, and Emily Watton for their expert assistance in bringing the book to its final form.

Introduction

Learn, strive, to know thyself.

Physician, heal thyself.
> Aeschylus (*c*.525 to *c*.456 BC): *Prometheus Bound*, verses 309 and 473–475

Our own pain teaches us to share in the sufferings of others.
> Johann Wolfgang von Goethe: *Goethes Werke*, quoted by
> Stanley W. Jackson (2001)

This book is about some of the most courageous and innovative clinicians and thinkers to lead the way in our exploration of the human mind. It grew out of my life-long search for ways to understand and help myself and others. Over a half-century of seeking and reading, I have come to realize that the theories and practices of many of these remarkable forerunners of ours are best appreciated in the context of their life experiences and the ethos of their time. Putting their life stories together, the theme "wounded healer" emerged as an important but hitherto neglected concept: We cannot fully understand a theory without understanding from whence it arose. This perspective has become an important cornerstone for my view on what we do and who we are, how our understanding of human nature has developed, and where we go from here.

The term "wounded healer" may be polarizing or confusing to many modern healthcare professionals who consider themselves neither as healers nor wounded. Ever since Europe emerged from the Dark Ages, Western professionals sanctioned by society as experts on matters of health and illness have progressively distanced themselves from terms like "healers" and "healing." In the late nineteenth century, major breakthroughs in biomedicine enticed the medical establishment to shift its attention from a person-centered to a disease-focused model, with technological fixes as the primary, if not exclusive, goal. In an effort to distinguish themselves from traditional healers, modern health professionals became detached from the original concept of healing, viewing it with suspicion. *But by minimizing their role as healers, health professionals distance themselves from the part of them that is most essential and effective. This disconnect has been one of the major challenges for modern healthcare* (Kleinman, 1988, 1991).

In addition, for the past century, the term "wounded healer" has been prominently associated with Carl Jung and his followers (Dunne, 2000; Merchant, 2012; Sedgwick, 1994), who developed and elaborated on the concept of the wounded healer archetype from an exclusively Jungian perspective. In this book, the term is used in its broader sense: knowing oneself, knowing one's limitations, weaknesses, hurts, and sufferings, is essential for all healers, all health professionals.

In an even broader sense, we might consider all of us wounded healers (Nouwen, 1972).

WE ARE ALL WOUNDED

Like it or not, we are thrown into this life of ours that is characterized by *duhkha*, or woundedness.

Some 2,500 years ago, at the age of twenty-nine, Prince Siddhartha Gautama abandoned his kingdom to search for Truth after realizing that, for himself and for all of us, there is no escaping *aging, illness*, and eventually, *death*.

This parable foretold the twentieth-century existentialists' idea of "thrownness." We are all thrown into this world, *blessed* and *cursed* at the same time with our *self-consciousness* and the awareness that our existence is finite, resulting in a pervasive sense of vulnerability and angst (Becker, 1997; Yalom, 2017).

On top of these ontological threats, we also live in a world full of dangerous pitfalls and undertows. The list of adversities is inexhaustible. Natural and man-made disasters may strike anywhere, at any time. Accidents, war, deliberate and random violence, child abuse and neglect, unemployment, discrimination, and poverty abound. No matter how sheltered our lives are, we have no hope of avoiding trauma and suffering. Ancient Indians called this predicament *duhkha*, one of the Four Noble Truths serving as the foundation of Buddhism.

We make valiant attempts to keep *duhkha* at bay, with varying degrees of success. But often we end up making things worse as well. We may err in overreacting, trying to run away, or just burying our heads in the sand. We may hide behind the façade of equanimity, seek artificial and temporary means to numb ourselves (e.g., alcohol, drugs, and other forms of addiction), or lash out at someone seen as weaker than us. While such strategies may succeed for a time, in the long run they boomerang back to hurt us.

Thus, on top of the ontological threats and the dangers lurking in the real world, we also suffer from self-inflicted wounds that can push us into regret, self-blame, and deeper despair.

WE ARE ALL HEALERS

Yet, no matter how wounded we are, we survive. We survive not only because of our innate capacity for denial and for self-soothing, but even more importantly, because we are in this together, and we care. It is ingrained in our nature – in our very genes – to care, to want those around us to hurt less, feel safe, feel whole. In other words, we have within us the urge to heal others, and we look to others to do the same for us.

This must be why healing practices have always been with us (Moerman, 1979; Dow, 1986; Jackson, 1999). Evidence of such practices can be found dating back to some 60 millennia ago, when our ancestors, *Homo sapiens sapiens*, emerged with the unique impulse to care for the old, the weak and the disabled (Fabrega, 1997). They fed and clothed them, keeping them company. They experimented with medicinal herbs, invented primitive surgical procedures (trepanation, bone-setting, bloodletting) and tried different methods of physical manipulation (massage, acupuncture). They also developed rituals, chants, and various forms of invocation for supernatural intercessions, for the purpose of soothing and alleviating suffering (Incayawar, Wintrob, & Bouchar, 2009; Kleinman, 1980; Torrey, 1986). Uniquely human are also the experiences of trance and possession, allowing some of us to enter into altered states of consciousness, during which healing may be achieved.

Etymologically, *to heal is to make whole* and *to care is to be present and grieve with those who are ill*. In this sense, *we all are (or should be) healers and caregivers*. However, since *healing* involves specialized knowledge and skills, all societies designate experts to be healers. They are called by different names in different cultures, ranging from the shamans in Siberia and Manchuria, medicine men among Native Americans, *Dang-ki* in Taiwan and southern China, *Mudang* in Korea, and *Voodoo* practitioners among the African diaspora. Although the rituals they perform and the paraphernalia they use may differ, they share the same goal of healing, and their effectiveness has been widely documented.

WE ARE WOUNDED HEALERS

If we agree that we all possess at least some instinct for healing and we are also more or less wounded, then it should be self-evident that all healers, whether ancient or modern, shaman or psychiatrist, are wounded healers.

The concept of the wounded healer does have ancient roots (Jackson, 2001; Rice, 2011). There are mythological tales around the world linking "woundedness" with the power of healing. *Asklepios*, the Greek god of medicine, was traumatized at birth by the tragic death of his mother. He was then raised and mentored by the wise centaur *Chiron*, who himself suffered eternally with an incurable wound from a poisonous arrow (Goldwert, 1992; Kirmayer, 2003). *Odin*, a principal Nordic god, sacrificed one of his eyes for the power of wisdom and healing (Davidson, 1964); *Ganesha*, the Indian elephant-headed god of wisdom and problem solving, suffered from unimaginable violence at birth (Brown, 1991); *Iron Crutch Li*, one of the most revered Taoist medicine gods, was crippled (Yang, 2008).

A vast anthropological literature, accumulated over the past century, convincingly demonstrates the role of psychological struggle and physical affliction ("dis-ease") in the making of traditional healers (Frank & Frank, 1993; Kleinman, 1988; Torrey, 1986). Prior to becoming healers, individuals have typically undergone prolonged periods of ill health, compelling them to look for ways to alleviate their own pain and suffering. With luck, they find established healers who accept them as apprentices. Passing the initiatory crises, they gradually learn the trade. Although the process and duration of the apprenticeship varies substantively across cultures, the role of physical and mental suffering in precipitating the search for self-healing, as well as the acquisition of healing power, appears universal.

WOUNDEDNESS AND HEALING IN MODERN MEDICINE

Compared to traditional healers, modern-day physicians are less likely to come to pursue a medical career as a result of their own illness. Instead, they more commonly cite intellectual curiosity, altruism, and influences from role models as motivating factors (Pagnin et al., 2013; Torres-Roman et al., 2018). Still, a significant percentage of health professionals do report being motivated to pursue this line of work by either a history of severe personal illness or the witnessing of ill health or death in their immediate family or community (Daneault, 2008). There are reports of a high prevalence of depression among health professionals. For example, a recent meta-analysis showed that the rate of depression ranged from 20.9 to 43.2 percent and increased with each calendar year (Mata et al., 2015).

For psychotherapists and mental health professionals in general, such links are even stronger (Ivey & Partington, 2014; Rippere & Williams, 1985; Straussner, Senreich, & Steen, 2018; Sussman, 2007; Zerubavel, & Wright, 2012). Researchers generally agree that rates of trauma, psychiatric issues, and substance-use disorders are much more prevalent in those entering these fields compared to in the general public. Following Jung's concept of the *Wounded Healer Archetype*, the consensus has been that in order to be able to help patients, clinicians must face their own adversities, and confront their own regret, confusion, anger, and grief. In this view, being in touch with one's own vulnerability and woundedness is crucial for the development of empathic understanding of the human condition and becoming a competent therapist. As Cecil A. Rice (2011), a talented group therapist, has said, "To be effective, therapists need some understanding of their vulnerabilities to facilitate their clients' healing and to prevent unrecognized woundedness from blocking that healing."

Similarly, in Abraham Verghese's novel *Cutting for Stone* (2009), the protagonist, a surgeon, muses, "My intent wasn't to save the world as much as to heal myself. Few doctors will admit this, certainly not young ones, but subconsciously, in entering the profession, we must believe that ministering to others will heal our woundedness. And it can. But it can also deepen the wound."

A BRIEF OVERVIEW OF THE BIOGRAPHIES INCLUDED IN THE BOOK

In order to examine the important issues discussed above, this book includes biographies of fifteen of the most influential pioneers of psychotherapy active in the first half of the twentieth century, who are grouped into two parts, reflecting the field's historical development.

Part I, "*Fin-de-Siècle* Vienna," begins with the triumvirates – Sigmund Freud, Carl Jung, and Alfred Adler – whose friendship, entanglements, and bitter feuds reverberated for a century and can still stir up emotional debates.

These are followed by the second-generation players of the psychoanalytical movement. They include: Otto Rank, of the "birth trauma" fame; Wilhelm Reich, who made valiant attempts to integrate psychoanalysis and Marxism; Ernest Jones, the proselytizer of psychoanalysis in the English world; Melanie Klein, founder of the school of Object Relation Theory; Anna Freud, one of the founders of child psychoanalysis and self-appointed guardian of Sigmund Freud's legacy; and Viktor Frankl, who survived Auschwitz and Dachau to develop the school of logotherapy, centering on the importance of "meaning" in relation to health.

Part II, "From Sea to Shining Sea," includes biographies of six pioneers in the mental health field who transplanted "healing practices of the mind" from Continental Europe to North America. Among them, William James and Milton H. Erickson's theories and practices reflect the maturation of American intellectual development around the turn of the century. Although Frieda Fromm-Reichman and Erik Erikson were born and educated on the other side of the Atlantic, their careers took off only after their immigration to the USA. Together with Harry Stack Sullivan, Margaret Mead, and Gregory Bateson, they led a distinctively American movement that has been called neo-Freudianism and interpersonal psychoanalysis.

In contrast to European thinkers of an earlier generation, the focus for these scholars was no longer only the "intra-psychic world," but more often the influences of family, society, and culture on behavior, adaptation, and health. Built on American optimism and pragmatism, they moved away from the earlier determinism reflected in the famous Freudian quote, "anatomy is destiny." Instead, they believed that individuals' mental health could be vastly enhanced by changing their environments. Such convictions served as the impetus for the promotion of community mental health, and at the same time paved the way for contemporary thinkers such as Erich Fromm to critically examine the role modern society plays in hindering human freedom.

WHAT CAN WE LEARN FROM THEIR STORIES?

What do these life stories have to do with us, as mental health professionals and those interested in mental health issues?

First of all, it may be comforting for us to know that, at least in some respect, our heroes are not that different from us. They share with us their *woundedness*, their human frailty. Their struggles to transcend their flaws and limitation may not lead to perfect or complete answers to our questions (nor should we expect this to be the case), but they serve as role models for us to continue our search, individually and collectively.

Too often when we think about *woundedness* and *healing*, we automatically assume they are dichotomous: One is either wounded or not wounded, healed or sick. Instead, they may be more usefully seen as a continuum. No matter how hard we try, the hurt from past trauma lingers on and our strivings for wholeness continue as a life-long process. Such a view helps keep us humble, making it more possible for us to draw on woundedness in the service of healing.

In addition, these life stories are also important in helping to deepen our understanding of various aspects of depth psychology. These include a healthy appreciation of the potential downside of traumatic life experiences, the importance of resilience and support, the situatedness of theories of depth psychology, the lure and danger of hero-worshipping, and the importance of the continuing search for our own path.

THERAPEUTIC CHALLENGES OF WOUNDEDNESS

While emphasizing the role of adversities in fostering empathy and striving, it should also be apparent that suffering does not guarantee healing power or creativity. Woundedness is a double-edged sword for those in the healing professions. More often than not, unresolved conflicts over pre-existing trauma can render mental health professionals vulnerable to vicarious trauma when working with patients who have been victims of trauma (Pearlman & Saakvitne, 1995). In such a situation, instead of helping patients to effectively deal with their trauma, therapists themselves become retraumatized. Laden with self-doubt and self-blame, the resulting ongoing emotional turmoil in the therapists can often lead to severe health consequences, and eventually, burnout.

Even more worrisome is the situation in which unresolved traumatic life experiences lead to therapists projecting their own inner conflicts onto their patients. Camouflaged with convoluted theoretical justifications, influenced by unresolved *countertransference*, they can fall into the trap of *acting out*, consciously or unconsciously manipulating and using their patients to solve their own intrapsychic conflicts. In extreme cases, this leads to sexual abuse or other forms of flagrant transgressions, causing further damage to their patients.

It is thus a balancing act, a dialectical process. Ideally, *knowing thyself* goes hand-in-hand with *healing thyself*. The stories of the pioneers included in this volume demonstrate that, by confronting one's own pain, the clinician is able to gain access into the patient's world, to be truly with him or her. At the same time, such clinical encounters enable clinicians to deepen and broaden their own self-understanding and self-acceptance. By demonstrating their own ability to cope with wounds in life, the clinicians become effective models for patients to emulate and learn from, in order to overcome their own problems.

THE ROLE OF RESILIENCE AND SUPPORT

To respond in a way that transforms vulnerability into strength, courage, ingenuity, and resilience are needed. As Sherwin Nuland (2007) said, "It is not the adversity itself that determines the shape of the future, so much as our response to the adversity." This is a transformation process that could be seen time and again in the life stories of the wounded healers, as well as others who struggled with and triumphed over their creative illnesses (Ellenberger, 1968).

In addition, personal strivings, no matter how heroic, are often not enough for overcoming adversity. Equally important is the availability of support and nurturance from those around: teachers, mentors, friends, colleagues, family members, and others. For those still in training for the healing professions, such support is particularly important. Although by virtue of having been selected into training programs they have already shown high levels of resilience and determination, struggling and coming to terms with one's own past is still a challenge. For trainees and practicing therapists to continue to grow and prosper, the profession as a whole should foster academic and professional environments in which it is safe for clinicians to acknowledge their challenges and receive support conducive to working through their problems.

THE SITUATEDNESS OF THE THEORIES OF DEPTH PSYCHOLOGY

Delving into the woundedness of the founders of the schools of depth psychology affords us a lens for understanding their theories and teachings. These life stories make it clear that their insights did not just materialize from thin air.

Rather, they arose from years of struggle that forced them to seek a way out, to make sense of their lives, to save themselves.

The life stories of Freud and Jung serve as good examples for this argument. Many biographers have pointed out that Freud's theories on the Oedipus Complex emerged only after the death of his father. The relevance of this connection is further deepened when we remember that, Jakob, Freud's father, had failed miserably both as a provider for the family and as a role model for Freud himself. Growing up in a family laden with poverty, shame, and secrecy, Freud spent more than half of his lifetime searching for a father figure to rescue him and help him to achieve glory and fame. Feeling abandoned time and again, like the baby Oedipus, he must have had great difficulties dealing with his patricidal fury when his aging father abandoned him for the last time, leading to the re-enactment of the ancient Oedipal drama, which eventually catapulted him into the development of the Oedipal theories.

The intense drama between Carl Jung and Sigmund Freud was no doubt another enactment of Oedipal conflicts, with Freud now playing the role of King Laius, desiring, and at the same time fearing, an heir for his intellectual legacy. Mirroring this, Jung was searching for a powerful father figure worthy of his admiration. Yet along with this there were also intense fear and rage.

However, even more powerful than this "father complex" was Jung's life-long yearning for his mother's attention and love. Almost totally neglected by a mother who suffered from chronic depression requiring frequent and lengthy hospitalizations, Jung grew up as a lonely boy craving a mysterious and unfathomable maternal love (Smith, 1996). It is not hard to imagine such yearning contributing to his fascination and ambivalence with the earth mother archetype and with the mystical world in general. At the same time, recognizing such intense craving for maternal love may also help us to be less puzzled by his voracious need for female admirers and the depth of his dependence on them.

Similar convincing cases can be made about most, if not all, of the pioneers in connecting the nature of their life's vicissitudes with the themes of their theories. Prominent examples include Alfred Adler's growing up under the shadow of, and feeling inferior to, a brilliant and successful older brother; Erik Erikson's life-long search for his real father and his own identity; and Harry Stack Sullivan's deep sense of alienation throughout his youth and into his adult life. Knowing how they were hurt and how they struggled and at times triumphed over the effects of their wounds, it becomes easier for us to see how they emerged from their attempts to make sense of the world they lived in and how the theories they have developed are of ongoing relevance to us.

HEROES IN PERSPECTIVE

It is a testament to the staying power of the ideas of these pioneers of depth psychology that, after close to a century, many scholars are still debating if they meant what they said, or if they practiced what they preached. Seeing them as "wounded healers" should help us to view their failings and self-inflicted wounds as cautionary tales, rather than betrayals. While we should not gloss over these less-than-ideal pictures of our heroes, or bend over backwards to provide excuses for their transgressions, we might keep in mind that many of the rules we now take for granted did not yet exist in their time. Some of their blunders might have come with the territory of their being pioneers of the field. Instead of judging them too harshly, we can see their mistakes, compromises, and even transgressions as examples alerting us to pitfalls to be avoided.

The concept of the wounded healer should also be useful for answering a mystifying question: How could these brilliant minds, full of agility and perceptiveness, become so rigid in their conviction of the absolute truth of their theories and how could they be so intolerant, even vicious, when the views of their former comrades or followers diverged from theirs?

If we approach their theories in the context of their life experiences, seeing them as the product of years of struggle to make sense of their own lives, the strength of their convictions and their reactions to threats to their hard-won "truths" start to make more sense.

This notwithstanding, despite the vehemence of their feuds, the minds of these original thinkers were much more subtle and flexible than appears at first glance. Throughout their lives, their thoughts continued to evolve. They may have pretended that their opponents had dropped off the face of the Earth, but they remained deeply attuned to what the others were doing. In this way, after decades of rejecting Adler's emphasis on aggression as an important part of human nature, Freud came to embrace the concept of "death instinct." Similarly, when Freud (1918) published *Totem and Taboo* in 1913, he reluctantly acknowledged Jung as an influence, even though *Symbols of Transformation* (Jung, 1912) had precipitated the schism between the two barely one year earlier.

LEARNING FROM THE MAESTROS TO FIND OUR OWN PATHS

Lastly, perhaps the most important lesson we can learn from these biographies is that theories have to be rooted in experience. Whether learning to deliver therapy, seeking therapy, or both, most of us yearn for definitive answers to the difficult questions that confront us. Naively and often unconsciously, we harbor hopes that someone holds the key for our salvation. The idea that the great figures of our field, those we have admired and sought to emulate, are flawed, are wounded healers, can be disappointing and disturbing.

However, perhaps more precious than the theories these forerunners left us with were the ways they were able to face their own traumas and suffering, and use their self-knowledge to save themselves and others. As quoted by Thich Nhat Hanh (1987), "A finger pointing at the moon is not the moon. The finger is needed to know where to look for the moon, but if you mistake the finger for the moon itself, you will never know the real moon" (McRae, 2000; Suzuki, 1932; The Śūraṅgama Sūtra Translation Committee of the Buddhist Text Translation Society, 2009).

As heirs of their traditions, our job is not necessarily to be their faithful followers, but to face our own difficulties and find our own paths. It is by being ourselves that we can best help ourselves and others. This is why rabbi Reb Zusha said at his deathbed (Buber, 1947; Mercer, 2016): "When I pass from this world and appear before the Heavenly Tribunal, they won't ask me, 'Zusha, why weren't you as wise as Moses or as kind as Abraham,' rather, they will ask me, 'Zusha, why weren't you Zusha?'"

Similarly, Hanshan ("Cold Mountain"), the reclusive ninth-century Zen monk poet, recorded his friend Shide ("Foundling") saying, "*Hanshan is Hanshan, Shide is Shide*" (Red Pine, 2000). And, *Linji Yixuan*, the eleventh Chinese Zen Patriarch, famously said, "If you run into Buddha, kill Him! If your Master is in your way, kill him!" (Fromm, 1960; Hanh, 1974; Wu, 2004).

May we grapple with and "kill" our intellectual forebears, so that we can benefit more fully from the gifts they have bestowed upon all of us.

PART I

FIN-DE-SIÈCLE VIENNA

1

Sometimes a Cigar Is Just a Cigar

Sigmund Freud's Addiction Problems

In the many pictures of Freud, the most noticeable detail are his piercing eyes. Second to that, it has to be the cigar, rarely absent from his hand. Freud was someone who cared very much about his appearance. Every morning, right after breakfast, a barber was already waiting there to make sure his hair and beard were trimmed to his satisfaction. Consequently, he was always fashionably dressed and well-groomed. This led me to assume that the cigar was part of his "persona": It was there as a prop to enhance his image as a philosopher deep in thought.

However, Ernest Jones (Freud Museum London, 2013; Jones, 1953), the author of Freud's only officially authorized biography, stated that on average he smoked twenty cigars a day.

How much nicotine was he exposed to if we convert that into cigarettes? Depending on the size and brand, each cigar is at least equivalent to ten cigarettes, with the larger ones approaching twenty (Clark, 2017). Thus, Freud's daily nicotine exposure was equal to between 200 and 400 cigarettes! Furthermore, since each cigar could last for up to an hour, twenty cigars a day would mean that he could have spent twenty hours a day smoking.

From the age of twenty-four to the last days of his life, for most of his waking hours, Freud's hand and mouth were rarely unattached from a cigar. Even after the diagnosis of oral cancer at sixty-seven, and after having endured more than thirty surgeries in the next sixteen years, to the point that he was barely able to eat and drink, he still didn't give up his cigar. Freud's dependence on nicotine is hard to surpass.

COCAINE AS A MIRACLE DRUG

Yet, when most people think about Freud's addiction problems, what comes to mind first is cocaine (Markel, 2011). For twelve years (ages 28–40), in addition to almost daily exposure to cocaine himself, Freud also actively promoted its therapeutic use. To make sense of how this could have happened, we need to go back to the time when cocaine was introduced to the modern world.

Cocaine originally came from coca leaves indigenous to South America, where for more than a thousand years it has been widely used for its stimulating effects. After the Spanish conquistadors subjugated the Inca Empire at the beginning of the sixteenth century, reports of the "magic effects" of the plant started to trickle back to Europe. Since the preservation and transportation of the leaves across continents and oceans was not easy, these reports were largely ignored until 1859, when cocaine was successfully extracted from the plant by the German chemists Albert Nieumann and Friedrich Wohler.

A few years later (1863), a French chemist, Angelo Mariani, added cocaine to wine (6 percent in Europe, 7.2 percent in the USA), and named it *Vin Mariani*. It was touted as a miracle drink that could cure a large number of diseases, in addition to enhancing one's physical health and mental prowess in general. The wine was a huge commercial success, used not only by prominent literary figures including Alexander Dumas and Arthur Conan Doyle, but even by Pope Leo XIII, who provided a public endorsement (Hamblin, 2013).

Twenty-odd years later, John Pemberton, a Confederate captain and pharmacist from Georgia, who sustained injuries during the Civil War and subsequently became dependent on morphine for pain suppression, stumbled on *Vin Mariani*. Surprised by the effectiveness of the concoction in curbing his addiction, he "improved" it and patented his product as "Coca Wine."

A year later, the Prohibition Act was enacted in the state of Georgia, banning the use of alcohol. In response, Pemberton took the alcohol out of the drink, added bubbles and other "secret ingredients," and called it *Coca-Cola*. It was heavily promoted as effective in curing common afflictions including headaches, dyspepsia, neurasthenia, and sexual impotence, as well as morphine addiction and many other maladies.

Although cocaine was eventually taken out of the cola, and the drink was no longer promoted as a panacea, Coca-Cola continues to be a popular beverage, enjoying wild successes in its marketing worldwide.

Pemberton's conviction of cocaine's therapeutic effect with morphine addiction, originating from his own personal experiences, was also supported by articles that had started to appear in medical literature around that time.

FREUD'S "ÜBER COCA"

Among these reports, the most thorough and convincing was a pamphlet by Freud (1884), titled "Über Coca." In this carefully crafted volume, Freud started with a review of the history of cocaine's discovery, its pharmacological properties, and relevant animal studies, and then went on to describe in detail his own experiences with the use of cocaine on many occasions. These effects included increased heart rate, improved attention, euphoria, and difficulties in falling asleep. Of note was his insistence that *cocaine was not addictive.*

Supplementing his personal experiences with observations on others given the substance by him (including his fiancée, Martha Bernays), he came to the conclusion that cocaine had great promise for treating various psychiatric and addictive disorders. This report earned him wide attention in academic circles, and also helped him to obtain grants from major pharmaceutical companies, including Merck and Park-Davis, making it possible for him to travel to Hamburg to be with Martha. Deeply infatuated, he had been writing long letters to her on a daily basis for over two years but had been unable to visit due to a shortage of funds.

In the following years, reports started to appear in medical journals showing that cocaine was not only highly addictive, but also associated with many severe side effects, including chronic rhinitis, nasal perforation, hypertension, and even stroke and psychosis. This notwithstanding, Freud continued to insist that cocaine's therapeutic potential far outweighed its risks, and ardently argued for its use.

Freud was actually the first to notice the potency of cocaine as a local anesthetic. He reported that, when put in the mouth, cocaine caused numbness on the lips and the tongue. However, he brushed this finding aside as he was not interested in surgical procedures. While he left Vienna to visit Martha, a good friend, Karl Koller, applied cocaine in cataract surgery and found it an excellent anesthetic. Koller's report was widely appreciated and noted by William Halsted, the "father of American surgery," who soon used cocaine as an anesthetic for various surgical procedures, achieving remarkable successes. In the process, Halsted himself also became a life-long addict, not only of cocaine but also morphine (Imber, 2010).

THE SEDUCTION OF COCAINE

Freud's interest in cocaine came partly from his search for ways to help one of his mentors, Ernst von Fleischl-Marxow. Fleischl-Marxow was a talented and innovative physiologist who had invented many instruments to measure electric conduction in the nervous system. He was also the first to demonstrate that the stimulation of different parts of the body led to changes in the brainwaves in distinct areas of the brain. Because of these achievements, he had been one of the most esteemed colleagues of the famed and influential Ernst Wilhelm Ritter Brücke, the head of the Physiology Department, achieving the rank of full professor in 1880 at the age of thirty four.

Remarkably, all of these accomplishments had been achieved by Fleischl-Marxow while he was suffering from constant excruciating pain that took a huge toll on him physically and psychologically. This problem started nine years earlier, when he accidentally cut his right thumb while performing an autopsy. The wound became infected, leading to repeated amputations. To make the matter worse, a recalcitrant neuroma developed on the stump, causing relentless pain that could not be relieved by anything but morphine. Unfortunately, as his tolerance grew, the dosage of morphine steadily escalated, eventually reaching an alarming level.

Having worked closely with Fleischl-Marxow at the physiology laboratory for years, Freud was intimately aware of Fleischl-Marxow's morphine addiction and deeply worried about its long-term consequences. Searching for a cure for his friend's condition, he came upon the idea of using cocaine, and rushed in an order to Park-Davis.

Cocaine turned out to be a "miracle drug," enthused Fleischl-Marxow. According to him, it enabled him to gradually cut down the morphine consumption until it was almost zero.

In this case, Fleischl-Marxow proved that the self-reporting of addiction patients is often unreliable, and world-renowned scientists are not exempt. Without warning, one day Fleischl-Marxow simply disappeared. Along with several colleagues, Freud rushed to Fleischl-Marxow's apartment. They broke open the entrance door to find a naked, delirious Fleischl-Marxow thrashing around. Taken quickly to the hospital, his condition improved only with a large dose of morphine. It turned out that Fleischl-Marxow had not only *not* weaned himself off morphine, but also continued to escalate the doses of cocaine, ending up taking huge amounts of both drugs at the same time.

This incident marked the beginning of Fleischl-Marxow's downward spiral. Weighed down by the double addiction, he gradually withered away and died seven years later, at the young age of forty-five.

FREUD'S TWELVE-YEAR COCAINE JOURNEY

This tragic event, however, did nothing to dampen Freud's fascination with and use of cocaine. For twelve years, from 1884 to 1896, he continued to take cocaine regularly and advocated for its therapeutic benefits (Masson, 1985). Believing that cocaine was only dangerous when misused, he used himself and his friends as guinea pigs, hoping to find the right dose range and regimen. One could argue that this itself is not necessarily an unreasonable approach. After all, as Paracelsus, the "father of toxicology," famously said, *Sola dosis facit venenum (Only the dose makes the poison)* (Ottoboni & Frank, 1985).

Lest we judge Freud too harshly, it is also useful to remember that, throughout the long history of modern medical research, self-experimentation has played an important role in advancing our knowledge. Mysteries solved in this manner include the discovery of a number of anesthetic agents, the danger of radioactive substances, the nature of nerve regeneration, and the transmission of infectious diseases, including cholera and yellow fever (Altman, 1987).

But, twelve years?

Considering the length and extent of Freud's exposure to cocaine, it would seem certain that he was playing with fire. Putting this together with his practically life-long exposure to huge quantities of nicotine, we might agree that he indeed had a major problem with addiction. Assuming this to be the case, the more intriguing question is what made him particularly prone to addictions?

Combing through events and experiences in his life, themes contributing toward his vulnerabilities start to emerge. They include: severe childhood trauma and loss; frustration and disappointments in career development made worse due to his unbridled ambitions; and professional, personal, and social isolation. It is hoped that a better understanding of what Freud had been up against all his life will help us to be more sympathetic regarding his addiction, as well as show how these difficulties might have played a role in shaping his career path.

FREUD'S TRAUMATIC CHILDHOOD

Traumatic childhood experiences have been consistently identified as a major risk factor for addiction (Dube et al., 2003; Ersche et al., 2012) and other psychiatric disorders (Copeland et al., 2018). Looking into Freud's childhood, there is no arguing that he was indeed repeatedly and significantly traumatized (Breger, 2000; Phillips, 2014). From birth, Freud was surrounded by family scandals, poverty, losses, and death. Freud's mother, Amalia Nathansohn, was the third wife of his father, Jakob Freud. Jakob's life prior to Freud's birth seems to have been in constant turmoil. After the death of his first wife in 1852, Jakob immediately married a woman known only as Rebeka. Three years later, when he married again, to Amalia, Rebeka was nowhere to be found.

At his birth, Freud already had two adult half-brothers, Emanuel and Philipp, a nephew one year older than him, and a niece of his own age. Two months before Freud's birth, his grandfather passed away. When Freud was six months old his mother became pregnant again and gave birth to a boy who died precipitously when Freud was two years old. From then on, Amalia became pregnant on a yearly basis, giving birth to five daughters and one son in eight years. Not having time for Freud, Amalia hired an "ugly" but loving middle-aged Catholic woman as his nanny (Masson, 1985). However, this nanny was fired when Freud was two-and-a-half years old, and disappeared from his life completely for reasons not specified (although there is rumor of her stealing silver utensils).

Around this time, Jakob became bankrupt and fled Freiberg (now Pribor in the eastern Czech Republic), first hiding in Leipzig, Germany, but shortly afterwards moving to Vienna, Austria, where he was soon joined by Amalia, three-year-old Sigmund, and one-year-old Anna. After moving to Vienna, Jakob was perpetually out of work and the family was constantly pressed for money, dependent on hand-outs from relatives. The whole family lived in a cramped one-bedroom apartment for several years before finally moving to a somewhat bigger unit.

While Jakob took his new family to Vienna, Freud's two married half-brothers escaped to Manchester, England, along with Emanuel's two children who had been Freud's only playmates (Krüll, 1986). Rumor has it that Philipp, his other half-brother, might have had an affair with his mother, Amalia, and that might have been the real reason for the brothers' abrupt moving away, taking along Johann and Pauline, Freud's childhood playmate.

When Freud was nine years old, his uncle, Josef Freud, was arrested for counterfeiting Russian rubles. Investigators raided Freud's house and found letters Josef had exchanged with Freud's half-brothers in England, implicating them as co-conspirators in the scam. The case against Emanuel and Philipp was eventually dropped, but Josef was sentenced to ten years in prison. The whole incident was widely covered in newspapers, causing further damage to the Freud family's reputation.

In sum, at a very young age, Freud was abandoned by his nanny, his brothers, and his only playmate. His elderly father was forever on the verge of insolvency and was unable to provide for the family. Throughout, the family was inundated with scandals and secrets. Growing up in such an environment could not have been easy.

"My Golden Sigi"

We may never know completely why, growing up, people turn out one way or another. But, according to popular psychology informed (or misinformed) by Freudian theories, parents are always to blame. In Freud's case, there might be some truth to it.

As the first born of Jakob and Amalia's union, Freud grew up as the favored child among his siblings, adored particularly by his mother, who called him "my golden Sigi" (Freud's first name was originally *Sigismund*). Many years later, his sister Anna still remembered vividly the unfairness of the differential treatment, reporting that the whole family was cramped into one room as the other room was reserved for Freud to study and to practice piano.

Accompanying such privileges was tremendous pressure for him to achieve and succeed in order to pull the family out of poverty and disgrace. Reflecting such expectations, Freud excelled in school and harbored ambitious dreams of glory and power, power to mold the world and change the course of human history, power to find and conquer new territories. The child Freud worshipped historical heroes such as Hannibal, Alexander the Great, Oliver Cromwell, and, above all, the Spanish conquistadors who subjugated the New World (Boehlich, 1992). That these were not passing fancies was shown in his insistence, when he was only ten, that his younger brother should be named Alexander. For the same reason, much later, he named his third son Oliver Freud, after Cromwell.

Entering college, such unbridled ambition led him to entertain a fantasy that one day there would be a bust on prominent display at the campus, inscribed with a quote from Sophocles' *Oedipus Rex*: "*Who knew the famous riddles and was a man most mighty.*" Even more candidly, at the age of twenty-nine, in a letter to Martha, then still his fiancée, he wrote that he had destroyed "all my diaries of the past fourteen years, with letters, scientific notes and the manuscripts of my publications." Why? Because he wanted to baffle his future biographers who would have to be busy grappling with his "Conception of the Development of the *Hero*," drawing wrong conclusions (Jones, 1953).

How does one go about finding the way to become a hero, a conqueror, especially for a Jew? Even though at the time the Austro-Hungarian Empire was at the threshold of Jewish emancipation, opportunities for young Jews were still limited, especially in fields such as politics and the military, which might lead to positions with *power over people*, in order to achieve his dreams of becoming a *hero* as traditionally defined.

At university, Freud drifted from law to philosophy, unable to find a path that might satisfy his ambition. Fortunately, he lived at a time when natural sciences were progressing at lightning speed. The emergence of germ theories and the development of vaccines and antiseptic procedures revolutionized the practice of surgery and medicine. Bolstered by exciting breakthroughs in comparative biology, organic chemistry, geology, and archeology, Darwinism provided a powerful paradigm for unraveling the secrets of life and of the human universe. Listening to the lectures of eminent research scientists based at the University of Vienna, Freud found a way forward. If *power over people* seemed out of reach, *power over nature* would seem to be a much better fit for satisfying his intellectual curiosity, and for offering him the possibility of achieving fame.

This led him to Brücke, who was at the forefront of the efforts to revolutionize the field of physiology by applying chemical and physical laws in biological research. A quiet, intense, driven man, unyielding in his scientific pursuits and convictions, extremely loyal to, and caring of, his colleagues, Brücke soon won Freud over, becoming his role model, mentor, and father figure. Later, in his autobiography, Freud wrote that in Brücke's laboratory he found "a sense of rest and satisfaction." In the next six years, he would spend days and nights working on exotic topics, including the morphology of the reproductive organs of eels and the structure and function of neurons of frogs, lamprey, and crayfish, in comparison to those of humans. Fervently pursuing these research projects in Brücke's laboratory, he neglected the clinical side of his education and delayed for three whole years his graduation from medical school.

Freud excelled in his laboratory research and authored a number of articles that were published in prestigious journals. His work was very much appreciated by Brücke, who was not prejudiced against Jews, which was still the case in many quarters of the Austrian capital at the time. However, the Department of Physiology had only two regular teaching positions, both already occupied. To make the matter even worse, there were several excellent senior researchers waiting in line who also coveted such a position, should one open up.

Advised by Brücke, Freud reluctantly started his clinical training. In the next two years, after rotating through surgery, internal medicine, and oto-rhinolaryngology (ENT – ear, nose, and throat), he entered the field of neuropsychiatry, where he found a new mentor in Theodor Hermann Meynert, a giant in the field, who also fostered the career of Sergei Korsakoff,[1] Carl Wernicke,[2] and Julius Wagner-Jauregg,[3] among many others.

Freud again worked exceedingly hard at Meynert's laboratory and made remarkable contributions to the field. These included the development of unique staining methods for brain tissues and investigations on the nature of aphasia. Unfortunately, competition for academic positions in this field was even more relentless and his training in neuroanatomy and neurophysiology did not distinguish him from his competitors.

Stymied from becoming a tenure-track professor at the university[4] and under mounting pressure to start and support a family, Freud saw no alter-natives other than entering into clinical practice, which had not been what he intended to do (Freud, 1963).

JOSEF BREUER, ANNA O., AND THE "TALKING CURE"

For the first decade of his practice, eking out a living in order to provide for a rapidly expanding family, as well as supporting his parents and sisters, was

---

[1] Korsakoff was a Russian neuropsychiatrist, known for his studies of alcoholic psychosis. Korsakoff's syndrome, named after him, is a condition characterized by profound amnesia and confabulation existing alongside relatively intact attention and consciousness.

[2] Wernicke was a prominent German neuropathologist who played a central role in localizing brain functions, especially speech. Wernicke's aphasia, named after him, characterizes patients who have difficulties understanding others' speech but can speak fluently, albeit lacking content or meaning.

[3] Julius Wagner-Jauregg succeeded Meynert and Richard von Krafft-Ebing as Chair of the Department of Psychiatry at the University of Vienna. He became a Nobel laureate in the fields of physiology and medicine in 1927 for his contributions in using malaria protozoans for the treatment of neuro-syphilis.

[4] Freud did remain a non-salaried faculty member at the university, first as a *docent* (lecturer) and later, in 1902, a *professor extraordinarius* (clinical professor). The latter was made possible with the intervention of one of his ex-patients, Baroness Marie Ferstel, who (supposedly) bribed the Minister of Education with a valuable painting (Crews, 2017).

a challenge. For years he worried about filling up his office hours and having enough income to make ends meet. Having a modest office in a building across from the *Rathaus* (City Hall), he soon shifted his practice to an apartment at the "famous" *Suhnhaus*,[5] rented initially with Martha's dowry, where they also resided for five years. In 1891, with the arrival of their third child, the Freuds moved to the more spacious Berggasse 19, a building made famous because it was where Freud lived and worked for the following five decades.

Out of financial necessity, Freud worked hard and could not afford to be picky, both in terms of patients and treatment methods. The therapeutic armamentaria at his disposal, as was true for other physicians at the time, were limited. They included electrical stimulation, hydrotherapy, rest, massage, nutritional manipulation (aimed at fattening the patients, who often gained more than 40 pounds), hypnosis, as well as the use of various potentially dangerous and highly addictive drugs, including morphine, chloral hydrate, and cocaine. He also referred patients to gynecologists specializing in performing hysterectomies and clitorectomies (Sheehan, 1981; Showalter, 1987), as well as procedures for inducing orgasms, either manually or with vibrators (Maines, 1999), for treating hysteria.

As is usually the case with most physicians starting a new practice, establishing a regular patient referral base was a huge challenge for Freud. In this he was lucky to have the help of Josef Breuer, his mentor and friend. Fourteen years his senior, Breuer was also Jewish. Like Freud, after working at the laboratories of both Brücke and Meynert, and authoring many significant research publications, he had also been unable to secure a regular teaching position at the university, and switched to a career of clinical practice. However, as a skilled and well-respected physician, he became the family doctor of many university professors, as well as the rich and powerful in Vienna, and had a busy and profitable practice.

Recognizing Freud's intelligence and talents, Breuer referred patients to him and provided financial assistance on many occasions without expecting repayment. In addition, Breuer also spent a great amount of time with Freud discussing various academic and clinical issues. At one of these get-togethers, Freud talked about the power of hypnosis in treating hysterical patients, which he had witnessed at the Salpêtrière Hospital while studying under Jean-Martin Charcot.[6] He was surprised that Breuer already had a great deal of

---

[5] Built on the site of the famous Ringtheater that had been burned down in 1881, with more than 400 casualties. Emperor Franz Joseph made this possible with his private funds and subsidized the rent to induce citizens with "worthy causes" to move in. The practical Martha persuaded a reluctant Freud to take up the offer.

[6] Dominating the emerging field of neurology in the late nineteenth century, Charcot is most well-known today for his work in hysteria and hypnosis. Freud studied with Charcot for close to five months with a fellowship in 1885–1886.

experience with hysteria[7] and had been using hypnosis to help such patients all along.

In the next ten years, their discussions crystalized in a book they co-authored, titled *Studies on Hysteria*. The book focused on one of Breuer's most remarkable patients, Bertha Pappenheim,[8] who was given Anna O. as a pseudonym in the book. She was the one who told Breuer that hypnosis was effective because it helped patients discover what they were unconscious of and did not want to know themselves. At some point, Bertha and Breuer found out that they did not even need to rely on hypnosis for this to happen. By just being able to talk freely, inhibition was reduced, allowing insightful material to emerge. Breuer called this *catharsis*; Pappenheim called it the "talking cure" and compared it to the sweeping of a chimney. These ideas became the foundation of practically all of the psychotherapeutic methods developed in the coming century (Kaplan, 2004; Launer, 2005).

Studies on Hysteria was well received and highly praised. But its publication also coincided with Freud's growing frustration and anger toward Breuer, eventually leading to the complete breakdown of their relationship. Part of this had to do with differences in their temperaments and theoretical orientations.

While Breuer agreed with Freud that traumatic life experiences represented important factors leading to the development of hysteria, and that sexual conflicts often plagued these patients, he could not go along with Freud's singling out sex as not only the predominant, but the *only*, cause of hysteria. Breuer insisted that other kinds of trauma could be equally damaging. He also did not want to brush aside the importance of genetic predispositions and neurobiological mechanisms that may underlie the condition.

Many years later, reflecting upon their conflicts, Breuer stated in a letter to a colleague that "Freud is a man given to absolute and exclusive formulations: this is a psychical need which, in my opinion, leads to excessive generalization" (quoted by Breger, 2009). Freud actually agreed with him, as reflected

---

[7] Due to the imprecise nature of the term, its historical roots, and its negative connotations, *hysteria* not only is no longer an official diagnostic category, but is generally not used in professional circles. However, during the late nineteenth century and early twentieth centuries, it was a widely used clinical label and a serious subject for research and intellectual discussion. The term is thus used throughout the book to reflect the historical reality.

[8] Bertha Pappenheim developed a wide variety of classical hysterical symptoms after her father fell ill and she became the main caregiver. Her condition further worsened after her father's death in the following year. Her condition fluctuated over the course of two years under Breuer's care, during which Breuer visited her at home on a daily basis. In 1882, the treatment was terminated abruptly. Although reported as "cured" in *Studies on Hysteria*, she actually continued to suffer from severe symptoms and was incarcerated most of the time at renowned psychiatric facilities until 1888 (age twenty-nine). However, she apparently become well once moved to Frankfurt, and became a productive writer of novels and plays, a vocal feminist, a leader in social welfare and reform, and the founder of the Jewish Women's Association, the largest charitable Jewish organization of the early twentieth century (Freeman, 1990; Kaplan, 2004).

in his letter to Fliess in 1896: "I believe he will never forgive that in the *Studies* I dragged him along and involved him in something where he unfailingly knows three candidates for the position of *one truth* and abhors all generalizations, regarding them as presumptuous" (Masson, 1985).

From our vantage point, Breuer's position seems completely reasonable, whereas Freud's might be regarded as one-sided, simplistic, *mechanistic*, and *reductionistic*. Yet, no matter how weary we may be about being misled by *reductionism*, it has been the driving force behind the remarkable progress in natural science in the past several centuries. It could thus be argued that it was Freud's single-mindedness in searching for *the one and only truth* that propelled the exploration of the unconscious mind in the years to come. Convictions and generalizations, whether right or wrong, are needed for us to move into previously uncharted water.

In this sense, Freud was not unlike Christopher Columbus, sailing west searching for India and instead finding the New World, paving the way for the *conquistadors* to alter the course of human history. And that was actually how Freud saw himself, a conquistador of the mind.

"NOTHING BUT A CONQUISTADOR"

In 1900, Freud wrote to his then friend and confidant Wilhelm Fliess: "I am actually *not at all a man of science, not an observer, not an experimenter, not a thinker.* I am by temperament *nothing but a conquistador*" (Goleman, 1985; Masson, 1985). The disclaimer about his not being a *scientist* and a *thinker* was peculiar and caused a great deal of speculation by Freudian scholars in the years to come. The denial of having been *an observer and experimenter* was even more puzzling. After all, in his youthful days, Freud had spent more than a decade working at "hard core" biological laboratories and making substantive contributions as well. Such vehement denials were also reflected in his life-long reticence about his earlier "biological" research activities. Publications from that period of his life were rarely referred to and were not included in his *Complete Works* (Strachey, 1953).

More telling was his insistence on being a *conquistador*. For most people, after having sacrificed so much comfort and worldly rewards for the sake of an academic career, the natural course to take would have been giving up the dream of becoming an adventurer, a conqueror.

But not Freud. The *golden Sigi* in him would not go away, and he held on to the belief that he would still one day become *a man most mighty*. Against all odds, he continued to search for ways to make earth-shattering discoveries. Rather like *Don Quixote*, the fictional character of Cervantes he deeply adored (Boehlich, 1992; Borch-Jacobsen & Shamdasani, 2012; López-Muñoz, Pérez-Fernández, Álamo, & García-García, 2017), Freud went on fighting one windmill after another, each time believing that he had seen through the disguise and slain the dragon. Like *Don Quixote*, each time he formulated a new theory, he went after it all the way, tried his best to convince others of its veracity, and was deeply disappointed and hurt when the "truth" of his findings was not appreciated. This was the case with his long romance with cocaine. It was even more evident when it comes to the famed "Freud's Seduction Theory" (Robinson, 1993).

Lest we dismiss Freud's ideas about sexuality and the "Seduction Theory" too readily as unbelievably naive and simplistic for us, let us remember that Freud lived in an exciting time when major scientific breakthroughs were taking place in various fields: elegant mathematical models were developed to predict electric and magnetic forces; Darwinian evolutionary theories provided a deceptively "simple" framework linking biodiversity with geology, paleontology, and embryology. In medicine, germ theories developed by Louis Pasteur and Robert Koch paved the way for identifying, treating, and preventing a large number of infectious diseases, including neurosyphilis, responsible for one-third of those incarcerated in asylums, masquerading as psychiatric patients.

So, if grand, unifying theories could be formulated to help us understand and deal with so many natural phenomena, why could it not be so in the realm of the human mind? Why should we not be able to formulate an all-encompassing theory that would help us get to the root of all cases of hysteria?

This was the background of Seduction Theory, formulated by Freud to solve the mysteries of hysteria. In three public lectures he delivered in 1886, he proposed that *all* hysterical and obsessive-compulsive patients had been traumatized by sexual abuse in their childhood, typically by their own fathers, but the memories of these events had been *repressed* because they were too painful to be retained in the conscious mind. However, suppressed or repressed, these memories continued to exist in the substrata of the patients' minds, which were later expressed indirectly as symptoms.

His lectures stirred up a great deal of animosity. Many of his colleagues, including his former mentor Meynert, regarded them as jokes. Although all abstracts of university lectures were published in conference proceedings as a rule, those for his presentations were conspicuously missing.

Freud was furious at his colleagues and "the establishment." However, the person bearing most of his anger was Josef Breuer. Isolated and dejected, Freud heaped all his anger upon Breuer, cut him off completely, and pretended that Breuer did not even exist whenever they passed each other on the street. This breaking up coincided roughly with the beginning of his "Splendid Isolation."

INTO THE "SPLENDID ISOLATION"

Starting in the mid-1890s, Freud's "Splendid Isolation" lasted for over a decade. He could have used the term as a jest, but the pain caused by such isolation was so raw, so plainly visible. As Ernest Jones (1955) said, "There is ample evidence that for ten years or so, roughly comprising the nineties, he suffered from a very considerable psychoneurosis ... His sufferings were at times very intense, and for those ten years there could have been only occasional intervals when life seemed much worth living ... In the depressed moods he could neither write nor concentrate his thoughts ... He would spend leisure hours of extreme boredom, turning from one thing to another, cutting open books, looking at maps of ancient Pompeii, playing patience or chess, but being unable to continue at anything for long, a state of restless paralysis."

Why so much misery?

For one thing, after having thoroughly offended his colleagues, and making an enemy of the clueless Breuer, Freud started having doubts about his Seduction Theory. His reasons for this change of mind, including the "impossibility of the high prevalence of paternal sexual abuse" and the relative rarity of such reports among psychotic patients less likely to repress their childhood trauma, were less than convincing (Izenberg, 1991). On the other hand, the Machiavellian motivation proposed by Masson (1984) and others, of Freud's need to "cover up the truth" in order to please his colleagues, runs counter to our image of Freud as a proudly independent thinker. Masson's accusation also does not make sense, since the theory he next came up with, "infantile sexuality," was every bit as shocking to his peers, if not even more so.

Once Freud shifted the focus of his attention from adult perpetrators of abuse to the fantasy lives of children, he stumbled into totally uncharted territories, leading to the development of the framework of psychosexual development. Again, one may take exception with the theory's hidden *biological, deterministic* orientation, but it did provide us with a workable model, totally new at the time. Freud the *conquistador* was not interested in ambiguities and qualifications, which he regarded as noise and distractions interfering with the construction of his new edifice. In the parlance of Thomas Kuhn (1962), he was not interested in doing "normal science" (elaboration and validation of theories). His passion was in making "paradigm shifts" (formulation of earth-shattering new theories).

The price to pay for such new discoveries was steep. If Seduction Theory was met with indifference and ridicule, *infantile sexuality* was dealt with as a scandal. Children were supposed to be innocent; childhood was supposed to be happy. Now Freud wanted to impute stormy *sexual* desires to them, making them struggle from the day they were born. If this was not cruelty, what was? And, how did these new insights help patients?

Thinking back about those years, Freud often raged against his colleagues and the powers that be in academia for marginalizing him, which was certainly true. But there was no denying that, to a large extent, Freud also brought the isolation and rejection upon himself. Further more, although undoubtedly very painful, such isolation actually might have freed him to express his creativity and productivity during this period of his life. No longer seeking his university colleagues' validation, he was free to explore the concepts of repression and the unconscious mind, both essential for the theory of *infantile sexuality* to make sense.

SOUL MATE

Freud survived his "Splendid Isolation" because he found a "soul mate" in Wilhelm Fliess, a flamboyant ENT doctor based in Berlin. Wilhelm Fliess shared with Freud two major beliefs: They both appreciated the important role "sex" played in health; and they were both regular users and active promoters of cocaine.

In their more than 300 correspondences spanning over 17 years (Masson, 1985), Freud was free to ramble about many of his ideas that were still being developed, share drafts of his papers, discuss patients' symptoms, and report the fluctuations of his own moods and his obsessive fear of impending demise. He was spellbound by Fliess' theories on bisexuality and on the links between nasal cavities and sexual organs. He also was convinced by Fliess that, just like women, men had their periods, although it was twenty-three instead of twenty-eight days.

Falling under Fliess' spell, Freud kept himself busy using his numerological calculation methods to determine how many more years he still had to live. Convinced by his that he had been suffering from various symptoms because something was wrong with his nose, he also asked him to perform several nasal operations on him.

Fortunately, there eventually came a turning point when Freud finally outgrew Fliess. This was probably bound to happen as Freud gradually re-emerged from his "Splendid Isolation," and needed less support and validation from Fliess. It was also precipitated by what happened to one of his patients, Emma Eckstein. Emma was a particularly challenging patient who hadn't improved after three whole years of therapy with Freud. At his wits' end, Freud asked Fliess to come to Vienna to perform an operation on Emma, hoping for a miracle cure of her hysterical symptoms. Fliess came and went in a breeze, leaving a long gauze hidden deep inside Emma's nasal cavity. Several days after the operation she started suffering from massive bleeding and almost died (Sulloway, 1992). Fortunately, the cause of the bleeding was eventually discovered, but, after the removal of the gauze, the bleeding persisted intermittently, and was followed by infection. Because of these complications, Emma was bed-ridden for several months. Freud did not seem to blame Fliess for negligence and even wrote to reassure him, saying: "I should not have made you come all the way to perform surgery in an unfamiliar setting." But this incident cooled his enthusiasm about Fliess' "magical cures," and he started to distance himself, eventually completely breaking off the friendship.

"MID-LIFE CRISIS" AND THE EMERGENCE OF THE MASTER

While struggling with his professional life, Freud was also under siege on the home front. Ten years after their marriage, Martha was weighed down not only by her own (and Freud's) high standard of homemaking, but also by the rapid arrival of six children. Their relationship was further complicated by the situation with Minna, Martha's younger sister, who moved in and occupied a small bedroom off the master bedroom, sharing with them a bathroom located on the opposite side. As a chronic insomniac, Minna used the bathroom often during the night, passing by their bed all the time. In Freud's letters to Fliess, he hinted at long stretches of abstinence. Although he blamed this on the lack of viable means for effective birth control, the living arrangement with Minna's constant presence could not have helped.

The relationship between Freud and his wife became strained, distant, and stale (Behling, 2005). After the birth of their youngest daughter, Anna, Martha suffered from postpartum depression, reflecting their marital discord.

The death of his father, Jakob, in 1896 was the straw that broke the camel's back. Several years later Freud wrote that he was surprised by the vehemence of "my reaction to my father's death – that is to say, to the most important event, the most poignant loss, of a man's life." Given his deep-seated ambivalence regarding his father, his grief must have been profound, and his reaction to the loss may have verged on pathological. It was thus no doubt a major crisis in his life. But it was far from the only one confronting him at the time.

Commenting on Freud's mid-life crisis, Jones (1955) said: "An admirer might be tempted to paint this in the darkest colors so as to emphasize by way of relief Freud's achievement of self-mastery . . . After all, in the worst times Freud never ceased to function."

Jones was right. Freud not only survived, but also thrived. With so many doors closed, what was left for him was his patients and himself. Applying his amazing power of observation to himself and to his patients, day after day, night after night, he gradually began to see that, above and beyond its role in causing pathological symptoms, the "unconscious mind" was also constantly operative in determining our daily behavior and acts, our fears and preferences, and even the contents of our dreams (Gay, 2006; Jones, 1953, 1955, 1957; Rieff, 1979; Tauber, 2010).

These observations and theorizations became the basis of a number of his most enduring contributions, including *The Interpretation of Dreams*, *Psychopathology of Everyday Life*, and *Jokes and Their Relation to the*

Unconscious. These publications in turn attracted a group of like-minded followers. Soon, the "psychoanalytic movement" was born.

Retrospectively, it is clear that if Freud's academic career had been "successful," if he had not been marginalized by his colleagues, if he had not broken with Breuer, and if he had continued to indulge himself in the morass of Fliess' nasal and "periodical" theories, Freud would not have been freed to wander into the realm of the "unconscious," leading the world in a brand new direction.

We might say that, at the age of forty, Freud was confronted by a "mid-life crisis" that led to his discoveries and contributions, reshaping the modern world. It seems like a "mid-life crisis" is not necessarily a bad thing, at least for some people, some of the time!

THE REVENGE OF THE CIGAR

It is commonly believed that the famous quote "Sometimes a cigar is just a cigar" came from Freud when a brave soul dared to question the symbolic meaning of his attachment to cigars (Quote Investigator, 2011). According to his theories, his dependence on cigars could be an expression of his ungratified oral need in his childhood (which no doubt had been the case). However, who would dare to apply such theories to the Master himself!

Yet, a cigar is indeed a cigar when it comes to its nicotine content. Once hooked, achieving abstinence or moderation can be very difficult. The problem is far from just the nicotine. Like cigarettes, cigars are made of tobacco, which contain numerous carcinogens. After forty years of continuous exposure to these toxic substances, oral cancer finally caught up with Freud.

Many surgeries and unsatisfactory dental fittings later, Freud continued to suffer from unbearable pain. He stubbornly refused the aid of opioids. We do not know if this was because he was guarding against his inclination toward addiction, but we are grateful all the same for his vigilance for the clarity of his mind, enabling him to stay productive until the last minute of his life, leaving us with ideas and theories that continue to inspire and confuse us, even after a whole century has come and gone.

2

A Most Dangerous Method

Jung and Freud, Entangled in Life and Death

I first saw the book *A Most Dangerous Method: The Story of Jung, Freud and Sabina Spielrein* (Kerr, 1993) on the New Arrivals shelf of a Borders bookstore in that 1993. Almost two decades later, following the release of the movie *A Dangerous Method* (Cronenberg, 2011), it resurfaced in most book outlets. I was puzzled by the omission of the word "most" in the movie's title. Does the omission make the title less threatening? Did the producer of the movie want to minimize controversial reactions from mental health professionals?

Although I had been fascinated and confused by the complicated relationships between Jung and Freud since my college days, what I had known about the topic was limited and superficial before reading the book. For decades, Jung was a fascinating mystery for me. Reading Jung was not unlike looking at flowers shrouded in mist. Kerr's book helped me to see Jung as a person, and to understand how his personal background influenced his ideas and theories.

"MEETING OF THE MINDS" IN THE ERA OF FIN DE SIÈCLE

Thinking about Jung's life and career, it is not unreasonable to see his first meeting with Freud in 1907 as a watershed year. Around that time, the theories of Freud, now fifty years old, had finally started to attract attention from the academic community. Along with the fame also came more intense controversy and hostility.

In contrast, although Jung was just over thirty, he had been working with one of the leading psychiatrists in the world, Eugen Bleuler, for years and was regarded as Bleuler's right-hand man at the Burghölzli Hospital, the premier psychiatric teaching hospital of the University of Zurich.

Jung was exceptionally energetic and talented, and his studies on word association had made him widely known by psychiatric and psychological researchers in Europe and the USA. The study was originally designed to collect comparative information on "normal controls" in their responses to a set of words, as compared to those collected from psychiatric patients. Jung and Bleuler hoped that such comparisons would help to elucidate how patients' thought processes might differ from those of "normals."

In the process of conducting the study, Jung was surprised by how little the "normal" subjects understood why and how their thoughts flew from one to another. Using a stopwatch to measure the galvanic skin response, he found that subjects' reaction times were very much affected by the emotions that were elicited by the words used in the study. These results suggested that many things were going on in the human mind that were outside our conscious awareness, and human behavior was often influenced by forces that were perhaps beyond our "rational" comprehension.

What was the nature of these forces? Bleuler suggested that Jung pay attention to Freud's publications. As an expert on psychopathology, Bleuler was at least as influential as Emil Kraepelin, later commonly regarded as the "father" of modern psychiatry. Schizophrenia, the term Bleuler coined for one of the most devastating psychiatric conditions, even replaced dementia praecox, the one favored by Kraepelin, to become the standard term for the condition for the coming century.

Born only one year later than Freud and Kraepelin, Bleuler also went to Paris in 1884 to study with Jean-Martin Charcot, a year before Freud's visit. There, just like Freud, he witnessed the dramatic power of hypnosis on hysterical patients. Although his work since returning from Paris had kept him busy in the psychiatric asylum systems where he did not primarily take care of hysterical or neurotic patients, he continued to be interested in the phenomena associated with hypnosis and hypnotic suggestion. He had read Freud's first book, *Studies on Hysteria* (Breuer & Freud, 1955), with great interest, and regarded it as a valuable contribution to the field. Freud's *The Interpretation of Dreams* (Freud, 1911), published in 1900, further convinced him that, although Freud was technically a neuroscientist and a neurologist in private practice, rather than someone with formal training in the field of psychiatry, his ideas were exceptionally creative and worth paying attention to.

Thus, Bleuler started organizing study groups to discuss Freudian theories, and he formally contacted Freud. Overjoyed, Freud suggested that he could become Bleuler's "long-distance" psychoanalyst, via written correspondence. This reflected Freud's eagerness to disseminate his ideas through the University of Zurich.

On the other side, Bleuler's intention was quite different. He entered the correspondence hoping to gain personal experiences of the new method in order to determine the soundness of Freud's theories and their practical utility.

In the following five years, Freud and Bleuler wrote regularly to each other. With little reservation, Bleuler provided a large volume of his personal and family materials, and detailed descriptions of many of his dreams. However, from time to time he complained about not having been able to understand Freud's analysis of his personal life and objected to Freud demanding total acceptance of his theories. In response to Bleuler's complaints, Freud suggested that these were signs of his *resistance*, a new idea that further baffled Bleuler. In addition to these differences were many other factors, leading to their eventual "breakup" in 1912. But, given all the differences in their backgrounds and orientations, the relationship was likely doomed from the beginning.

It was during those ten years of "honeymoon" between Zurich and Vienna that Jung was transformed from a skeptic to a devotee of the Freudian project. Reading *The Interpretation of Dreams* for the first time as recommended by Bleuler, Jung at first thought it was an outsider's mumbo jumbo. In 1904, he half-heartedly tried Freud's "talk therapy" on a very challenging patient (Sabina Spielrein, discussed later) and was surprised by its results. Even two years after that, he still remained unconvinced as to Freudian methods' place in the care of patients. In the preface of his book, *The Psychology of Dementia Praecox*, published in 1906, he praised the "excellent conceptions" of Freudian theories but also emphasized that theories should not be turned into dogmas, and specifically stated that he was unable to agree with the idea of "infantile sexuality."

Urged by Bleuler, he went to Vienna in 1907 to pay Freud a visit. He was totally unprepared for what was to happen and was surprised by how much he clicked with Freud. From one o'clock in the afternoon until two the next morning, the two of them talked nonstop for thirteen hours. Many years later, when Jung recalled this once-in-a-lifetime "meeting of the minds," he said: "Freud was the first man of real importance I had encountered; in my experience up to then no one else compared with him. There was nothing the least trivial in his attitude. I found him extremely intelligent, shrewd, and all together remarkable. And yet my first impressions of him remain somewhat entangled; I could not make him out." (Jung & Jaffe, 1962).

Before taking his leave, Jung again expressed his doubt regarding the validity of the theory of "infantile sexuality," but he readily "lost the argument." Prior to his departure, when Jung also gathered up his courage to talk about his fascination with the soul and his own psychic experiences, Freud demanded that he "should not throw away the theories on sexuality," and he "should not waste his life on things that could not be seen and touched."

Thus began the life-long entanglement between Jung and Freud. Over the next five years, they exchanged more than 700 letters (Freud & Jung, 1994), passionate and unreserved, but at the same time also calculating and manipulative.

OEDIPUS FOUND LAIUS, OR WAS IT THE OTHER WAY AROUND?

At the time they met, Freud was searching for a "son." Conversely, whether Jung knew it or not, he had also been looking for a "father" for many years. They found what they wanted in each other. It's no wonder that from the moment they first met their relationship was so intense, and it soon became all-consuming. To Freud, Jung was a "gift from heaven." He was amazingly smart, full of energy, and even at such a young age he had already started to achieve international fame.

Even more importantly, Jung was not Jewish. He was the one who would be able to prove to the world that the fledgling psychoanalytic movement was not just a brand of "Jewish psychology," but was universally applicable to people with divergent cultural roots.

At the other end, why was Jung searching for a father? For an answer to this question, we need to look into Jung's childhood.

As an only child, Jung had a lonely childhood (Bair, 2003). Although he had three older brothers, they all died in infancy. His father was a not-very-successful country pastor, but his mother came from a patrician family in Basel, and she never liked living in the countryside. She was chronically unhappy and constantly in and out of hospitals for problems nobody ever understood, gone for months at a time. Jung was dropped off at her parents' place and taken care of by a spinster aunt. Even when his mother was at home, she was withdrawn and distant, often cloistering herself in her own room, refusing to leave home for any reason (Smith, 1996).

Even though his grandfather on his mother's side was a famous minister, almost all the members of that family were gifted with psychic power, and they often got together to discuss their experiences of possession by spiritual beings, as well as other supernatural phenomena. Jung envied his cousins' ability to communicate with the deceased, but he was also frightened by such experiences. Vacillating between believing and questioning, he was unable to make up his mind one way or another (Lachman, 2010).

During childhood, Jung's main support had come from his father. But when he entered adolescence and started to search for the meaning of life and the mystery of the universe, he was disappointed by his father's answer: "He told me not to think, just believe."

Disillusioned, he distanced himself from his father and the church. At the age of twenty, when his father was on his deathbed, Jung was so preoccupied with his observation and recording of what the "ghosts" possessing his cousins did and said that he was not able to be with his father in the last moments of his life.

In 1907, Jung might not have known that for quite some time he had been searching for an "ideal father," but looking from the outside it seems clear that this had long been the case, consciously or unconsciously. His search ended with Freud. In many of the letters he wrote to Freud, he went out of his way to please the older man, often so blatantly solicitous and syrupy the reader could almost feel his longing and heartache. On several occasions he even came out to admit that he had homosexual fantasies about Freud.

At times Freud chided Jung mildly in his letters, either because Jung over-interpreted Freud's theories or because he could not resist expressing his fascination with spiritual phenomena and metaphysical issues. Whenever that happened, Jung retreated immediately, apologizing profusely for straying away from Freud's ideas. Thus, even though he proclaimed being completely candid with Freud, he often needed to hide his thoughts, keeping part of what was going on in his life away from Freud in order to avoid criticism.

Why was Jung so accommodating to Freud? One might think that he needed Freud to help promote his career. But that was just not the case. Although Jung was still relatively young at the time, he was already well situated academically, and did not need Freud's support to move forward. On the contrary, it was exactly his involvement with Freud that fatally stalled his academic career. This is reflected in what he said in his memoir (Jung & Jaffe, 1962): "When I became acquainted with his work, I was planning an academic career . . . But Freud was definitely *persona non grata* in the academic world at the time, and any connection with him would have been damaging in scientific circles."

It was true that he became the president of the newly established International Psychoanalytic Society because of Freud's support (Freud originally wanted him to be president-for-life, but was forced to withdraw this proposal due to opposition from his Viennese followers), but it was not as if Freud had another choice. Compared to his Vienna circle, Zurich at that time was much more open and international. Even before Alfred Adler rebelled and left in 1911, along with almost half of the members in Vienna, Zurich had already become much more prominent in the psychoanalytic movement, with more members, who were also more talented and active. It would not be far-fetched to say that at that time Freud needed Jung more than the other way around. So, it did not matter how jealous Freud's Jewish followers were, Jung was Freud's only choice as his heir apparent.

WHO FAINTED?

But, just as the concept of the Oedipus Complex implies, a powerful son is the biggest threat to the father. It is therefore no wonder that in Freud's letters to Jung there was also a great deal of scheming and distortions of reality. Such incredible tension was most clearly and dramatically revealed in Freud's two fainting episodes (Becker, 1997).

The first time Freud fainted in front of Jung was when they were on their way to the USA to lecture at Clark University (Worcester, Massachusetts). While they were waiting at Bremen for their transatlantic voyage, Jung became fascinated by the recently discovered "bog men" unearthed in many parts of Northern Europe. Jung speculated that they were the ancestors of modern Europeans. On the ship, he continued to be obsessed with these mummies, and brought thee topic up often in his conversations with Freud. One day after dinner, when he did it again, Freud said abruptly, "You are so interested in these dead people because you have a death wish toward me." Then he fainted.

Why did this happen? Maybe Freud was thinking that these bog men were Aryans, not Jewish. So, by focusing on them, Jung was distancing himself from Freud, his Jewish "father."

The American tours were successful for both of them. At Clark University, Freud received an honorary doctoral degree. A number of leading American psychologists, including William James (see Chapter 15), participated in the event. Freud's five lectures, delivered in German, were immediately translated into English and published in the *American Journal of Psychology*.

In addition to speaking at Clark University, Jung was also invited to lecture at Fordham University in New York. The success of his lectures led to an invitation to return as a visiting professor for six weeks in the coming year, which he accepted with gusto.

On their voyage back to Europe, the conflicts between Freud and Jung resurfaced and worsened. While on the ship they kept analyzing each other's dreams, and, according to Jung, at one time when they were talking about a particular dream of Freud's, Freud suddenly stopped, became quiet for a long while, and then said that he could not reveal something about himself because he needed to protect his own authority.

Just like many couples who do not get along, the conflicts between Jung and Freud submerged and resurfaced time and again, eventually leading to Freud's second fainting spell in 1912. After this, their fights came out in the open. Several sharp and curt letters later, Freud finally made up his mind to "break up" with Jung.

The famous second fainting of Freud's also had something to do with archeology. It took place at the psychoanalytic conference in Munich, with many leaders of the psychoanalytic movement in the room. After lunch, someone started talking about the Egyptian Pharaoh Akhenaten (reigned 1353–1336 BC; named Amenophis IV before the fifth year of his reign), who had changed the state's religious practices. For the first time in human history, the young pharaoh asserted that there was only one god, and thus started the tradition of monotheism.

When the father complex was brought up as an explanation for the pharaoh's motivation for the changes, Jung protested vigorously. He argued that the innovation was due to Akhenaten's creativity and originality, not just a result of his rebellion against his father. He went on to say that Akhenaten had great respect for his own father but felt compelled to destroy his father's idols for the sake of the "Truth." Furthermore, Jung said that, even though the other pharaohs did not dismantle their progenitors' statues, without exception they all erased their predecessors' names and replaced them with their own, wiping out traces of their elders.

Immediately after Jung finished his thoughts, Freud slipped from his chair and became unconscious. Jung picked him up and placed him on a couch. It took quite a while for Freud to regain consciousness, upon which he said: "If death could be this sweet, why not?"

In reality, between the two of them, it was Jung who was more prone to fainting. At the age of twelve, after having been beaten up by a classmate, he started having frequent fainting spells and was thought to be epileptic. What is amazing is that in the drawn-out process of his "rebelling" against his "father," Jung was not the one to fade out. One might speculate that at the time he was too busy fighting and had no inkling of how serious it was going to be once he was deserted by his "father."

BLAME EVERYTHING ON THE SIREN

But, of course, anyone is free to blame the siren, the femme fatale, the Helen bringing down Troy. The siren in this case was a young woman, Sabina Spielrein (Carotenuto, 1982; Kerr, 1993; Launer, 2014), who became Jung's first test case for trying out psychoanalysis soon after her admission to the Burghölzli Hospital in 1904. The eighteen-year-old Sabina was a petite, brainy, sentimental, and exotic Jewish girl from Crimea.

Jung was surprised that, with Sabina, psychoanalysis indeed worked miracles. Sabina's recalcitrant hysterical symptoms quickly disappeared. However, at the same time, she also fell madly in love with him. As a newlywed who cared about his own reputation, Jung did not know how to respond to this alluring young woman. He successfully suppressed his desires, and instead persuaded her to enroll at the University of Zurich to study medicine.

Several years later, Sabina again became Jung's patient and again immediately fell in love with him. She fantasized about bearing a child of his, with mixed Jewish and Aryan blood, who would grow up to be the savior of the world. Jung vacillated between lust and guilt. Caught between bliss and self-blame, he was unable to pull himself away because "she had taken his unconscious into her hands."

The stormy affair continued for seven months, and might have persisted further, save for the intervention of Jung's wife and Sabina's mother. Deeply hurt, Sabina wrote to Freud to ask for help, but Jung categorically denied any of her accusations, instead blaming her for trying to seduce him, claiming that anything she said was pure fantasy. Freud stayed neutral, not wanting to offend either party. However, several years later, after he had "broken up" with Jung, and after Sabina was married and pregnant, Freud said to her: "At the end, we are and remain Jews. The others will only exploit us and will never understand or appreciate us."

What had happened with Jung between these two encounters with Sabina? Although there are no definitive or simple answers, Otto Gross (Heuer, 2016) certainly played an important role. Not yet thirty, Gross was already widely regarded as a genius in psychoanalytical circles. Passionate and perceptive, he won people's trust as soon as they met him. He was also very much a playboy, a drifter, and a morphine and cocaine addict. Using cafes and bars as his "offices," day and night he rubbed shoulders with *avant-garde* writers and artists, administering therapies on the spot and on demand, for free. The cafes and bars also provided him with platforms to seduce multitudes of glamorous women from high society, including the von Richthofen sisters.[1]

Otto was the only son of Hans Gross, an internationally renowned expert on criminology. Watching Otto's speedy descent into hell, Hans became increasingly alarmed, and stepped in to intervene. When he wrote to Bleuler and Freud at the same time to ask for help, both recommended Jung. Although Jung strongly disliked Gross at the time, he could not say no to these father figures of his, and reluctantly admitted Gross into the Burghölzli Hospital.

Soon after Jung started analyzing Gross, their relationship reversed. They found that they had many things in common: both worshipped Nietzsche and Freud, and both held the faith that psychoanalysis was going to revolutionize the world. In this process, Jung learned something new from Gross that shocked him, but also kept him spellbound: Gross convinced him that, whether you look at it from the evolutionary or psychoanalytical angle, untethered sexual freedom was part and parcel of human nature. Monogamy, said Gross, was imposed by society and was the source of misery and illness for individuals.

When you put two geniuses together, there is no way to tell who is going to influence whom. In this instance, Jung lost the contest. He lost, first of all, because his "patient" Gross eventually jumped over the hospital's fence and

---

[1] Baronesses Else von Richthofen and Freida von Richthofen (Green, 1974). Both had affairs with Otto Gross around the same time while married to others. Freida later deserted her husband and three children and ran away with the famous writer D. H. Lawrence. She was the inspiration for his controversial novel, *Lady Chatterley's Lover*. Else was the first female German social scientist with a PhD in economics. She had been married to Edgar Jaffé (an industrialist and economist who later served as Germany's minister of finance), with three children, when she fell in love with Gross and had a fourth child. She later had an affair with Max Weber, one of the founders of modern sociology, and Max's younger brother, Alfred Weber, with whom she lived after Jaffé's death. Alfred is known as one of the founders of modern economic geography.

escaped after six months of incarceration, leaving Jung holding the bag. More seriously, even though Gross was physically gone, the idea of polygamy had become deeply rooted in Jung's mind. Was Jung "brainwashed" by Gross? Or had such inclinations long been dormant in Jung's mind, Gross having only served to remove the inhibition?

Gross did not really win after all. His health and life went steadily downhill after his escape, and he ended up destitute a few years later. Homeless and broken, he died in the gutter in Berlin (1920).

JUNG'S COLLAPSE AND RECOVERY

When Freud decided to "break up" with Jung, Jung was still the president of the International Society of Psychoanalysis. In addition, as editor-in-chief of the Society's journal, he wielded enormous power. In order to carry out the *coup d'état*, Freud's most faithful followers organized a Secret Committee (Grosskurth, 1991) (see also Chapters 4 and 6),[2] whose first task was to persuade branch societies to leave the international society. But most member societies were confused about what this situation was really about, and they remained equivocal and indecisive. Even at the fourth International Psychoanalytic Conference, held in Munich in September 1913, Jung was re-elected president (he received more than fifty votes, but some twenty delegates abstained from voting). Those who voted for Jung were not necessarily his sympathizers, but they felt all Jung wanted was for the Society to tolerate different opinions and voices, and that there was nothing wrong with such a policy.

Yet, soon after this victory, Jung abruptly quit his position and withdrew completely from the organization. Why?

Jung had not expected himself to be so fragile. His self-confidence suddenly disappeared after his "rejection" by Freud. All of a sudden, he realized that he did not really know who he was.

He had firmly believed that since antiquity, "mythology" was indispensable for human existence. Now he found that he had no idea what the myths were that were sustaining modern men, let alone his own myths. He was no longer a Christian, but he did not yet have a belief system to bolster his existence.

---

[2] After Jung broke away in 1912, Ernest Jones recommended to Freud that he should create a group of loyal psychoanalysts who would privately discuss any question of departure from "any of the fundamental tenets of psychoanalytical theory." The group initially consisted of five members – Jones, Sándor Ferenczi, Otto Rank, Hans Sachs, and Karl Abraham – all of whom were given a golden ring by Freud. Max Eitingon was added to the committee in 1919. The committee was dissolved in 1924 over the dissension involving Rank and Ferenczi but reconstituted the same year with the addition of Anna Freud.

No matter how hard he tried, he was unable to find answers to these fundamental questions. Becoming increasingly anxious and irritable, he started experiencing auditory and visual hallucinations. Everywhere he looked, he saw corpses being burned in furnaces – the dead, whose souls had already been released, perished again and again. He saw floods rushing from the North Sea, all the way up the Alps, putting the whole European continent under water (except Switzerland, because the flood somehow pushed the Alps even higher). Countless corpses floated every which way, along with enormous amounts of garbage. Then the flood turned into blood.

Soon afterwards, World War I erupted, and many of his hallucinations became reality. One night he dreamed of himself murdering Siegfried, one of the most worshipped heroes in German mythology. In his mind, this meant that he should die. Waking up, he found a loaded gun on his nightstand.

Over the next few years, the hallucinations and nightmares kept coming. As a patient, he was scared to death; as a physician, he knew he was on the verge of free fall; and as a scientist, he was busy recording the details of these visions and dreams. These documents were later compiled into several obscure and strange books, including *The Seven Sermons to the Dead* (Jung, 1916), which remained unavailable to most of his followers, let alone the public, until many years later.

However, the most puzzling and amazing opus was a handwritten book called *Liber Novus*, commonly referred to as *The Red Book* because of its red leather covers. For a long time this book had been kept a secret, rarely seen by outsiders, but in 2009 it was published and made available to the general public (Jung, 2009). Weighing more than 10 lb, the book contains more than 400 folio-sized pages, each crowded with line after line of carefully calligraphed, multi-colored verses. In addition, there were more than 100 large panels of vivid, multi-colored illustrations made with gouache paints, pregnant with symbolism and not easily deciphered by the uninitiated. No matter what you make of it, even just flipping through the pages one is awed by the boundless vitality and creativity of the author.

In this way, writing and painting provided support and rescued him, sustaining the connection between his inner and outer worlds. With these activities, he was able to examine and restructure his experiences and memories, through which he continued to search for order and meaning. And this must be why and how Jung was eventually able to escape from his "madness."

Progressing in this manner, he gradually came to believe that, rather than being a victim of frightful visions and horrific dreams, he was actually an exceptionally brave soul intentionally engaging in a process of "active imagination" in order to understand his "real" self and enter a more elevated realm of his life. By voluntarily jumping into that dark, bottomless chasm, he entered the world of the deceased and was "reborn." It hardly matters whether this narrative was "true" or a product of retrospective justifications. What is important is that to him this view was meaningful and uplifting.

Jung later said that during those years he had lost almost all of the things that were most dear to him. Rejected by his mentors and confidants, he lost his university position and social status. Fortunately, he still had his family and his patients. One could say that these were more than enough, and Jung was indeed a lucky man. His wife, Emma Jung (Clay, 2016), stood firmly by him all her life. Their five children were all healthy, intelligent, and likable. Coming from a well-to-do family, Emma made sure that the family never had to worry about financial concerns. They not only lived in a luxurious mansion, but her fortune provided the means for Jung to build a "primitive stone house" with no water or electricity, at the lakeside twenty miles from town, which he used as a retreat where he could meditate and be in touch with nature (Dunne, 2000).

Mad or not, he remained charismatic to his patients, especially female patients, and continued to be regarded internationally as one of the most talented psychotherapists. Many of his patients were women of wealthy backgrounds and huge fortunes, including Fanny Bowditch Katz[3] and Edith Rockefeller McCormick.[4]

In order to receive treatment from Jung, they moved from the USA and settled down in Zurich, staying there for years, if not decades. Edith's husband, Harold Fowler McCormick, heir of Cyrus McCormick's business and fortune, was "ordered" by his father-in-law, John D. Rockefeller, Sr. (considered the richest American of all time), to get Edith back to America. Yet, once in Zurich, Harold realized that he also needed therapy from Jung, and wrote to Rockefeller to explain why he and Edith, as well as all three of their children, needed to stay in Switzerland to continue their therapies. As an astute industrialist and businessman, Harold's summary of the essence of psychotherapy was succinct and to the point, but it failed to convince his even shrewder and more intelligent father-in-law, who refused to donate to the cause of the Jungian movement. Yet Rockefeller was no match to his daughter Edith, who obtained a huge loan from Rockefeller's banking friends for such a purpose, eventually forcing her father to foot the bill!

In addition to financial support, Jung's patients also worked hard advocating for his brand of therapy and served as conduits for Jung to connect with power brokers in the English-speaking world (Noll, 1997).

Jung's charisma with women contributed to the success of his practice, but it also repeatedly brought him trouble. Soon after Sabina left Zurich, he started another affair with Toni Wolff, a former patient turned colleague.

---

[3] Cousin of James Jackson Putnam, the "father of American neurology."
[4] Daughter of the oil tycoon John Davison Rockefeller, and the daughter-in-law of Cyrus McCormick, the inventor of the mechanical reaper.

Toni was half-Jewish and also came from a rich family. Before becoming Jung's patient, she had been chronically depressed and was constantly suicidal. Soon after entering therapy with Jung, she was miraculously "cured," but she was also transformed into his indispensable, "around the clock" assistant. Many a time, when Jung became horribly agitated, incoherent, and on the verge of total collapse, Toni was the only person who was able to calm him.

This complicated relationship triangle between Jung, Emma, and Toni took quite a few years to be more or less sorted out. Eventually, Emma came to the conclusion that she needed Toni to help "stabilize" Jung, and they reached a compromise: Toni started coming to dinner with the whole family once a week, and Jung was free to spend weekends with Toni at the stone house retreat.

There is no way for us to know how they handled this arrangement. While we may agree with Jung's depiction of himself as a hero exploring the virgin landscape of the psyche and the soul, we might also take note of the fact that his "heroic journey" was made possible only because of the sacrifices of the people around him (Jung & Jaffè, 1962).

DIALOGUES BETWEEN QUANTUM PHYSICS
AND THE REALM OF THE SOUL

All through his long life, the biggest complaint Jung had about Freud was that Freud's mind was dominated by nineteenth-century science, which was linear and deterministic. He disagreed with Freud's view of the unconscious, which was limited to that of the individual. By so doing, Jung thought that Freud completely neglected the craving and exploration of the soul that is the essence of all of us.

Jung agreed with Freud that consciousness was only a very small part of each individual's mind. However, behind or below Freud's "individual unconscious," there was the even more important and powerful "collective unconscious" which was the root of people's existence, and the source of meaning in our lives. Furthermore, this "collective unconscious" was tuned to the rhythm of the universe. In order to find our place in the universe, to be in touch with our soul and to live a meaningful life, in Jung's estimation we needed to pay attention to this "collective unconscious."

Does this make sense? Is he right? I would be the first to admit that, as much as I remain fascinated by him and his thoughts, I am even more often confused by him. His writings remind me of the concept of Tao and the macrocosm–microcosm correspondence in Chinese traditions. They also bring to mind the *Anitya* ("impermanence") in Buddhism, the *Atman* ("real self") revered in Hinduism, the metaphysical aspects of alchemy, and the teachings of early Christian Gnosticism.

Like Jung, I have been deeply fascinated by these esoteric traditions. Yet, after trying for many years, I have come to the conclusion that it will never be possible for me to fully grasp the meaning and reasoning of these ideas and practices. This does not mean that I have given up on them. They represent valiant efforts to grasp the mysteries of the universe, and these mysteries attract me, but after so many years of trying to unravel their secrets, I am resigned to leaving them as mysteries.

However, to say some phenomena or theories are "mysterious" does not mean that they are not "real." In truth, if we look at any of the "scientific" theories that we without a doubt regard as true (such as the concept of gravity), we would soon realize that they are equally "mysterious."

Like Freud, most of the time we still live in a world constructed by Newton and Galileo. The formulations and equations proposed by them feel "real" to us because they were taught in schools (and we were "brainwashed"). It also helps that we could readily test the "validity," or at least the utility, of these theories (for example, apples really could fall from trees to hit our heads).

But I am of the opinion that many of the contemporary concepts governing our physical world, such as the Theory of General Relativity and quantum physics, are beyond anyone's comprehension, with the exception of rare mathematical geniuses. Nevertheless, we have no doubt that these concepts are "real," because they foretold the horrendous power of the atomic bomb and they enabled us to construct nuclear reactors to generate electricity.

Even more bizarre to me are the concepts of black holes, the big bang, dark matter, and string theory. However, since they are essential for the advancement of physics and astronomy, who am I to say that they are not real?

And then we come face to face with the *Heisenberg Uncertainty Principle*, which says that the results of observations and experiments can never be independent of the one doing the observation. Such uncertainty is inherent to the nature of whatever is being observed, not just because of chance (probability) or the limitations in experimental methods.

If this is the case (and it has to be), then the human mind and the universe are indeed tightly linked together. Without the mind behind the observer, there is no outside world. So, it turns out that Jung is right after all, along with many philosophers and mystics who proposed similar ideas before him.

Was the convergence between Jungian psychology and modern physics purely coincidental, or did they interact and inform each other? Between 1909 and 1912, Jung and Einstein often got together for dinner, giving them ample opportunities to exchange ideas. The issues they discussed and agreed upon include the idea that the concept of *time* being lineal and unidirectional (from the past to the present and on to the future, not the other way around) does not exist objectively but is purely a construction of the human mind.

Even more convincing evidence of such exchanges can be seen in Jung's relationship with Wolfgang Pauli, the 1945 Nobel Laureate. Pauli was another of the rare geniuses who became known as an expert on the Theory of Relativity when he was merely eighteen. He went on to make significant contributions to the development of quantum physics. Unfortunately, at the age of thirty-two, when he was at the height of his career, tragedies struck: his mother committed suicide after divorcing his father and Pauli proceeded to fall in love with a bar singer of ill repute, ending in a devastating divorce.

Pushed into a severe depressive state further complicated by alcoholism, he found his way to Jung's clinic. Their physician–patient relationship quickly evolved into an enduring friendship. In their constant correspondence, they talked about alchemy, paranormal psychology, and the mysteries that link the mind (and soul) with the physical world (Lindorff, 2004). While Jung was searching for the human soul with the help of quantum physics, Pauli found inspiration for scientific innovation in Jung's theories of archetypes.

So, it really seems that the mind and the physical world are entwined and inseparable, even if we continue to puzzle over how this could have taken place.

THE PROPHET BECAME A WISE OLD MAN

Jung's ideas on human growth and the vital importance of the soul came at the right time for us living in the twentieth century and beyond, devastated by one catastrophe after another and no longer able to derive comfort from traditional religious institutions and belief systems (Jung, 1933). In this age of pervasive anxiety, fear, and distrust, Jung points to a new path that shows promise. With his insight and his charisma, he provided us with new meaning for our suffering, making us believe that if we can confront our shadows, it is possible for us to eventually be in touch with our "true self" and find our soul. His writings inspired a new generation of mythologists, including Joseph Campbell (Campbell, Moyers, & Flowers, 1991), the world-renowned expert in comparative mythology and religion, who in turn had a significant impact on contemporary thinkers, religious leaders, and the general public.

Then came the 1960s, with various brands of New Age movements, transpersonal psychology, and schools promoting self-actualization, Jung's ideas became even more popular and relevant. Even Alcoholics Anonymous (AA) can trace part of its origin to Jungian ideas. Bill Wilson, its founder, corresponded with Jung, and was encouraged by him to explore the spiritual aspect of recovery (McCabe, 2018). The apparent success of the AA stimulated the development of similar movements for the care of those suffering from all kinds of addictions, including Narcotics Anonymous (NA), Gamblers Anonymous (GA), and even Internet and Technology Addicts Anonymous (ITAA). Through these organizations, the lives of tens of millions have been touched. With all these influence on these movements, Jung's contributions to the welfare of humankind is hard to measure.

Surprisingly, Japan turned out to be a fertile land for Jungian psychology. Hayao Kawai, the first Japanese Jungian psychologist, devoted his life to synthesizing Jungian theories and Buddhism, and to making them palatable for the Japanese. He also played a key role in inventing and promoting sandbox therapy, an ingenious nonverbal approach using miniatures in a sand tray to help patients express their imagination and their subconscious or unconscious conflicts and motivations. His efforts not only made Jung understandable and acceptable for Asian therapists and patients, they also attracted a large number of "Western" thinkers and therapists to examine Buddhist thoughts and practices, who, in turn, brought Buddhism-inspired therapeutic approaches to Western societies, benefiting an increasing number of "Western" patients (Kawai, 1996).

After the death of Emma in 1955, Jung spent most of the last six years of his life in his lakeside stone house, which had by that time been expanded into a two-story building and was no longer as primitive as he once wanted it to be. Many admirers came to visit, hoping to lay eyes on him, or exchange a few words. Because of Jung, for a time Lake Zurich became a tourism hotspot. People rented boats and rowed them to the lakeside retreat, getting as close to the stone house as possible. When the weather was good, they could sometimes see him chopping firewood or carving stone statues. Once in a while, he might even raise his head and wave warmly to these uninvited "visitors."

Perhaps it is not difficult to imagine that, after so many setbacks and so much striving, he had finally found his home and his destiny. He became what he had always wanted for himself: a wise old man.

3

We Are Abel: We Are Cain

Alfred W. Adler – Founder of Individual Psychology

When we think about pioneers of psychotherapy, the three masters that naturally come to mind are Sigmund Freud, Carl Jung (Kerr, 1993), and Alfred Adler (Stepansky, 1983). They lived and worked in Central Europe, close to one another, and their personal and professional lives overlapped and entwined. Compared to Freud and Jung, Adler might not have appeared as charismatic or audacious, and his ideas might not have appeared as groundbreaking. However, these ideas have permeated all aspects of the field of mental health (Adler, 1931; Bottome, 1957; Stepansky, 1983), and his influences on practicing clinicians remain profound and enduring.

ABEL AND CAIN

It was just Adler's luck to have to live in the shadow of older brothers all his life. Born in a middle-class Jewish merchant family in Vienna, he had an older brother coincidentally also named Sigmund, who was good-looking, bright, and likable. Sigmund Adler excelled at school with ease and became a successful industrialist who was generous and caring to his younger siblings all his life.

It was not easy to grow up in the shadow of such a "perfect" older brother. To make the matter worse, Adler was sickly throughout his childhood. For a long time he was confined to bed due to spinal tuberculosis, diagnosed when he was two. Then, his younger brother died at birth when Adler was just three. Soon afterwards, he was twice hit by cars, each time narrowly escaping death. These events further unsettled him, leaving him with a deep-seated sense of the fragility of life. At five, he was hospitalized for pneumonia not responding to treatment. He eventually survived, thanks to the compassionate care of a young doctor. That was when Adler made up his mind to become a doctor – to help others, as others had helped him.

Another vivid childhood memory he had was having to pass through a huge graveyard to go to school when he was six. This daily walk frightened him a great deal. To overcome this fear, he decided one day to force himself to stay in the cemetery, running up and down, until he was totally exhausted. This experience, he thought, completely erased his fear of the tombs and the dead.

Were these childhood memories all objective facts? Adler did not think that was necessarily the case. Decades later, when he mentioned this incident to a schoolmate, his friend was completely taken aback and argued that there was never a graveyard anywhere close to their school. Dumbfounded, Adler went back to the school to prove his schoolmate wrong. But there was indeed no graveyard anywhere in sight! This experience convinced him that childhood memories were not always reliable. It also taught him that, "real" or not, "memories" weren't something to trifle with: That "manufactured" memory did help him to overcome his fear of death.

BORN TO BE A DOCTOR

Adler was not a "good student" by any traditional definition. He didn't do well under pressure or his poor performance made him feel inferior to others. But inferior or not, he was determined to enter medical school, and so he redoubled his efforts to make sure it would happen.

But medical school disappointed him. He found out that most of his internationally renowned professors did not care about their patients. Instead, what interested them was getting the diagnosis right. Often what they did at the hospital was wait for, and perhaps even wish for, the patients to die so that they could perform autopsies to get to the "real" answers, to prove their original hypothesis right.

Nevertheless, it was an exciting time for medical advances. Following Robert Koch's discovery of bacteria, infection as the cause of diseases became all the rage. Everyone's focus was on the identification of pathogens that made people sick. Instead, the question intriguing Adler most was, "What kind of environment makes it easier for patients to be exposed to these pathogens, and what weakens or enhances their resistance to infection?"

He found that bacteria were but a small part of the equation. What was far more important was how patients were exposed to them. The answer to this question was clearly poverty and poor working environments. This led him to read books by Marx and other socialist thinkers. Soon, he also started to attend meetings of socialist movements around town.

After medical school and one year of obligatory military service, he stayed at the Vienna University Hospital for another two years to receive training in internal medicine and ophthalmology, with some exposure to the field of neuropsychiatry. He then opened a clinic in a low-income community where he worked with patients from all strata of society, including street circus performers. These firsthand experiences served as the basis for his commentaries and special reports, which started to appear regularly in popular newspapers and magazines. Using common, easy-to-understand language to discuss pressing medical and public health issues, his writings caught the attention of his medical colleagues as well as the general public.

However, the young Adler was no Che Guevara.[1] He was not interested in revolutions. What he wanted to do was to use his medical background to educate patients and the public. In his articles, he looked at issues from divergent angles, emphasizing that diseases and health were not just determined by biological processes. Even more important were social and economic factors, in addition to an individual's life history and childhood experiences.

In a sense, Adler was ahead of his time, and could be regarded as a pioneer of social medicine, preventive medicine, and environmental health. For example, in a pamphlet he published in 1898, titled "Health manual for the tailoring trade" (Silver, 2009), he documented the high prevalence of various health problems among tailors and seamstresses, including lung diseases, gastrointestinal conditions, eye problems, and arthritis. He also identified factors responsible for these ailments, such as malnutrition, overcrowding, poor sanitation and ventilation, long work hours, poor postures, and poor lighting. He then went on to talk about why these problems had been neglected for so long, and what interfered with efforts toward eradicating these awful conditions. The pamphlet has remained a classic until this day.

LOVE KNOWS NO BORDERS: LONG-DISTANCE RACE OF AN ODD COUPLE

As much as Adler tried to stay away from politics, he had to thank his early involvement with socialist movements for meeting Raissa Timofeivna Epstein, the love of his life, who nevertheless also became a main source of headache and heartache that seemed to never end.

Raissa was born and raised in a super-rich Russian Jewish family. She left the comfort of her opulent life and went by herself to Zurich to study at the university. While there, she became involved with the women's suffrage movement, which took her to Vienna, where she ran into Adler. He fell immediately and desperately in love with her, and twice made the long trip to Moscow, eventually persuading her and her family to accept him. They were married in 1897.

Passion and love notwithstanding, their marriage turned out to be full of ups and downs. Raissa was an extremely independent, idealistic, and driven

---

[1] Ernesto "Che" Guevara was an Argentine physician, author, revolutionary, guerrilla leader, and a leader of the Cuban Revolution. Executed by CIA-assisted Bolivian forces, he became an enduring global symbol of countercultural rebellion.

young woman with a strong personality. In Vienna she was an active member of the women's movements, befriending many leaders of the Communist Party.

Because of her, Adler became a good friend of Leon Trotsky, later to become "Father of the Red Army." During the seven years when the Trotskys were exiled in Vienna, the two families saw each other often, spending many pleasant weekends together. In addition, Adolph Abramovich Joffe,[2] another future leader of Soviet Russia, became Adler's patient for his addiction problems and also studied psychoanalysis with him for a time.

Despite all these contacts and influences, Adler remained adamant that he would stay clear of politics, which greatly dismayed Raissa. On top of their different approaches to politics, Raissa was also unable to adjust well to marital life in Vienna. Although an exceptionally beautiful woman, she never cared about clothing or appearance. She was also a straight shooter who said whatever she whatever came to her mind, not caring if she might offend or hurt others. Frustrated by the subtlety and indirectness of the communication styles of the Viennese, she displaced her anger toward Adler, often accusing him of being unnecessarily evasive and even purposefully misleading.

The relationship deteriorated to the point that Raissa "ran away" in 1914, taking their four children with her back to Moscow. Soon after, the crown prince of the Austro-Hungarian Empire was assassinated, pitting Russia against Austria and Germany, and triggering World War I. Adler sent many telegrams to her, urging her and the children to return home immediately, without revealing the real reason for this urgency. Raissa thought he was pressuring her to give in and refused to budge.

When she finally found out the real reason for his demands for her return, all routes between Moscow and Vienna were blocked. She was eventually able to obtain special permission from the tsar and returned safely to Vienna with their children, more than five months after the war broke out.

Of their four children, the second daughter (Alexandra Adler) and the only son (Kurt Adler) became psychiatrists who continued to promote Adler's teachings. Alexandra was later also noted for her contributions in research on posttraumatic stress disorder.

---

[2] Joffe came from a well-to-do Jewish family in Crimea and became one of the leaders of Russian revolutionaries. As a close friend of Leon Trotsky, he was also co-editor of *Pravda*, the official newspaper of the Communist Party of the Soviet Union. After the October Revolution, he led the Soviet's efforts to end hostilities with Germany and also played a key role in ending wars with various other countries surrounding Russia. In 1923, as Soviet's ambassador to China, he signed the *Joint Manifesto of Sun and Joffe* with Sun Yat-sen, the Founding Father of the modern Republic of China. The manifesto served as the blueprint for the ill-fated collaboration between the Chinese Nationalist and Communist Parties. In 1927, Joffe committed suicide after Trotsky's expulsion from the Soviet's Communist Party.

Their oldest daughter, Valentine Adler, took after her mother. She joined the Communist Party at the age of twenty-one, and married Gyula Sas (a.k.a. Giulio Aguila), one of the leaders of the Hungarian Communist Party. In 1933, she clandestinely entered Russia to be reunited with her husband and to contribute to the cause of communism. Unfortunately, they were caught in the power struggle between Stalin and Trotsky following the death of Vladimir Lenin and were exiled in 1937 to a Gulag labor camp in Siberia, where they both perished.

Despite all these obstacles and tragedies, as well as continuous conflicts caused by differences in their personalities, Adler and Raissa were able to respect and support each other throughout their lives. This was in sharp contrast to Jung's repeated infidelities and Freud's ossified and distant relationship with his wife. In this sense, at least, one could say that the Adlers' marriage was quite successful.

A WHOLE DECADE OF "MEETING OF THE MIND," A WHOLE DECADE OF RIVALRIES

Adler and Freud first met in 1902, and they finally went their separate ways in 1911. In those ten years, the two "comrades-in-arms" managed to evolve into deadly enemies. How did this happen?

The answer depends on who you ask. Freudians were convinced that Freud was the injured party who was treacherously betrayed by Adler. Adlerians, on the other hand, stressed that Adler had never been Freud's student, so there was no betrayal at all. Their view was that, as a friend and a colleague, Adler labored at establishing and promoting the Vienna Psychoanalytic Society, only to be brutally expelled from the organization at a most critical moment.

Looking back, it may not be that important to decide who was right. What was clear was that, given the very different life goals and professional orientations, they were never meant to be close allies, and they were doomed to split from the very beginning.

The publication of *The Interpretation of Dreams* in 1899 ended Freud's stage of "Splendid Isolation." Of those who were moved by the book, Adler was one of the most ardent. After reading it, he wrote an enthusiastic review, doing his best to defend Freud against his detractors. A few years later (1902), Wilhelm Stekel,[3] an ex-patient of Freud's turned fervent follower, proposed to Freud that they invite a few like-minded physicians to meet regularly at

---

[3] As one of Freud's earliest students and colleagues, Stekel was also one of the five founding members of the Viennese Psychoanalytic Society. He was an expert on sexual dysfunction as well as the symbolism of dreams and made significant contributions to the content of the second edition of Freud's The *Interpretation of Dreams*. After breaking up with Freud in 1912, he started his own clinic in Vienna. He committed suicide in 1940, shortly after moving to London.

Freud's house on Wednesdays, which gradually became more formalized and was later known as the famed Wednesday Psychological Society. The five founding members included Freud, Stekel, and Adler, plus Max Kahane and Rudolf Reitler, both practicing physicians in Vienna.

Since Adler was not close to the other members, Freud made a special effort to write a courteous invitation letter, asking him to take part in these events. The letter was apparently special for Adler, who carried it with him all his life so he could show it to whoever asked about his relationship with Freud. For Adler, it proved that, from the beginning, he had been a friend and colleague, not a student, of Freud, as commonly misperceived.

At the beginning, they were just a loosely structured group. The survival and expansion of the group speaks volumes about Freud's personal charisma. It also reflects the passion of the members regarding the importance and potential for exploring the realm of the "unconscious," perceived as a vast virgin land that was still "terra incognita."

Thus, they could be regarded more as an adventure group instead of an exploration team. At the outset, there was no particular consensus among group members for the direction of their explorations. They ventured out on their own and came back together to share what they had found. During the first few years, all members seemed to enjoy and benefit from such gatherings. It was indeed a luxury to have a group of like-minded people to bounce off thoughts and ideas with one another.

But, as is true for any organization, over time the need for structure became increasingly important for members whose backgrounds and orientations were quite divergent. When the Wednesday Psychological Society first started, most basic psychoanalytic tenets had not yet been formulated. Over the next few years, Freud gradually developed his psychosexual developmental theories, including infantile sexuality and the Oedipus Complex. These ideas did not go over well with Adler. He did not believe that the most important challenge for young children was the gratification of "sexual needs," however defined. Instead, Adler thought that the central developmental task for children was the unfolding of the *self*, enabling the child to define herself or himself by interacting with various environmental (physical and social) constraints. In this process, the key task was the management of the pervasive "inferiority complex." This condition, deeply ingrained in all of us because of our long infancy and childhood, is characterized by our needing to depend on our elders, with whom we were indeed "inferior." In the long process of maturation, infants and children strive to develop the ability to control the environment in an effective and appropriate manner, in order to avoid or lessen the pervasive sense of inadequacy and helplessness. Adler called this process "compensation." Appropriate compensation, under this theory, was seen as the basic ingredient of mental health, whereas excessive ("over-compensation") and inadequate compensation would lead one to maladjustment.

Freud's deterministic frameworks asserted that, right from our infancy, we're constantly pushed by our various "drives," and we are thus squeezed by the "pleasure principle" on the one hand and the "reality principle" on the other. In contrast, Adler's "self-instinct" emphasizes individuals' agency: We are always looking into the future, making decisions and choices. Along with this sense of agency, we are also responsible for the consequences of our choices and decisions.

Adler and his followers weren't shy to say that this sense of autonomy, this sense of being the master of one's actions, was perhaps "fictive." But fictive or not, such a sense of agency is deeply ingrained and hardwired in our brains, pushing us to take actions. In other words, our behavior is goal-oriented and our imagination of the future not only determines the action we take, but also shapes our perception of ourselves at the present time, as well as our assessment of our past. In this sense, *the future determines the past*.

To Freud and his followers who were anxious to promote the "psycho-sexual" theories, Adler's concepts sounded like irrelevant noise. Were all these notions not just common sense? Did the emphasis on the autonomy of self and self's responsibility not sound suspiciously like moralistic preaching? Was Adler just paying lip service to the importance of the unconscious while promoting ideas that would distract people's attention from it? In Freud's and his followers' eyes, Adler was becoming more and more like a dangerous traitor.

On top of these theoretical arguments, racial conflicts and pervasive anti-Jewish sentiments were another, at least equally powerful, undercurrent. During the second half of the nineteenth century, the rapid industrialization and urbanization of Europe caused a huge shift of the population from the farms and small villages to big cities. While the majority of people remained poverty stricken, some managed to enter the middle class. In Adler and Freud's Vienna, half of the city's residents were "migrants" (from all corners of the vast Austro-Hungarian Empire) and descendants of migrants. A large proportion of the newcomers were Jewish. They worked hard, excelled in schools, and soon became prominent in business, manufacturing, and education. Recognizing their contributions to society, the Imperial Court issued edicts to loosen restrictions on Jews, aiming at minimizing discrimination. But at the beginning of the twentieth century, such rapid changes led to waves of backlashes, with the "natives" and right-wing groups demanding the restoration of many of the anti-Jewish traditions and practices. Partly reflecting such changes, psychoanalysis came to be regarded as a "Jewish psychology." Since Freud and his followers at the time were all Jews, they were very much threatened by this shift in the wind.

From the inception of the Wednesday Psychological Society, Freud was worried about this issue, and felt pressured to reach out to Christian communities. Specifically, he felt the need to find an "heir" (not just a spokesperson) who was not Jewish. In 1906 he thought he had discovered such a person in Carl Jung, who had started corresponding with him and had tried Freud's therapeutic method on patients. The following year, Jung came to visit Freud from his native Switzerland, and they talked for thirteen hours. From then on, Freud saw Jung as his son, his "Crown Prince," his official heir.

Indeed, Jung seemed clearly the future of psychoanalysis. Under his leadership, Burghölzli Hospital in Zurich, Switzerland, soon became the major center for the training of psychoanalysis, attracting enthusiastic psychiatrists from all over the world. Such a development was deeply threatening to Freud's colleagues in Vienna, including Adler, who felt left out.

"ONE MOUNTAIN CANNOT ACCOMMODATE TWO TIGERS"[4]

At the First International Congress on Psychoanalysis held in 1909 at Nuremberg, Freud proposed that Jung be appointed president-for-life, triggering strong reactions from the Viennese contingents. They held a meeting in secret to discuss the issue. Somehow, Freud got wind of the gathering, barged in unannounced, and angrily dressed them down. Eventually a compromise was reached, making Jung the president for a term of two years. But widespread resentment was again triggered when Freud insisted on establishing a new rule stipulating that all publications by the society's members be first approved by the newly installed president.

In order to appease his Viennese colleagues, Freud nominated Adler to be the president of the Viennese Psychoanalytic Society. Adler happily accepted the appointment and put his heart into it. He negotiated with the city to obtain tax-exempt status for the society. During his one-year tenure, the Society's activities were greatly expanded and discussions in meetings were increasingly more lively and scopes were broadened. The membership also doubled, from twenty-one to forty-three.

Then, seemingly out of the blue, several members started to question Adler's position vis-à-vis Freud's basic tenets, particularly in regard to the theory of "infantile sexuality." In January 1911, Adler delivered two major speeches, trying his best to demonstrate the links between his and Freud's ideas, arguing that there were more similarities than differences. But it seemed that Freud had already made up his mind to expel Adler. He called Adler a coward, and said he was afraid of accepting the importance of "sexuality" in the human psyche, criticizing Adler for watering down concepts of psychoanalysis and replacing them with superficial ideas.

---

[4] An old Chinese proverb.

After several explosive debates, Adler resigned from his post as president but continued to attend the regular Wednesday meetings. However, he stopped participating in discussions. After the summer vacation, when the meetings resumed, he was surprised to find his name missing in the newsletter that had thus far been edited by him. This was the straw that broke the camel's back – he resigned from the Society to start his own Thursday Study Group.

Many members did not want to choose sides and attended both meetings. When Freud put an end to this, forcing them to choose one or the other, half of the membership left him and went away with Adler. This rupture, in effect, concluded the first major schism of the psychoanalytic movement.

In a recently published book titled *Cassandra's Daughter*, Joseph Schwartz (1999), an expert on the history of psychoanalysis, stated that even if Freud and Adler had the best of intentions, there was no chance that they could continue to collaborate together due to the marked differences in their theories, as well as their backgrounds.

As the first born, Freud was worshipped and indulged by everyone in the family, making him believe that he was exceptional and was destined to become famous, with the power to change the whole world. He was elegant in his speech and impeccable in his manners, always well-dressed and groomed, thanks to his wife Martha's meticulous attention to these matters. He thrust himself into Vienna's high society and most of his patients and friends were rich and famous. After medical school, he struggled hard to establish a research career in the laboratories and was deeply wounded at not being able to gain a full-time tenured professorship, entering private practice only reluctantly and continuing to be more interested in research than taking care of patients.

Freud was a perfectionist. His writings were typically revised multiple times, resulting in products that were tightly structured and cogently presented. He was also prodigious in letter-writing. His correspondences were persuasive. Using the pen as a weapon, he was effective in convincing colleagues and students to side with him.

In many ways, Adler was the opposite of Freud. As the second son, he was constantly outshone by his older brother, also named Sigmund, and knew from early on that competition was part of life, no matter how much he hated it. He cared little about his appearance and did not go out of his way to impress others, but he enjoyed socializing and made friends easily with people of all kinds and stripes. He cared more about how to help and educate patients and was not overly concerned about his academic status or the construction of a perfect theoretical system. He was happiest delivering speeches and communicating with others face to face, and was less interested in spending time and energy writing and publishing.

Considering how different they were, it was indeed remarkable that they had been able to work together for so many years and learn so much from each other.

EACH TO HIS OWN

After breaking with Freud, Adler continued to develop his own theories, which eventually evolved into a school named "Individual Psychology." His productivity demonstrated that no matter how traumatic the year 1911 was for him, he was able to continue to stand on his own two feet, fulfilling his own destiny. Remarkably, even though he and Freud stopped communicating with each other, they continued to occupy an important role in each other's minds. Throughout their lives, whether knowingly or not, they continued to influence each other.

The Oedipus Complex occupies a central position in Freud's theories and its significance and universality was the focus of debate between Freud and his critics. Ironically, during Freud's long professional career, "Oedipal conflicts" kept on repeating themselves, often leading to serious and at times lethal outcomes. But what was different between Freud's case and the Oedipal legend was that Freud as the "father" was not killed by his "sons," but survived and "won" the fights. In contrast, many of his followers turned competitors did not fare well. Otto Rank (Taft, 1958) and Wilhelm Reich (Sharaf, 1983) died lonely deaths. Sándor Ferenczi[5] perished prematurely after being marginalized. Viktor Tausk,[6] who played a crucial role in supporting Freud after his "breakup" with Adler and Jung, felt neglected by Freud, and ensured the success of his suicide by hanging and shooting himself at the same time (Roazon, 1969). The other two founding members of the Wednesday Psychology Society, Stekel and Max Kahane, quit the Society after Adler. They also ended their lives with suicide. Even Jung suffered from a psychotic-like state and remained on the verge of suicide for several years after leaving Freud.

In comparison, Adler was far less traumatized. After World War I, he resumed his regular schedules and lifestyles, working with patients, delivering lectures, and helping to set up new child guidance centers. As years passed, his fame spread internationally, and he started doing more and more lecture tours in England and the USA. In the 1930s, he received an invitation to teach at the Long Island Medical School, and convinced Raissa to leave the increasingly unstable and dangerous Vienna. They immigrated to the USA with their

---

[5] Ferenczi was a Jewish Hungarian who joined Freud's psychoanalytic movements very early on and made significant contributions. He was the mentor of Ernest Jones and Melanie Klein. He was distanced by Freud after he started to experiment with shorter-term therapy and advocate for a more active role for therapists.

[6] Viktor Tausk was one of the first to apply psychoanalysis to psychotic patients.

family (minus Valentine Adler) and thus escaped Nazi persecution just in time.

For Adler, leaving Freud was the easy part. Explaining how he differed from Freud was a more difficult task. For that reason alone, Adler continued to pay close attention to what Freud was up to. In contrast, Freud largely ignored Adler after the "separation," at least on the surface. Yet many of Freud's later ideas showed Adler's influences. For example, his concept of the "death drive," focusing on the aggressive and competitive side of human nature, overlapped with Adler's "inferiority complex."

In the twilight years of his life, as Freud started to tackle the mechanisms people needed to harness their "libido," he also became more receptive of the concept of the "self." Such explorations eventually led to the establishment of "ego psychology" by his daughter, Anna Freud (Young-Bruehl, 1988), and her colleagues.

Adler's influences on Harry Stack Sullivan (Perry, 1982), Frieda Fromm-Reichmann (Hornstein, 2005), Karen Horney, Erich Fromm, and other interpersonal theorists and neo-Freudians were also visible in how they focused their attention more on the "here and now" rather than the past. They also tended to emphasize the importance of social and cultural forces in determining individual behavior. All in all, Adler's impact on the field of psychoanalysis and psychotherapy appears to be more profound than meets the eye.

Indeed, we have reason to believe that Adler and Freud continued to live in each other's minds long after they went their separate ways. For the rest of his life, Adler continued to carry the first letter he received from Freud, using it as evidence that he had never been Freud's student. How powerful and precious that letter must have been! And when Freud heard that Adler passed away at the Scottish town of Aberdeen, what blurted from his mouth was: "What a way for a Jew boy to die in such a remote place! He had gone a long way." One might well wonder if Freud revealed a measure of jealousy or was this an expression of admiration? We have no way of knowing and it may not even be important after all.

4

Fear of Death and Trauma of Birth

Otto Rank's Tragic Saga

The first time I heard about Otto Rank, more than forty years ago, I thought he was a joke. It had been hard enough for me to accept that my neurosis came from the Oedipus Complex. Now Rank expected me to blame everything on the trauma I might have experienced at birth. If he was not crazy, who was?

But right around that time, we were entering the era of the hippies and the so-called "counter-culture." Many new therapies emerged along with the New Age movement and quite a few were inspired by Rank's theory of "trauma of birth." Whether called Primal Therapy, Primal Integration, Rebirthing–Rebreathing or Prenatal and Perinatal Psychology, their central goal was to encourage (some might say coerce) patients to "recover" their memories and emotions at the moment of their birth, in order to again experience the intense ordeal of fear, helplessness, and anger caused by being forcefully expulsed from the warm and secure wombs of their mothers.

Using hypnosis, meditation, suggestion, and group pressure, these therapies aimed at facilitating the "conscious recall" of these "primal" images and sensations. Such "primal memories," buried in the deepest strata of our existence, are like the djinn or genie who has been confined in the bottle for so many years. Once released, its power would be formidable. Consequently, once the memories of the "primal" trauma were brought out in the open, the pain they caused could be overwhelming and unbearable, often leading one to uncontrollable screaming (Crosby & Crosby, 1970).

Arthur Janov, founder of Primal Therapy, called this reaction a "primal scream." In his theory, the right kind of therapy should be able to help patients comprehend, process, and integrate these disruptive emotions and thus free them from harmful effects originally caused by the trauma of birth (Crosby & Crosby, 1970).

For someone as dense as myself, such theories have continued to seem as fanciful as the so-called "past-life regression" (Spanos, Burgess, & Burgess, 1994). I assumed that, as the first to argue for the power of "birth trauma," Rank is to be blamed for misleading many people over so many years.

What went wrong with Rank? The British psychoanalyst Ernest Jones had a simple answer – he claimed that Rank was just crazy (Lieberman, 2010). Whether deliberately or unintentionally misleading, Jones stated that Rank had struggled with serious psychiatric conditions all his life, was frequently suicidal, and eventually did commit suicide.

However, if this were the case, how was Rank able to stay by Freud's side for more than twenty years, serving as his competent secretary and right-hand man?

FEAR OF DEATH

Many years later, urged by my mentor Milton Miller, I decided to dive into Ernest Becker's classic, *The Denial of Death* (Becker, 1997). To my surprise, many of the issues that had puzzled me for years had already been addressed in this book. Becker cited Rank often and had only the highest regard for his creativity and insight. He was especially moved by Rank's thoughts on our "fear of death," as well as our "fear of birth." Becker's lavish adulation of Rank convinced me that there must be something about Rank that I had missed.

Becker's exposition on "fear of death" was partially rooted in the theory of evolution. He proposed that of all the ways that we differ from other animals, the most important was the constant awareness of our own existence. Our ancestors from Africa (*Homo sapiens sapiens*)[1] were not equipped with sharp teeth, lacerating claws, or armor-like skin. In terms of physical prowess and endurance, they did not even compare well with hominids or Neanderthals (*Homo sapiens Neanderthal*). The main reason they were able to compete with other species was the highly developed sense of their own existence that allowed them to remember the past and imagine the future. In addition to sharing the capacity of implicit (procedural) memories with other species, their explicit (episodic, declarative, or narrative) memories permitted them to systematically and consciously explore their past experiences and learn from their "mistakes." At the same time, their ability to project their conscious mind into the future enabled them to plan ahead and formulate strategies to guide their actions.[2]

But these advantages are also sources of our burden and sorrow. Our pristine, specific memories force us to confront the fact that many of the

---

[1] When *Homo sapiens sapiens* burst out of Africa about 100,000 years ago, they encountered Neanderthals who had moved out earlier and adjusted to the harsh environment of Eurasia during the previous ice age. Neanderthals were physically stronger than our ancestors and had larger brain capacities, implying that they might have had language capabilities. Recent genomic research indicates that there was significant interbreeding between *Homo sapiens sapiens* and Neanderthals, and on average about 4 percent of our genes come from the Neanderthals.

[2] Explicit memory allows us to recall specific events that happened in the past, whereas implicit memory is mostly outside our consciousness. For example, when we walk, we do not think about how to put one leg ahead of the other.

people we loved and things we enjoyed are gone. This could lead to a profound sense of loss and sadness. On the other hand, along with our boundless capacity to imagine the future, we are confronted by the fact that nothing is guaranteed in life. The understanding that "one day we will no longer be here" becomes an overwhelming challenge for our *sapient* forebearers. This awareness leads to fear that could overwhelm and paralyze us.

How then, do we escape from this bottomless dread that was so aptly depicted by Sartre (1956) in his play *No Exit*? For this deliverance, we have to thank our ability for repression and sublimation. As explained by Becker, after satisfying their basic physiological needs such as food and clothing, the central task of every *Homo sapiens sapiens* was to find ways to deny "death," even if just for a short while. These "methods" could be religious or spiritual (such as ancestral worship, faith in the Almighty God, or mythical experiences of merging with the universe). They could also be in the realm of passion (sexual ecstasy, devotion to greater causes), interpersonal (care and love for family and friends), social (sense of belonging to a worthy group or cause; achieving lasting fame by performing meaningful work), and artistic (being creative for the joy of creating and exploration, rather than practical gains) (Watson, 1989).

What is the common thread of all these "noble" activities? One answer is that they enable our "mind" to overcome our "body." By so doing, we are no longer confined by our "selves." Getting the *self* out of the way, we no longer need to worry about "death" or "annihilation."

Thinking along this line, it becomes clear that all these "death defying" or "death denying" efforts are actually the foundation of cultures and civilizations. They rely heavily on symbols, value systems, and beliefs. Beliefs are often imposed upon us, but they are also generated through our active "choosing." We rely on these beliefs to escape from the *"Fear and Trembling"* (Kierkegaard, 1971, 1986) caused by the thoughts of death.

Unfortunately, belief systems are typically dichotomous, forcing us to choose sides, and thus leading to intolerance. This may be why Becker (1997) called them *"the vital lies."* We cannot survive without them, yet we need to be vigilant to avoid being trapped by them. Caught in such a dilemma, we could easily be crushed. Compared to this kind of struggle, the frustrations and conflicts caused by unfulfilled libidinous drives may seem trivial.

THE TRAUMA OF BIRTH

What about the "trauma of birth"? It turned out Rank never proposed that we should experience "birth" a "second time" in order to undo "damage" sustained at our birth. His concept of "trauma of birth" was *metaphorical*. "Birth" is but the beginning point for numerous "separations" we need to go through in our lives in order to grow and move forward.

Starting from birth, we are constantly facing separation. Separation is painful, but without it, there is no growth. Leaving the womb is the necessary step before the infant can start to breathe; and understanding that breasts do not belong to you is the first step for infants to develop the concept of their separate identity.

All through a person's life, moving forward is not possible without giving up something at the same time (and death is the ultimate *moving forward*). It is hard enough to be separated from one's parents, family, and friends, or to leave one's childhood. Giving up part of one's original self in order to grow is even harder and is at the heart of many of our psychological problems, according to Rank.

Lao-Tzu famously said: "The reason we have a lot of trouble is that we have *selves*. If we had no *selves*, what troubles would we have?" (Cleary, 2003; Feng, 1972). To *exist* ("to have my *self*") is to have to deal with the "fear of death" and the "fear of birth" at the same time. We fear birth because we fear separation and individuation. We fear death because we do not want the "self" to evaporate, to merge with the "infinite." Coping effectively with these fears is what Rank's thoughts are all about.

Becker said further: "We demand the impossible: We don't want to be alone, yet we also don't want to be encumbered by others."

WAS OEDIPUS REALLY A MURDERER?

As it turned out, dealing with "merging" and "separation" were exactly the problems with which Rank had the most trouble. This was also why it had been so hard for him to leave Freud. The process of leaving started with Rank's publishing of *The Trauma of Birth* (Rank, 1929) without consulting any of his colleagues. For sure, he dedicated the book to Freud, and expected to be praised for this "magnum opus." He argued that the book in no way deviated from Freud's teaching. All he did, in his estimation, was expand Freud's ideas from the stage of the Oedipus Complex (focusing on father–son conflicts) to earlier stages (conflicts between desires for independence and fear of separation).[3]

But this was not what Freud and other members of the Secret Committee (Grosskurth, 1991; see also note 2 in Chapter 2) perceived. After the initial shock, they were furious. Such a colossal "revision" must have been percolating in Rank's mind for a very long time, so why did he hide it for so long and then publish the book without any forewarning?

Initially, Freud only complained about the book's lack of structure and clarity. Criticism of Rank's deviation from "the accepted truth of the Oedipus

---

[3] This focus on the "pre-Oedipal" stage later became the starting point of both object relation theory and self-psychology.

Complex" came much later, which led to the accusation that Rank had discredited Freud's teachings and replaced them with his own.

While accusing Rank of "patricidal" intent, Freud also wanted to show his magnanimity, and suggested that this had happened only because Rank had not really been formally "analyzed" by himself, even after their having worked closely together for so many years. As predicted by Freud, Rank realized his "mistakes" every time his analysis started, rescinded his theories, and profusely apologized to Freud and members of the Secret Committee. But as soon as the analysis stopped, he "relapsed." This process went on for quite a few rounds, until both Freud and Rank were exhausted and called it quits.

Why was their separation so difficult? In order to answer this question, we need to go back to Rank's personal and family backgrounds.

HOW ROSENFELD BECAME RANK

Rank was born in 1884 in a downward-spiraling Jewish family in Vienna, with Rosenfeld as his last name. Although his father held a good job as a jeweler, the family was financially strained due to the father's alcoholism. The lack of resources meant that the family could only afford to support the higher education of Rank's elder brother, who eventually became a successful lawyer. In contrast, Rank was sent to a trade school, to be trained as a locksmith.

Exceptionally bright but also extremely shy and introverted, he was isolated and lonely throughout his adolescence, suffering from frequent bouts of severe depression. During one of these episodes, he bought a handgun, intending to use it to kill himself. Remarkably, the presence of the gun reminded him of the joy of life in this world, and he changed his mind at the last minute (Taft, 1958).

During this period, he spent all his spare time reading, finding solace in the writings of Søren Kierkegaard, Arthur Schopenhauer, and Friedrich Wilhelm Nietzsche. His interests in philosophy and the arts made it possible for him to survive his adolescence.

His chance encounter with Freud's The *Interpretation of Dreams* was *the* turning point in his life. After reading the book, he quickly completed his writing of a book titled *The Artist*, in which he applied Freudian theories to studying the creative processes of various artists. Gathering up his courage, Rank presented his manuscript to Alfred Adler, his family doctor. He was pleasantly surprised when Adler showed great interest in the book, and immediately recommended the manuscript to Freud. In turn, Freud had the book circulated among members of the Wednesday Psychological Society.

The timing could not have been more perfect for Freud and Rank. Freud was just starting to ponder how his theories could be applied to history, literature, art, and philosophy. Impressed by the book and its twenty-one-year-old author, he not only invited Rank to become a member of the society but also hired him on the spot as his secretary and librarian. With Freud's encouragement and financial support, Rank went back to finish high school and then went on to the University of Vienna to study psychology, eventually graduating with a doctoral degree in 1912. From then on until their "breakup," other than the short time when Rank was sent to Poland for military service, he was constantly by Freud's side, searching for background literature, editing and co-authoring manuscripts, and organizing conferences. Most of Freud's letters, including those for the members of the Secret Committee, were channeled through him. Rank also wrote two chapters for the second edition of *The Interpretation of Dreams.*

In 1920, Freud started referring patients to Rank for therapy. With direct clinical experience, Rank gained even more confidence, and gradually developed his own ideas.

Why did Rank decide to publish *The Trauma of Birth* secretly? Why did other members of the Secret Committee react so strongly to this "transgression"? Most likely the crisis was precipitated by the diagnosis of Freud's oral cancer. In 1923, a leukoplakia was identified in Freud's mouth, which proved malignant. Surgery was recommended. Unfortunately, the operation came close to dispatching Freud from this world. Rank was the first to learn of the bad news, and he was the one to convey the message to Committee members. Since Rank was the only one physically close to Freud, other members became alarmed of the possibility of Rank taking over the leadership of the psychoanalysis movement if Freud did not survive the cancer or its treatment. They did not want this to happen, especially as Rank was the youngest member of the group and the only non-physician.

We might not be able to say for sure what motivated Rank to publish his book without going through the customary channels, but it would not be unreasonable to propose that this was a classic case of the Oedipus Complex in action. The illness and the possible impending death of the "father" represented an overwhelming threat to his beloved "son," who came to realize that his "father" was not invincible and could disappear any time and cease to protect him. In this situation, Rank may have considered his best option was to protect himself by taking action. Since leaving was a hard thing to do, an easier way out might be to make the "father" angry enough to kick him out.

Could this be the reason that in 1924, while Freud was trying to regain his health, Rank distanced himself by undertaking his American lecture tours and publishing his book? Be that as it may, the value of the book should not be discounted just because its genesis may have reflected his intra-psychic conflicts. Motivations for human behaviors are complex, "over-determined." The value of creative activities is not necessarily diminished just because part of the driving force is rooted in unconscious factors.

"KING LEAR" FIGHTING BACK

Thanks to luck and willpower, Freud not only escaped death from the surgery but lived for another fifteen productive years. Recovering from the operation, he was dismayed to find that the one person who had been constantly by his side, sharing his ups and downs for the past twenty years, had more or less deserted him.

During that whole year, Rank continued traveling back and forth across the Atlantic Ocean and didn't write much to Freud. Regarded as Freud's favorite student, he was warmly welcomed everywhere he went. But he no longer wanted to be Freud's mouthpiece. He was more enthusiastic about promoting his own theories on the trauma of birth than his teacher's views on sexuality.

Accusations of his "rebellion" abounded, leading to his ostracism. He was treated as *persona non grata* and shunned by all branch societies. All his analysands were asked to go through another full course of analysis, so as to undo the "damage" caused by him. The ostracism was so complete that even his best friend, the mild-mannered Ferenczi,[4] pretended not to recognize him when by chance they passed each other at the Penn Station in Manhattan.

What hurt even more was that his young wife, Beata Rank-Minzer, a recently minted lay analyst, also sided with Freud without blinking.[5] Assaulted from all sides, Rank moved constantly, from Paris to New York to Philadelphia, searching for a stable base in which to operate and survive.

The thoroughness of the expulsion was such that one can find no trace of Rank's contributions in Freudian books after 1924. Although Rank's ideas on the importance of the bond between the mother and the child during the "pre-Oedipal" stage preceded the development of the object relations theories of Melanie Klein and her colleagues (see Chapter 7), this fact was also rarely mentioned.

RANK'S "REBIRTH"

The exiled Rank lost his "father," his "brothers," and his family, literally and symbolically. For a time, he also lost his direction. Luckily, this did not last long.

By losing everything, he gained a new life. Ironically, one might well wonder if this was not the best example of his theory on the "trauma of birth."

---

[4] The two of them co-authored The *Development of Psychoanalysis* in 1923, advocating for a more active role for therapists, advising them to pay more attention to the present instead of the past, to be more expressive, and to not prolong the course of therapy unnecessarily.

[5] Beata Rank-Minzer later moved to Boston and became a key member of the Boston Psychoanalytic Society.

No longer having to labor as Freud's secretary, editor, and office manager, Rank found a new sense of freedom, and time to do what he really wanted to do. Freed from the need to censure his ideas, his creativity was no longer tethered and he could finally fully express whatever he had in his mind.

In a span of less than six years (1926–1932) he completed and published some of his most important books, including *Truth and Reality*, *Will Therapy*, *Double*, *Psychology and the Soul*, *Beyond Psychology*, and *Art and Artist*. His theories included a patient-centered approach, emphasis on encouraging autonomy and self-development, belief in patients' self-healing potential, focus on the "here and now," and the therapeutic potential of brief psychotherapy. His ideas on pre-Oedipal mother–child relationships subsequently stimulated the development of the schools of object relation and self-psychology.

Even more importantly, Rank's ideas strongly influenced later masters of psychotherapy, including Carl Rogers, Rollo May, Paul Goodman, and Irvin Yalom. In this sense, Rank was the precursor of a number of major contemporary schools of psychotherapy, including client-centered therapy, humanistic therapy, existential therapy, and gestalt therapy.

As an example, Carl Rogers, commonly regarded as one of the most influential American psychologists of the twentieth century, invited Rank to New York to deliver a series of lectures in 1936. Rogers later said, "I became infected with *Rankian* ideas," which revolutionized the way he thought about psychotherapy. Goodman and Fritz Perls, founders of gestalt therapy, said that Rank's ideas were "beyond praise." Rollo May said: "I have long considered Otto Rank to be the great unacknowledged genius in Freud's circle."

Leaving Freud and his psychoanalytic circle also freed Rank to return to the topic that had long fascinated him: How do artists find their inspirations, how do they create art, and how does the art move us? According to him, artists use their creativity to temporarily "step out of the frame of the prevailing ideology." By getting out of the constraints of society and the "self," they were able to feel closer to nature and the universe and to have a sense of merging with the "infinite."

Similarly, when we look at a product of art, we become so absorbed in it we forget our "self" at the moment. That feeling of temporarily merging with the artist's vision can produce a sense of merging with the *infinite* and the *universe* so powerful that it helps to alleviate our sense of separation, isolation, and alienation.

These ideas influenced many prominent artists in the twentieth century, including Annais Nin[6] and Henry Miller, who were both starving artists

---

[6] Annais Nin and Henry Miller were two important writers active during the mid-twentieth century. They were both prolific in their writings, exceptionally brave in their exploration of new territories

struggling to find their bearings when they first met Rank in Paris. Nin said in her diaries that Rank helped her to be "reborn" and that she owed her life to him. Through Nin, Miller became Rank's patient. Miller's notorious best-seller, *Tropic of Cancer*, was first published thanks to Rank's financial support.

Leaving Freud also enabled Rank to find his "Brave New World." He fell in love with America. Mark Twain became his new guru and spiritual guide; *The Adventures of Huckleberry Finn* became his bible. Following Mark Twain's footsteps, he was free to roam the vast, seemingly endless American landscapes. Crossing prairies, rivers, and snowy mountains, he finally reached the even vaster Pacific Ocean. In the last summer of his life, he married his new love in San Francisco.

Sadly, three months after embarking on his California dreams, having overcome so many obstacles, with a new life ahead of him, he died at the age of 55. However, his death had nothing to do with what was reported by Ernest Jones, the influential British psychoanalyst who speculated that Rank finally killed himself. Rank did not will his death; his life was cut short by a severe allergic reaction to a sulpha drug.

The one who committed suicide was Freud. Just five weeks before Rank's unexpected death, Rank heard that Freud ended his life with dignity, having suffered enough from his terminal cancer. At his death bed, Rank reportedly said: "What kind of a joke this is! Why do I have to go meeting him again so soon?"

and challenges against traditions and conventional moral codes. Their writings often include graphic narratives of sexual scenes. Although they were lovers, Nin was also in love with Miller's wife, June Miller. Their entanglements were recorded in detail, which were scattered across the eleven thick volumes of Nin's diaries. The story became the inspiration for the movie *Henry & June* (1990).

5

From Character Analysis to Cloud Busting

Wilhelm Reich; the Lonely Prophet

In 1974, when I first arrived in Seattle, I hardly knew anyone, everything was new and unfamiliar, and the loneliness was almost unbearable. One day, by chance I wandered into a used bookstore on a side street by the university campus. It turned out to be very well stocked, with some fine books I didn't know existed.

I was elated by the sight of books stacked from floor to ceiling. They reminded me of the used bookstores I frequented so often during my college days in Taiwan. The bookstore made it easier for me to bear the onslaught of waves of homesickness.

One day, while I was busy browsing through the books, a thin volume fell off the shelf. Picking it up, I noticed that the cover featured a middle-aged man with a full head of white hair, holding an infant in his arms, who must have been barely one year old. They were smiling warmly at each other. This was my first encounter with *A Book of Dreams* (Reich, 1973), written by a young man by the name of Peter Reich.

The blurb inside the book said that Peter was Wilhelm Reich's young son, and that Wilhelm Reich was a psychiatrist who died in a federal prison in 1957, when Peter was only thirteen years old.

A psychiatrist in prison? That piqued my curiosity. The introduction of the book said that prior to his imprisonment, he had been involved with numerous lawsuits with the Food and Drug Administration (FDA) and that eventually he was arrested for the illegal transportation of medical equipment across state lines. But this was not why he was sent to prison. He ended up there because of a charge of contempt of court.

I was confused. Why did this Wilhelm Reich, whoever he was, run afoul of the authorities? I went to the university's library to look it up and found that Reich was not only a *bona fide* psychiatrist, but also a psychoanalyst. He was known in the 1920s as a favored protégé of Freud's. But why, and how, did a psychoanalyst get into trouble with the FDA?

WHEN FREUD MET MARX

To answer these questions, we have to go back to the year 1918, right after the end of World War I.

At the age of twenty-one, Reich had just returned to Austria from the warfront in Italy and was newly enrolled in the medical school of the University of Vienna. By chance he attended one of Freud's lectures and was immediately taken in by Freud's theories on "sexuality." One year later he finally had a chance to visit "the Master." The meeting went extremely well, ending in his being invited to join the Psychoanalytic Society.

Freud and his colleagues were so impressed with the young man that in 1924, just two years after Reich's graduation from medical school, he was appointed the training director at the Vienna Ambulatorium.[1] He worked in that capacity until 1930. During those years, he was nicknamed "Freud's pet" (Sharaf, 1983; Turner, 2011).

However, in 1930 Reich was forced to resign from the Viennese Psychoanalytical Society and leave Vienna. This happened because, in addition to being a psychoanalyst, he was also a believer in Marxism and a leader of the Austrian Socialist Party. He was convinced that the two major intellectual and social movements should be merged and he worked diligently to try to make such a union happen.

According to Marx, in feudalistic and capitalist societies the ruling class was able to exploit and abuse the masses only because the oppressed did not have the will to rebel and fight for their rights. But why were people unable to rise up to address all the horrendous injustices they endured? And, how could they be aroused to liberate themselves? Reich thought that Freudian theories provided the answers to these fundamental questions.

According to Reich, people were restricted and paralyzed because, starting from their infancy, their sexual drives were completely and continuously inhibited and repressed. They became used to submitting to the power of authority embedded in patriarchal and hierarchical systems. Such suppression and brainwashing were so extreme that they did not even know what their own rights were and were unable to fight for them.

Reich reasoned that this is where the new insights coming from psychoanalysis could play a critical role in social reform. He was convinced that in order for the oppressed to be liberated, they needed to first be freed from sexual oppression. To make this happen, he organized a department for sexual education within the Socialist Party to promote healthy sexual attitudes and behaviors. These efforts included the promotion of the use of contraceptives, the right to abortion, and the general elevation of women's status.

---

[1] Outpatient clinic.

These activities shocked the society's leaders and those in charge of public security. They had already been nervous about talks of "sexual liberation" on the university campus. How could they now let Reich spread such "dangerous ideas" to the general public? Even worse, they found out that Reich was targeting his efforts at adolescents and young people because of his belief in early intervention. This triggered a panic, and rumors started to circulate, accusing Reich of being a pedophile. Facing such controversies, the socialists expelled him from the party. They wanted to choose their battles and did not want to draw unnecessary attention to themselves. At the same time, psychoanalysts felt Reich's efforts were premature and decided to distance themselves from him. Rejected by both sides, Reich decided to leave Vienna to search for greener pastures.

DR. REICH BESIEGED

Moving to Berlin in 1930, Reich found a city in turmoil. The Great Depression led to accelerating inflation and sky-rocketing unemployment. Those who had lost their jobs and livelihoods joined either the Communist Party or the Nazi Party, looking for radical solutions. Many paramilitary groups were formed, and their members prowled the city, looking for fights.

But for Reich, Berlin was just the right place. There he found many like-minded analysts and left-wing thinkers, including Erich Fromm and other young scholars who later became the backbone of the renowned Frankfurt School.

Reich found a home in Berlin where he was able to practice his brand of psychoanalysis, and at the same time actively engaged in political activities as a member of the German Communist Party. In three short years, he completed and published some of his most influential books, including *Character Analysis*, *Dialectical Materialism and Psychoanalysis*, and *The Mass Psychology of Fascism*.

But his relentless promotion of "sexual liberation" and his unreserved criticism of both Hitler and Stalin soon caught up with him. He had expected attacks from the Nazis, but he was surprised by the Communist Party's decision to drive him out as well.

Facing threats of violence, he left Berlin in a great hurry. Seeking safe haven, he first went to Copenhagen, Denmark and then tried Stockholm, Sweden. But his reputation preceded him. Both countries were uneasy about his controversial theories and were also worried about his corrupting their youth with wild talks of sexual liberation.

While searching up and down for a place to move to, he sustained another major blow, this time from the International Society of Psychoanalysis, which took away his membership.

Unexpectedly, Norway opened its door and Reich was able to breathe easily in Oslo, at least for a short while.

HOW TO HELP PATIENTS DISARM THEIR
"WHOLE-BODY ARMOR"

During his five-year stay in Norway, Reich was again extremely productive. He developed and promoted a new therapeutic method called "vegetotherapy," and established a scientific laboratory to search for the source of the life force he believed to be central to the healing of patients.

Vegetotherapy represented a natural extension of his earlier works discussed in the book *Character Analysis*, which convincingly described how intra-psychic conflicts (which he believed to be due to sexual inhibition) could cause tension and imbalance of muscles in the whole body, leading to various health problems. It was as if such patients' bodies were totally trapped in thick armors, limiting freedom and ease of movement. To help reduce such bodily tension, he developed a method using his hands and fingers to "talk" directly with patients' bodies, assisting them to shed their restricting shields and become more in touch with their inner selves.

Such practices went totally against one of the most basic tenets of psychoanalysis and psychotherapy: the avoidance of direct bodily contact between the therapist and the patient. Reich not only disregarded this most sacred "commandment," but even instructed his patients to be naked during the therapy session. This made complete sense to him. For him, clothes were camouflage, serving the function of hiding oneself from others, and consequently also from oneself. They were the visible shells we wore that would have to be removed for treatment to ensue.

Looking back from our current vantage point, we can easily say that this is common sense. Otherwise, how could massage therapists do their work? But in Reich's time, European societies were still very much influenced by Victorian values, in which bodies were not supposed to exist. Reich's practices collided head-on with prevailing social codes, and his motivations were easily seen as prurient in nature, leading to all sorts of rumors that spread like wildfire.

WHERE IS THE SOURCE OF THE LIFE FORCE?

Rumors notwithstanding, patients flocked to Reich seeking magical cures. With the substantive income generated from his practice, and donations from people who had benefited from his treatment, Reich was able to set up a sizable, well-equipped laboratory at the University of Oslo. Using the most advanced biological research methods and equipment, he set out to search for the basic substances that sustained life and made healing possible.

After much trial and error, Reich thought that he had finally found what he was searching for. He did this by lumping sand, iron, grass, gelatin, and animal tissue together, and heating the mixture with an electric torch. When it reached 500°C, bright glowing blue vesicles suddenly emerged. He believed these to be the rudimentary forms of life and named them "bions." In petri dishes, he observed that these bions grew and proliferated. When he showered the bion-containing liquid on flowers and shrubs, they apparently grew and grew! Taking it one step further, Reich fed the bions to the mice in his laboratory, and the creatures reportedly became supersized and disease-resistant. He reasoned that if this was not the source of life, the spring of eternal youth, what was?

Prominent physicians and researchers rushed in from all over the world. Some came to study "vegetotherapy," while others wanted to take part in this new scientific venture. They wrote enthusiastic praises in magazines and newspapers that supported the importance of Reich's new findings.

Unfortunately, his growing fame also attracted the attention of leaders in medical and scientific fields, who became increasingly frustrated by Reich's arrogant rejections of their pleas to moderate his fantastic claims. Reich would not budge. Desperate, they petitioned the Norwegian government to deny the extension of Reich's visa.

These requests triggered strong reactions from academic leaders. Even though many of them also questioned Reich's research methods and conclusions, they were even more worried about the use of political power to settle academic disputes. They also thought that it would be very unfair to Reich – deporting him back to Germany would be akin to a death sentence at the Nazis' hands.

Fortunately, at that moment, one of Reich's American admirers found a teaching post for him in New York. He left Norway in the nick of time, just before it was invaded and occupied by Hitler's forces. Ironically, Reich might have those "traditional" scientists to thank, who went out of their way to boot him out, which saved his life!

Safe in the New World, Reich was infused with even more energy than before. Not long after his arrival, he bought and remodeled a sizable house in Queens, New York. He remodeled one of the upstairs bedrooms, converting it into a therapy room, and made the whole first floor and basement into his office, meeting rooms, and laboratories. His clinical practice soon started to thrive in this new setting, and his "bionic elixir" was as bright and as potent as before, working "magic" with plants and animals.

TAMING OF A MAN WITH AN ABUNDANT LIBIDO

Reich's personal life also went through a number of changes around this time. He had been estranged from his wife, Annie Pink, a fellow psychoanalyst, since leaving Vienna almost a decade earlier. Although Pink had also immigrated to the USA with their two children before his arrival, they opted for divorce rather than reunion.

While in Berlin, Reich fell in love with Elsa Lindenberg, an accomplished dancer, dance therapist, and socialist. Lindenberg accompanied Reich to Denmark and then Norway, but refused to follow him across the Atlantic. Although still in love with each other, the relationship had been strained by Reich's frequent affairs, leading to intense jealousy and domestic violence.

In Queens, he was introduced to twenty-nine-year-old Ilse Ollendorf, who became his bookkeeper and laboratory assistant (Ollendorf, 1969). She soon moved in and became an indispensable part of his household and his life, providing him with a measure of stability. When they finally got married, Peter, their only son, was already two years old.

LIBIDO WAS TRANSFORMED INTO ORGONE

When Freud first proposed the concept of "libido" in his book *Three Essays on the Theory of Sexuality* (Freud, 1920), he saw it as something akin to electricity. Believing that libido was physiological in nature, he hoped that it would soon be quantifiable with scientific instruments. However, frustrated at not being able to pin it down in a concrete manner, Freud gradually abandoned the idea of its being a physiological phenomenon.

According to Freud, libido was a kind of energy that was attached to different parts of the body at different psychosexual developmental stages: oral, anal, phallic, and genital. The last stage, the genital period, was regarded as the most mature phase of human development, providing the foundation for good mental and physical health. But it was not clear how this most highly desirable genital stage is defined and achieved.

Not clear, except to Reich, who thought the answer was self-evident. The basic factor, he reasoned, had to be with the capability to achieve orgasm. This function, he believed, was essential for releasing the tension caused by the build-up of the bioelectric energy that was the libido. This release would lead to achieving a state of homeostasis and balance that was important for the promotion of health and prevention of diseases. In Reich's mind, since the energy or life force associated with orgasm is so fundamental and so all-encompassing, it should not just be called libido. Thus, he created a new term for it: *orgone*.

But where did the life force, or orgone, come from? Reich thought it had to come from outside. But where from? And how did it happen? To answer these questions, he and his followers bought a 280-acre farm in the town of Rangeley, Western Maine, on which they built a well-designed laboratory, a library, and an astrological observatory. He named this new farm "Orgonon."

An astrological observatory? What, one might wonder, did it have to do with psychiatry? It turned out that Reich had come to the conclusion that our orgone energy came from the sky. In order to understand how the energy coming from the natural world was converted to orgone energy, he started to spend a great deal of time in the observatory, using high-powered telescopes to observe the Earth's atmosphere.

After several years of hard work, Reich and his followers accumulated tons of data, which they believed contained the answers they sought. Armed with their exciting new findings, they constructed a new device, called the "orgone accumulator." This was a large box that looked like a small shower room when seen from the outside. Patients went in totally naked, in order to absorb the energy that had been accumulated by the machine from the natural world.

Soon Reich and his followers alleged they were able to demonstrate that the orgone accumulators indeed helped enhance patients' immunity, leading to significant improvement in their health. These results were published by their own Organon Research Institute, with articles, pamphlets, and books reporting studies conducted on microorganisms, cells, tissues, animals, human volunteers, and, finally, patients. They convinced many professionals, as well as the general public, of the efficacy of the contraption. Responding to increasing demand, Reich and company also designed orgone blankets that were portable and less expensive. These instruments, large and small, soon became hot items on the market, with demands coming from all over the country.

Reich's success led to unwanted attention that eventually became his undoing. In 1947, Mildred Edie Brady, a well-known writer famed for protecting consumers' rights, got wind of this new "miracle cure" and published a well-researched and extremely caustic review of the orgone accumulator (Brady, 1948). She pointed out that Reich's findings had never been corroborated by independent laboratories, and the new device had never been peer-reviewed or approved by the FDA. Thus, she suggested that the selling and promotion of these "medical devices" was not only unethical, but also illegal.

She asked how the medical and psychiatric communities could have allowed this to happen and she registered her displeasure with the professional authorities for their *laissez-faire* attitude toward such an embarrassing "fraud."

At first, Reich thought that Brady was just another of Stalin's agents, who had been harassing him since his days in Berlin. In 1939 he had been detained for several days at Ellis Island by the Federal Bureau of Investigation (FBI) for his complicated relationship with communists. He had believed that this happened because informers sent by the Soviet Union alerted the FBI to his past political activities. Since he had already been cleared by the FBI, he did not think anything would happen with Brady's report. He was thus surprised when the FDA took Brady's complaints seriously. FDA agents swarmed Organon, looking into anything they could lay their hands on. They combed through his records and scrutinized his publications. Soon, FDA agents started to follow him around while spying on Orgonon. During a surprise visit, they found 250 orgone accumulators, which they confiscated as evidence. During their investigation they interviewed a large number of Reich's female customers, insinuating that these women had been using the device as a cover for providing sexual services.

Reich was defiant and uncompromising. He acquired a large stock of firearms and ammunition, and had his supporters patrol the perimeter of Orgonon to keep out suspicious characters.

In 1956, an FDA agent posing as a customer approached one of his students, Michael Silvert, asking for a batch of Orgone accumulators to be sent from Maine to New York. Silvert was arrested and Reich was sued by the government for illegally transporting medical devices across state lines. At the time, Reich was in Arizona with his teenage son, Peter, and knew nothing about the charge or the order for him to appear in court. His absence was ruled as contempt of court, for which he was eventually sentenced to two years' imprisonment. Around the same time, the FDA also finally obtained approval from the federal court to confiscate and destroy all orgone accumulators and any books related to the device. They did not find much in the State of Maine, but had a windfall in New York that resulted in the public burning of four tons of books at the busiest intersection in Manhattan.

The lawsuits dragged on for several years, during which time Reich insisted on not hiring lawyers as he believed he was the most qualified to speak on the issues involved. He demanded that judges read all of his publications in order to be well informed and impartial. He insisted that he had the inherent right to explore natural phenomena, which should not be stopped by anyone wielding political power. Even if his theories were eventually proven wrong, it was no reason for him to be hanged, he said.

WHEN A PSYCHIATRIST BECAME A RAINMAKER

Why did Reich go to Arizona? He went there to make rain and end a drought. He believed he was able to do that because he had designed a machine called "*the cloudbuster.*" Cloudbusters, about the size of small anti-aircraft guns, are made from an array of parallel hollow metal tubes connected at the rear to a series of flexible metal hoses. Reich claimed that when he aimed the pipes at areas of the sky, they would draw the orgone energy out of the atmosphere and cause the formation of rain clouds. As a "proof," he pointed out that, in Maine, it did bring a drought to an end and averted a crisis for local strawberry farmers.

With donations from grateful farmers, Reich and his colleagues shifted their attention to the American Southwest, where a persistent dry spell had devastated the whole region. Bringing with them several of the most advanced cloudbusters, they set about to change the threatening weather pattern, hoping that the success of such a large-scale expedition would bring them sizable donations to solve Orgonon's funding problems.

Not many people knew at the time that these cloudbusters were designed to serve multiple functions. Their original purpose actually was not rainmaking but was for the identification of something he called deadly orgone radiation (DOR), which Reich believed to be the ultimate cause for all kinds of illnesses. In addition to causing ill health, DOR also negatively impacted the environment in general, causing desertification (the process of desert formation due to changes in weather patterns). It was primarily for the purpose of neutralizing DOR that he designed these gigantic machines. He called this work "cosmic orgone engineering."

Who or what was responsible for these DORs? Reich had come to believe that DORs were the work of aliens who had come from outer space to help Stalin and his cronies fight against him. He further believed that these alien forces had already infiltrated different branches of the American government, including the FDA and FBI, all the way to the top echelon. But the president and the secretary of the air force were supposedly aware of what was going on and they were secretly protecting him. This was why airplanes were flying around wherever he went.

During the last few years of Reich's life, many of his students, friends, and patients distanced themselves from him because they were frightened by the "scandals." Most of the time, Reich was left to fight his war alone, with the exception of Peter, who became his most important assistant. Trusting, loving, and worshipping his father, Peter put all his mind and heart into learning how to operate the multifunctional cloudbuster. Improving his ability to identify and fire at the intruding UFOs, Peter's proficiency and dedication earned him the title of sergeant of cosmic orgone engineering, and he was soon promoted to the rank of a lieutenant by his father. Reich warned Peter that Soviet Russia was plotting against him, with the FDA and FBI persecuting him at the same time. He also told everyone still in his circle that at any moment he could be arrested, imprisoned, and even murdered.

These predictions, unfortunately, turned out to be partially accurate. In March 1957, Reich was tried in his absence and given a two-year prison term. Whenever Peter went to the prison to visit Reich, he always told his son to be brave but also to remain tender in his heart and not be ashamed if he had to cry. His last letter to Peter, dated October 1957, seemed to be full of hope, indicating that he was likely to be paroled in a few weeks. But a few days after that, in the middle of the night, he suffered a fatal heart attack and quickly passed away.

Growing up, Peter completely blocked out most memories of his father and his childhood. He did well at school, graduating from Boston University with a master's degree in public health. He traveled widely and made friends all over the world. But he always appeared distant, remote, and unable to talk to anybody about himself. He was also haunted by nightmares that refused to go away.

WAS DR. REICH PSYCHOTIC?

Two psychiatric evaluations were conducted on Reich while he was in prison. The first psychiatrist indicated that Reich had suffered from egomania and persecutory delusions. In contrast, the second expert reported that his basic personality was within the normal range, but he suffered from temporary psychotic symptoms due to stresses. Did he?

There seems no doubt that he was psychotic at least some of the time while imprisoned, but the question remains unanswered whether this was a relatively new development, or whether he had been psychotic for a long time.

Ever since Reich's break with Freudian psychoanalysts, rumors of his earlier hospitalizations for a psychotic condition had been circulating among his former colleagues. To this day, however, no records have been found of such incarcerations and treatments.

Irrespective of whether he had been treated earlier, reports about his bizarre behavior grew substantially during the last years of his life. The belief in UFO visits may not necessarily be a sign of psychosis, since it is widely shared by millions of otherwise "normal" people (Pasulka, 2019; Sagan, 1995). But the idea that the president and the secretary of the air force were his secret allies and would come to his rescue was harder to fathom. It was thus speculated by some of his biographers that he had long been suffering from paranoid schizophrenia, or at least a delusional disorder.

Reviewing his life history, it seems more likely that he had a bipolar disorder. Throughout his life, Reich was exceptionally energetic, self-confident, and impulsive. He was also said to be easily irritable. These are traits compatible with a bipolar diagnosis. His complicated and multiple love affairs were reflections of his hyper-sexuality, another symptom of mania. It was thus likely that, just as is true with many "geniuses," he lived in a hypomanic state for most of his life. This condition afforded him boundless energy and creativity without interfering with his ability to function until near the end of his life.

In addition to bipolar disorder, Reich's "strange" ideas and behaviors might also have roots in his childhood experiences. Reich was born in a small town right at the border of the Austro-Hungarian and Russian Empires. His father was an extremely strict and unforgiving person. Although born a Jew himself, he prohibited his children from having contacts with anything Jewish. When Reich was ten, he accidently found that his mother was having an affair with his tutor. According to his autobiography, written many years later (Reich, 1988), for months he hid in the closet, secretly listening to and even watching these sexual escapades. Such experiences elicited in him all sorts of emotional responses: anger, sympathy, envy, and jealousy. When the affair was exposed, the tutor ran away and his mother committed suicide by swallowing pesticides. Soon afterwards, his unforgiving father started going to the frozen lake nearby, "fishing." He eventually caught pneumonia and passed away.

To make matters even worse, at the end of World War I, both the Russian and Austro-Hungarian Empires collapsed, the borders were redrawn, and Reich and his brother lost their inheritances.

However we look at it, there is no question that Reich was severely traumatized during his childhood, which must have exerted major impacts on his personal and professional life.

WILHELM REICH'S LEGACY

During the five years I was in training in Seattle in the 1970s, I never heard of Wilhelm Reich from other psychiatrists. He was not mentioned in the courses on psychotherapy or in psychosomatic medicine or the history of psychiatry. Many years later, when I became fascinated with him and his struggles and brought it up with my colleagues, all I got was blank stares and silence. This led me to believe that Reich is even more embarrassing than lobotomy for the field of psychiatry, so much so that he was in effect wiped out of collective memory.

But did he really disappear without a trace? Twenty-some years later, when I accidentally saw his books on prominent display in a souvenir shop in Ashland, Oregon, I was astonished. This was followed by something even more surprising: The salesperson told me that she was a devoted Reichian herself. She mentioned that Ashland was not just famous for its annual outdoor Shakespearean plays, it was actually a "mecca" for alternative healing, where Reich's theories and practices are still very much alive. In fact, on the hillside not far from town, there is a major Reichian institution named "Natural Energy Work," which has been active in publishing books and organizing workshops for the purpose of promoting Reich's legacy. Of course, they also manufacture and market orgone accumulators and blankets, as well as other related products.

A search on the Internet showed that Ashland was not the only place where Reich remained popular. Similar organizations exist in many parts of the country, competing for the market for orgone accumulators. Some of them also manufacture and sell cloudbusters.

Among these Reichian organizations, the largest and the most authoritative has to be the Wilhelm Reich Infant Trust, located at the Orgonon campus in Rangeley, Maine. The Trust has long been active in editing and publishing Reich's books and pamphlets. It also organizes annual Reichian conferences and provides various training courses and workshops.

Somehow, Orgonon became recognized as an official historical site, and has evolved into a tourist spot. Every day, visitors come to pay their respects at Reich's grave and statue, where they are awed and mystified by the remains of one of his humongous cloudbusters. Many are so impressed that they are motivated to write online about their impressions, commenting on Reich's life and ideas.

Reich has also continued to have a major impact on many writers and artists. Notables include Norman Mailer, Saul Bellow, and J. D. Salinger. All these prestigious authors mentioned that they had benefited from vegetotherapy. In addition, Reich's ideas on sexual suppression and social injustice had a significant influence on contemporary thinkers such as Michel Foucault.

However, what really convinced me of Reich's continuing relevance in the modern world was what I saw at the City Lights Bookstore, the famous landmark in San Francisco. While visiting the bookstore, I was surprised to find that in its basement there was a whole wall of books related to Reich, proving that he remains of interest to a large group of readers more than half a century after his tragic death.

PETER REICH'S NIGHTMARES

After a major accident leading to multiple fractures and surgeries, Peter woke up from general anesthesia only to be assaulted further by intense nightmares. With therapy, he gradually regained many of his childhood memories. The recovery of his memories eventually freed him from the burden of having to play the role of his father's sergeant or lieutenant, even if only at the unconscious level. Peter no longer needed to be part of Reich's mission to save the universe by fighting flying saucers, Soviet Russia, and the federal government at the same time. His nightmares finally receded.

As a friend of Peter, Kate Bush, the British singer, was deeply moved by his life story and wrote the song "Cloudbusting" (Bush, 2010). She also produced a video to accompany the song, with the actor Donald Sutherland as Wilhelm Reich. The song and the video are on the web and can be downloaded any time for free. In this way, Wilhelm Reich continues to live on "the cloud," possibly for eternity, reminding us of his passion, struggles, and tragedies.

6

Ernest Jones
Freud's Wizard

Ernest Jones was the first English-speaking psychoanalyst, and a crucial figure in the development of world psychoanalysis. In the early 1910s, after the "defection" of Alfred Adler and Carl Jung, Jones became one of Freud's most ardent supporters. He was the founding president of the British Psychoanalytic Society and served as president of the International Psychoanalytic Society for twenty-some years (1922–1925; 1934–1951).

It was mostly because of him that Freud and his family were able to escape the Nazis at the last moment. In his old age he became the only official biographer of Freud, creating an opus divided into three volumes, each more than 500 pages long. This tome continues to be regarded as a classic and a valuable source for references for understanding the history of psychoanalysis.

MERLIN'S DESCENDANT

Jones was a Welshman through and through. Although the Welsh were defeated by the English in the thirteenth century and Wales have been an integral part of the UK ever since, the Welsh kept their culture and traditions alive for many centuries. Even toward the end of the nineteenth century, when Jones was born, Welsh was still a widely spoken language in the region.

Along with the Scots, Irish, and Cornish, the Welsh have been regarded as the "aborigines" of the British Isles. They are descendants of the Celts[1] who had escaped assimilation by the invading Anglo-Saxons arriving in the fifth

---

[1] Celts were the inhabitants of continental Europe and the Britain Isles from 3000 BC. They introduced bronze and metal working to the area. Although much remains unclear regarding their cultures and lifestyles, it was believed that they held firm beliefs in animism and the power of magic. They erected many outdoor structures comprising huge slabs of stone, measuring up to two meters tall and one meter in width and depth; the most famous is the Stonehenge, in southwestern England. It is believed that these structures served religious purposes, probably involving human sacrifice at the dawn of the spring equinox. The Celts were conquered by the Romans about 2,000 years ago, and then were invaded by wave after wave of migrating Germanic tribes, including

century. The Welsh people have been commonly regarded as a "happy-go-lucky" nation, who tend to be superstitious, imaginative, musical, artistic, glib, and even untrustworthy, a common prejudice of dominant groups towards the oppressed.

The famed legends of King Arthur and the Knights of the Round Table originated from tales of Welsh resistance to the invading Anglo-Saxons. Merlin, often regarded as the most mystical and fascinating figure in these stories, was seen as a wizard with supernatural power who aided King Arthur in his conquests. This was why the author of a recent biography of Jones titled the book *Freud's Wizard* (Maddox, 2006).

However, when Jones was born, Wales was in the middle of seismic transformations. During the Industrial Revolution, Great Britain needed an unlimited supply of coal, which was abundant in Wales. Industrialists moved their factories to Wales to be close to the energy source. Consequently, the once remote and tranquil Welsh countryside was rapidly transformed into industrial towns.

Reflecting such changes, both of Jones' parents came from families who climbed up the social ladder. From farmers and pastoralists, they became blacksmiths, ship carpenters, and foremen, and eventually "white-collar" workers. Jones' father, a good example of such upward mobility, was an autodidact who taught himself to become an accountant and was eventually promoted to the position of factory manager.

Entering the "middle class," the elder Jones started to live mostly in the English-speaking world, which gradually molded his identity. In contrast, growing up in the countryside, Jones' mother remained more fluent in Welsh and preferred to talk to Jones in her mother tongue, calling him Myrddin (Merlin in Welsh). But Jones' father saw English as the language of the future and insisted that he be registered as Alfred Ernest. This was how he came to be known as Ernest Jones.

Although both of Jones' parents grew up belonging to Welsh-speaking Baptist churches, his father insisted that they should use English when praying at home. When Jones was nine years old, the Church of England came to town. Jones' father immediately converted to that faith, while his mother resisted such a change by just staying at home, praying privately on Sundays. Caught in between, Jones became an atheist.

Although Jones' Welsh was not fluent, his accented English betrayed his Welsh origin. He tried hard to hide this and was able to do so by the time he entered college. But since Jones was the most common surname in Wales, it was hard for him to hide his Welsh origin, no matter how hard he tried to get rid of his Welsh accent.

the Anglo-Saxons. Other than Wales, Scotland, and Ireland, small pockets of populations still exist in Europe (such as Brittany in France) who use languages derived from Celtic.

One might say that Jones was a typical example of a marginal man. He grew up in a town flanked by bucolic hinterland on one side, and bustling industrial compounds on the other. His mother stuck to her roots in Welsh-speaking Baptist traditions, whereas his father had no compunction in metamorphosing into a British gentleman. The young Jones was sometimes Welsh, sometimes English. This made it possible for him to switch between different identities with relative ease. Many years later, when he became one of the most powerful figures in the field of psychoanalysis, some of his critics labeled him a cunning and unreliable opportunist, mistaking the relative fluidity of his identity as evidence of duplicity.

Jones was an exceptionally intelligent child, always at the top in academic performance. His teachers' only complaint of him was that he was too talkative. But soon this drawback was turned to his advantage as well: He became an excellent debater, easily outsmarting his opponents and winning many medals and commendations.

At fourteen, he was awarded a full scholarship from a well-endowed public school, and became financially independent from his parents. In that liberal and accommodating school setting, he read widely, was exposed to many different schools of thoughts, and was particularly impressed with T. H. Huxley's[2] writings, which converted him into a life-long Darwinian.

Reaching the age of sixteen, Jones greatly disappointed his teachers by turning down a scholarship from Cambridge. Instead, he elected to enter a new local medical school, and two years later transferred to the University of London for clinical courses.

On the brink of the twentieth century, modern medicine was progressing at lightning speed, and vaccinations became widely available to the general population. Research in epidemiology shed light on the cause and prevention of various infectious diseases such as cholera and typhoid fever; Joseph Lister invented sterilization in surgical procedures, saving countless lives. Pioneers in neurology, such as Jean-Martin Charcot,[3] explored the neuroanatomical and neurophysiological bases of neuropsychiatric disorders. Paying special attention to the enigma of "hysteria," they suggested that the human mind and emotions need not be shrouded in myth, but could be investigated with scientific methods.

Jones was excited by all of these developments. He studied hard, often to the extent of sacrificing food and sleep. He saw himself as a man of science and

---

[2] Huxley was a famous British biologist who lived during the time of Darwin and was the foremost promoter of Darwinism.

[3] Charcot was the most famous and most influential French neuroscientist in the late nineteenth century. He identified and systematically described a large number of neurological disorders, and thus has been regarded as the father of modern neurology. He also made groundbreaking discoveries on the phenomenology and treatment of hysteria and a number of other major "psychoneurosis." Thus, he was also called "the Napoleon of neurosis." Freud was a student with him from early October, 1885–to the end of February, 1886 and regarded him as one of his most important mentors.

he was fully devoted to what he was doing. His diligence and mental agility were duly noted by his teachers, many of whom were at the forefront of the field. Although barely older than twenty, he was already full of self-confidence, convinced that his future was boundlessly promising.

YOUNG AND RECKLESS

When Jones graduated from medical school in 1902, his plan was to spend a year or two at a regional hospital to garner additional clinical experience and then he would be ready to return to his alma mater, the University of London, to pursue an academic career, and become a tenured full professor in due course. It was beyond his imagination that in the next ten years there would be one setback after another.

In those ten years, first in England and then in North America, he was repeatedly accused of "behavioral indiscretion" and fired from his positions. Not only that, he also barely escaped being gunned down. What went wrong? Was he just unlucky or was there something seriously wrong with his character?

If we look closely, it would seem that, in addition to whatever defects or blind spots he might have had, he got into trouble so often because he was arrogant, prideful, competitive, and addicted to the limelight. Offended and outshone by him, his colleagues and coworkers resented him and would not come to his rescue when he got into trouble. And he got into trouble he did, often, usually because he was excessively solicitous to those he was attracted to. His attention and capacity to make someone feel special typically led to misunderstandings. This was particularly problematic with women, whom he felt a compulsion to charm. The charmed ladies would often fall under his spell, and many were madly in love with him, repeatedly complicating his life.

In 1903, he was fired by a small regional hospital for repeated truancy. He claimed that there were medical emergencies with his girlfriend that demanded his full attention. He had no idea what kind of trouble he was getting himself into, finding out too late the gravity of the situation. This record followed him wherever he went, so much so that he was unable to obtain another full-time job, despite having passed one medical qualification examinations after another, with flying colors. He was thus forced to make do with a number of part-time jobs, criss-crossing the city of London. Gone was the dream of returning to university and becoming a professor.

Two years later, Jones' father came up with funds for him and his good friend Wilfred Trotter,[4] a neurosurgeon seven years his senior, to set up

---

[4] Wilfred Trotter was a famous British neurosurgeon who also made prominent contributions in social psychology. He was later appointed honorary surgeon for the king and became a fellow of the London Royal Society of Science. His book *Instincts of the Herd in Peace and War* was very influential in the development of crowd psychology and marketing. He was Jones' brother-in-law.

a medical practice on a street studded with many famous physicians' offices. Jones settled down, but only for a short while. Another scandal soon erupted. This time he was doing language assessment at an institution for people with intellectual disabilities when four children accused him of indecent behavior. Although the court ruled against the accusation (due to people's belief at that time of the unreliability of the testimony of those with intellectual disabilities), Jones' reputation was further tarnished.

It was around this time that Trotter introduced him to Freud's writings. He immediately became fascinated with Freud's new ideas. At the same time, David Eder,[5] a physician tutored by Jones for his medical degree examination, introduced Loe (Louise Dorothea Kann), a very rich Jewish Dutch heiress with opioid addiction problems, to Jones. They soon fell in love and started living together.

With Loe's financial support, Jones was able to attend a medical conference in Amsterdam in 1907, where he met Carl Jung (Kerr, 1993) and Otto Gross. Following the conference, he went on to Munich to be a visiting physician at the famed psychiatric hospital of Emil Kraepelin,[6] where he studied descriptive psychiatry for one month. Following that he went on to Zurich to visit Jung, and met Brill,[7] who was also visiting at the time.

In March 1908, Jones again ran into trouble, after becoming known as a follower of Freud. This reputation led to Jones being consulted on a case that had puzzled many doctors at a hospital where he was working on a part-time basis. A ten-year-old girl had been admitted due to a sudden paralysis of her

---

[5] Eder was a Briton of Jewish descend. He was originally a general practitioner. While serving as a military surgeon during World War I, he witnessed and treated numerous cases of soldiers suffering from "shell shock," which piqued his interest in the psychological problems related with life events, as well as the possibility of using psychoanalysis to help these patients. He read widely on the emerging literature in the field and translated works by Jung and Freud. In addition to becoming a Freudian psychoanalyst, he was also an active member of the Zionism movement and spent long stretches of time in Palestine. He also established a training farm in Kent for young Central European Jewish refugees.

[6] Kraepelin was arguably the most famous and most influential psychiatrist in the late nineteenth and early twentieth centuries. He actively promoted the use of objective observations and longitudinal follow-up in studying the phenomenology and classification of major psychiatric syndromes. He was the first to differentiate manic-depressive disorder (bipolar disorder) from schizophrenia (then called dementia praecox). His influences are still recognizable today. He is often regarded as the father of modern psychiatry.

[7] Brill was born in Austria but went by himself to the USA at the age of fifteen, supporting himself through high school and college, eventually graduating from the School of Medicine, Columbia University, at the age of twenty-eight (in 1904). He then went to Baltimore to study psychiatry with Adolf Meyer, then to Zurich in 1907 to study psychoanalysis with Eugen Bleuler and Carl Jung at the Burghölzli Hospital (at the time, Jung was still regarded as Freud's heir apparent), and started translating books by Freud, Jung, and Bleuler into English. He founded the New York Psychoanalytic Society and the American Psychoanalytic Society and kept both apart from the International Psychoanalytic Society. He defied Freud's intent to include none-MD members in psychoanalytic societies and was instrumental in ensuring that membership of the mainstream American psychoanalytic organizations were limited to those with medical training. His influences on psychoanalysis as well as on the whole field of psychiatry peaked between 1929 and 1936.

right arm. Since there was no neurological basis for her paralysis, Jones was asked to try the "psychoanalytic method" to see if the etiology of this condition could be clarified. Jones found out that just prior to the onset of the paralysis, an older boy who had been the girl's playmate attempted to do something "inappropriate," and the girl used her right arm to push him away. The paralysis emerged right after the incident. Jones was excited about the apparent psychological link and reported this back to his supervisor. However, once back in the ward, the girl told ward attendants that Jones "talked dirty" to her. The director found out that similar complaints had been lodged against Jones before and had to let him go. This scandal sealed the deal – Jones was no longer able to stay in London.

Luckily for Jones, right at that time, William Osler[8] (Launer, 2016) and Charles Clarke[9] were in London to recruit teaching staff for the young medical school at the University of Toronto. They were impressed with Jones' resume and also enjoyed their interviews with him. Although the neuropsychiatric clinic would not be ready for another two years, Clarke hired Jones on the spot, giving him an interim position at Clarke's sanitorium to function as a psychiatrist there.

HAMLET IN TORONTO

Although Loe and Jones never went through an official wedding ceremony, Jones came to regard Loe as his wife and wanted Loe to go with him to Toronto. However, Loe had serious misgivings about living in the "wild" New World, especially Canada. The trip was therefore postponed for six months. Jones took the time, as part of his preparation for the new job, to visit many of those he admired. His first stop was Salzburg, to attend the First Congress of the International Psychoanalytic Society. This was where he finally met Freud. Listening to the three-hour lecture by Freud on the case of the *Rat Man* (Mahony, 1986), he fell into a state of rapture.

After the conference, he and Brill went back to Vienna with Freud in order to attend some of his famous Wednesday night meetings. Then the two future leaders of psychoanalysis in North America went together to Budapest to visit Sándor Ferenczi.[10] Jones went from there to Munich alone, where he

---

[8] Osler was a Canadian physician. While working at McGill University and the University of Pennsylvania, he became a world-renowned exponent for bedside clinical teaching. He was widely regarded as the force behind revolutionary changes in modern medical practice. He has been called the father of modern medicine.

[9] Clarke was a Canadian psychiatrist who came from a family with several generations of involvement in running asylums. He devoted his entire life to the improvement of psychiatric education and care and was among the first to promote community mental health. He was the founding chair of the Department of Neurology and Psychiatry at the University of Toronto. The Clarke Institute, with a long track record in excellence in addiction research, was named after him.

[10] Ferenczi was a Jewish Hungarian who became Freud's colleague and follower early in the development of psychoanalysis. He drifted away from Freudian thoughts in his old age due to his

studied biological psychiatry with Kraepelin during the day and was "analyzed" by Otto Gross at his old haunt, the Stephanie Café, in the evening. Stephanie Café was where Gross socialized with and provided "psychoanalysis" for many artists and literature luminaries, including D. H. Lawrence and his own wife, Frieda von Richthofen.

Jones soon realized how hopelessly addicted Gross was to both heroin and cocaine. Gross' decadent lifestyle and complicated amorous relationships alarmed him. In May of that year Gross was coerced into hospitalization at the Burghölzli Hospital in Zurich to be treated by Jung. Gross later escaped from the hospital and returned to Munich, even more hopelessly sick than before (see Chapter 2). It appeared that during the time that Gross was away, Jones – who was requested by Gross to "treat" Gross' wife Frieda – became "excessively attached" to her. In his autobiography, written many years later, he spent pages reminiscing about the fine time he had with Frieda during that period.

From Munich he returned to London, after making a short detour to again visit Jung. After a short rest, he was on the move again, going to Paris, where he stayed for six weeks to study with Charcot's student, Pierre Marie.[11] After this, he felt he had learned all he needed to learn, had made all the connections that were important, and was ready for his major move.

Loe finally agreed to accompany Jones to Toronto, along with her two maids, as well as Jones' two sisters. Just prior to departure, in a letter he wrote to Freud, he jokingly said that he was going with his full contingency of a "harem." There might be a certain degree of truth in this statement, as he did later develop an intimate relationship with Lina, one of the maids.

Jones and others of his household did not adjust well to the new environment. Jones described Toronto as a desert when it came to culture and academia. Although this was certainly a gross exaggeration, it did reflect the degree of his loneliness there. Yet loneliness might not be a totally bad thing for an academician. Jones was finally able to focus on his work with fewer distractions, and had a prodigious output of journal articles, focused mostly on neurological topics.

At the same time, he started to promote ideas from psychoanalysis in many professional and public meetings. For his own intellectual sustenance, he grabbed at any opportunity to go to Boston. His passion and energy lessened the skepticism of many academic leaders who were suspicious of psychoanalysis. Jones was especially proud of the fact that he persuaded James

differing views on the need to focus on the here and now, and his belief that brief analysis had its place as part of the therapist's armamentarium. He exerted major influences on Otto Rank, Carl Rogers, and Jaques Lacan.

[11] Marie was Charcot's most accomplished student, and was famous for his pioneering works on the pituitary gland and the neuroendocrine systems. He was one of the discoverers of the Charcot–Marie-Tooth disease, which was named after him and Charcot.

Jackson Putnam, the 62-year-old leading neurologist in North America at the time, to become a full-blown supporter of Freudian theories.

Another major event in the autumn of 1909 was the visit of Freud and Jung to North America. After hearing so many rumors about psychoanalysis, North American academic leaders finally saw Freud in person. They were surprised to find that he was not wild at all, but was actually extremely self-disciplined. This proved to be immensely reassuring. Freud's and Jung's lectures at Clark University in psychoanalysis and the word association method proved to be huge successes, paving the way for future development of psychoanalysis in the USA and Canada.

Jones was exalted after a long talk during a two-hour walk with Freud, which further consolidated his devotion to psychoanalysis. At the same time, Freud gained real appreciation of the potential of North America as a fertile ground for psychoanalysis, and he viewed Jones with even higher regard. After the visit, the two of them started to correspond on an ongoing basis.

Encouraged by Freud, Jones started working on a psychoanalytical inter-pretation of Shakespeare's *Hamlet*. In the play, Hamlet's uncle murders Hamlet's father and marries Hamlet's mother. As the crown prince, Hamlet seeks revenge for his father, but throughout the play Hamlet continues to show profound indecision, which has puzzled and fascinated readers for several hundred years.

However, when Jones looked at the story from the angle of the Oedipus Complex, he did not find the story puzzling at all. Since, according to Freud's theory on infantile sexuality, Hamlet already had strong unconscious desires and drives to kill his father and possess his mother, he might feel a tremendous amount of guilt when his uncle did the deed, in essence fulfilling his own unconscious wishes. Revenge for his father would in a symbolic sense mean the negation of his own act. At the same time, since his uncle was a father figure to him, killing his uncle would also symbolically be another patricide. And, to the extent that Hamlet identified himself with his uncle, this would also amount to suicide. Although Jones' other writings were often criticized as superficial and not creative, this particular exposition on Hamlet was seen as an exception.

Far away from his homeland, Jones continued to exhibit tremendous ability to charm women. Although he had not been formally accused of any incidents during his tenure at Toronto, there was no shortage of rumors. There were also many letters of complaint, expressing at the same time the writers' craving and infatuation with him. A particularly puzzling event involved a woman who followed him all the way from Toronto to Chicago and attempted to kill him with a pistol. Jones was shaken to the point that he hired a twenty-four-hour bodyguard. He also offered to pay $500 dollars (equivalent to one year of his salary) to the woman, leading people to question his self-proclaimed innocence.

Unfortunately, after seven years, his relationship with Loe started to deteriorate. Loe's opioid addiction worsened, and her depression deepened to the point that she started contemplating either committing suicide or leaving Jones. In 1911, Jones went to Weimar to attend the Third Congress of the International Psychoanalytic Society and complained profusely to Freud about Loe. He was surprised when Freud offered to treat Loe and even more surprised to find that she readily accepted the offer.

Following a promotion to the rank of associate professor with tenure, Jones' credentials were good enough for him to return to England and start a new career there. Accordingly, he took his "harem" back to Europe.

ONE—TWO PUNCH

Upon returning to London, Jones was pleasantly surprised to find that his reputation as an expert in psychoanalysis had preceded him, and many patients were already waiting for him. His psychoanalytic book, *Papers on Psycho-Analysis*, as the first of such books in English, proved to be very popular and was for a long time in high demand, leading to several reprints and revisions. With the book, Jones' reputation soared further.

In a different sense, Jones' return to Europe was also timed perfectly. In that year, Alfred Adler and Wilhelm Stekel[12] left Freud, taking *Zentrablatt*, the Society's official journal, with them. The rift between Jung and Freud had been evident for quite some time, and the final breakup was expected to happen any moment. With Jung as the president of the International Psychoanalytic Society and the editor-in-chief of its journal *Jahrbuch*, the loss was next to unthinkable.

SECRET COMMITTEE

Facing these challenges, Jones proposed that a Secret Committee be organized, with membership including Karl Abraham,[13] Otto Rank (Lieberman,

---

[12] Stekel was one of Freud's earliest supporters and students, and a member of the Vienna Wednesday Meetings from the beginning. He made extensive contributions on the symbolic meaning of dreams and was involved in Freud's original writing of The *Interpretation of Dreams*. He also made significant contributions in clarifying issues related to the field's understanding of sexual dysfunction and "perversions." After breaking with Freud, he established his own practice and publication endeavors. He moved to London and committed suicide by overdosing in 1940.

[13] Abraham was a Jewish German. He met Jung while receiving psychiatric training at the Burghölzli Hospital in Zurich and became interested in psychoanalysis. In 1907, he went to Vienna to study with Freud and, in 1910, he founded the Berlin Psychoanalytic Society. He served from 1914 to 1918 as the president of the International Psychoanalytic Society. Many German and British psychoanalysts were trained by him.

2010), Hans Sachs,[14] and himself. To protect Freudian orthodoxy, each member of the committee pledged to *never* deviate from Freud's teaching. In order to achieve this goal, the committee members would communicate regularly with circular letters that were shared with all members and each member promised not to publish anything without it having first being reviewed by all the other members. They also were responsible for watching out for any hint of potential betrayals, alerting each other for anyone suspected of "heresy."

To provide members of the Secret Committee with a sense of special status and esteem, Freud made identical rings with a Greek letter intaglio and gave one to each of them.

The committee functioned in secret for many years before it finally fell apart with further defections and deaths of some members. The existence of the committee remained unknown to outsiders until many years later. When the story finally emerged, it elicited a huge outcry, as such a practice was certainly not compatible with the idea of academic freedom (Schneiderman, 1991).

YOU WIN SOME, YOU LOSE SOME

Once analysis started, Loe improved quickly. But while under analysis with the Master, Loe met another Jones (Herbert "Davie" Jones), an American poet whose father was also in treatment with Freud at the time.

At the same time, while waiting for Loe to be cured and return to him, Jones started an affair with Loe's maid, Lina. These "quadratic" entanglements persisted until the spring of the following year, when everything finally exploded. Loe terminated her seven-year relationship with Jones.

After fretting over the potential damage to Jones for a short while, Freud decided that this new development was good for both Jones and Loe. To provide some consolation, Freud nominated Jones to be the chair of the Secret Committee, and also recommended that he go to Budapest for a short analysis with Ferenczi, which lasted for two months. As expected, Ferenczi reported phenomenal success when the analysis ended. Jones returned to London feeling refreshed and renewed and was able to get along with Loe even though she had already married the other Jones. Loe also insisted on paying for the renovation of Jones' clinic, and personally supervised the work to ensure it turned out well.

---

[14] Sachs was originally a lawyer. After studying the psychoanalytic literature for many years, he finally became a member of the Vienna Wednesday Meetings in 1910 and became the editor-in-chief of *Imago* in 1912. After moving to Berlin in 1920, he became a key member of the society there and played an important role as a therapist and a training analyst. His students included Erich Fromm and Michael Balint. He immigrated to Boston in 1932.

The thirty-five-year-old Jones remained extremely popular and prosperous. His charms, especially with women, easily triggered and facilitated "transferences," the effect of which was that many of them stayed up late, night after night, often writing ten pages or more of passionate letters to him. Fortunately, Jones seemed to finally have become more able to define and uphold his boundaries with his patients, and thus managed to not cause any major scandals. However, his co-habitation with Loe's former maid, Lina, continued to elicit gossip.

This notwithstanding, when the eighteen-year-old Anna Freud came to England for the first time, Jones threw himself into a romantic pursuit without hesitation (see Chapter 8). Forewarned by Loe and her father, Anna kept her distance from him.

LADY OF THE LAKE, CAME AND WENT

In the ancient Welsh fairytales, Merlin lost everything after he fell in love with Nimuë (also known as Viviane), the Lady of the Lake. She learned all of his magic tricks and then used them against him. She either imprisoned him in a stone cellar with no exit or exiled him to faraway forests.

Jones, the modern-day Merlin, met his Lady of the Lake in 1917 in the person of Morfydd Owen,[15] a beautiful twenty-five-year-old woman, also from Wales. She was fluent in Welsh and proud of it. She was also a prodigy – a gifted pianist and composer.

Their union was short and tragic, but tragic in a manner that was the opposite of what happened to Merlin and Nimuë. In this case, the one who suffered and evaporated was Morfydd, while Jones survived, in a fashion.

Jones ran into Morfydd at a social gathering for the Welsh and instantly fell in love with her. Keeping up his intense and passionate pursuit, day and night, he proposed marriage two weeks after their first encounter, and set the date of their wedding two weeks later. He probably would have done it earlier, but needed time to find a job and living quarters for Lina.

Jones could not wait. He insisted on a civil marriage while his future in-laws were still on their way to London. This deepened the in-laws' misgivings, already worried about Morfydd's musical career being compromised by the union. They turned out to be right, as Jones insisted that the newly-wed couple spent most of their leisure time in his country house, fifty miles away from London, making it difficult for her to participate in musical events.

---

[15] Morfydd came from south Wales. Her parents were both amateur musicians. She started studying piano at a very young age, and from sixteen years old onward she started studying soprano and composition. She composed more than 180 music pieces in her short life, many of which are still widely appreciated.

Unfortunately, Jones' fairytale marriage did not last. Not long after their marriage, Morfydd developed acute appendicitis while they were visiting Jones' retired father, living far out in the countryside. An emergency operation performed on a kitchen table by Jones, with little support and inadequate equipment, led to complications that took her life. Jones watched her slip away in despair. The loss and grief crushed Jones and the guilt associated with doubts about whether he had mishandled the situation continued to pain him in the years to come.

CLIMBING TO THE TOP

Fortunately, Jones was able to find salvation in work. With the continuing expansion of his fame, he had more patients than he could handle. The number of psychoanalysts in England also increased gradually, leading to a need to establish a separate society in the country. As the founding president of the society, he started to develop connections with leaders of both the political and business worlds.

Although World War I had ended, the collapse of the Austro-Hungarian Empire and the widespread demoralization in Germany made it hard for psychoanalysis to continue to thrive in German-speaking countries. Realizing the importance of the English-speaking world for the future of the movement, Freud and his followers started thinking about the need to publish in English. It fell upon Jones to set up a journal for such a purpose, which was called the *International Journal of Psycho-Analysis*. With this added responsibility, Jones' plate became more than full. This might have been a good thing for him, as being busy took away the time he might have dwelled on his grief.

For four years, with the war raging, communications were completely cut off between London and those on the other side of the conflict. Although members of the Secret Committee were able to send messages to one another, it was with great difficulty, and was haphazard at best. Thus, at the end of the war, the first priority for Jones was to reestablish channels of communication. Unfortunately, the signing of the peace treaty dragged on and British citizens were not allowed to enter "enemy territory."

In the spring of 1919, Jones was finally able to get in touch with Ferenczi, Rank, and Sachs. Unexpectedly, this led to Jones settling down with a life-long companion. This happy development occurred because of his need for a bilingual secretary to help him undertake the increasingly taxing editorial work. It so happened that Sachs was recuperating from tuberculosis in Switzerland, and his girlfriend at the time had a younger sister, "Kitty" Katharina Jokl, who had just graduated from the University of Vienna with a PhD in economics and was looking for a job.

During the slow process of Kitty's visa application to come to England to take a job as Jones' secretary, Jones and Kitty corresponded often and gradually their relationship began to take on a romantic tone. In the fall of that year, when Jones finally obtained permission to visit Vienna, he first went to Zurich to meet Kitty, and immediately fell in love. Already with a great deal of practice, he knew the tricks for winning the heart of a young lady. Fifteen days later, Jones wrote to Kitty from Vienna, saying: "Dear Sweetest Kitty, I do not believe that there could be anyone in Europe who is happier than me."

Jones was also very happy that, after almost six years of estrangement, he finally got to see Freud again. Wartime hardship had taken a toll on Freud, who had lost a great deal of weight. But Jones was even more surprised that, this notwithstanding, Freud appeared handsome, energetic, and caring. Jones took Freud's and Rank's families to the best restaurant in Vienna, and they finally were able to have a good meal, after so many years. This made everybody very happy.

Returning to Freud's residence, they were greeted by Ferenczi, who had just arrived from Budapest. Planning for the future of the movement, Freud suggested that Ferenczi should transfer the presidency of the International Psychoanalytic Society to Jones, to which Ferenczi readily agreed. Freud also recommended Max Eitingon[16] to join the Secret Committee. Emerging from these meetings, everyone was infused with a new sense of purpose and optimism.

For Jones, another major event during this visit was that he got a chance to take a close look of Anna Freud. Afterwards, he told Kitty that he was surprised at how cold, exacting, and distant Anna's voice was, and he was so happy that Kitty was totally the opposite of Anna.

YOU ARE YOUR FATHER'S SAVIOR

From 1934 to 1938, the political situation in Austria continued to deteriorate, and everyone predicted that it was only a matter of time before Germany invaded the country. While most psychoanalysts started to look for ways to escape, Freud stuck to his plan to live and die in Vienna, overriding the wishes of everyone else around him.

On March 14, 1938, the inevitable finally happened: Without firing a shot, Hitler occupied the whole of Austria. Jones was beside himself.

Pulling all the strings he could, he was able to find a flight to Prague, which had not yet been invaded by the Germans. From there he managed to

---

[16] Eitingon was a Jewish Russian from an opulently rich family who migrated to Germany when he was twelve. Like Abraham, Eitingon also went to Zurich's Burghölzli Hospital to be trained by Jung, and after that moved to Vienna where he received analysis from Freud for five weeks. He moved to Berlin after World War I, working with Abraham to establish the Berlin Psychoanalytic Society and a formal system for the training of psychoanalysts. He also served as director of Berlin's Psychoanalytic Polyclinic. He served as president of the International Psychoanalytic Society from 1927 to 1933. In 1932, he suffered a stroke. The next year he moved to Palestine and founded the Jerusalem Psychoanalytic Society.

charter a Cessna two-seater airplane, zooming directly to Vienna. At touch down, he dashed for the Psychoanalytic Publishing Company, only to find the place already ransacked and Freud's eldest son, Martin, arrested. This apparently was going to be his fate as well. However, even with his barely workable German, his cunning and persuasiveness overwhelmed the German soldiers, who decided to let him go.

Reaching Freud's residence, Jones again came face-to-face with the Germans, who had already confiscated all the valuables in the house and taken Anna Freud away. Although Anna and Martin were later released, there was no doubt that the arrest of Sigmund Freud was just a matter of time. The question was not whether it would happen, but when.

But the most immediate obstacle to Jones' rescue mission was not the Germans – it was Freud himself. He argued with Freud for five days and five nights, but nothing he said made a dent on Freud's determination. In desperation, he finally told Freud that Vienna as he knew it no long existed. In doing so, he accomplished what no one else had been able to do: He persuaded the frail, 82-year-old Freud, who had been fighting a losing battle with his cancer and who knew he was soon going to die anyway, to leave his beloved Vienna and move to London.

With his personal connections, including his close friendship with people such as the Lord Privy Seal, Jones was able to secure the necessary approval for the resettlement of Freud's own and his personal physicians' families. In addition, Jones worked day and night to help many other psychoanalysts get to England and obtain licenses to practice. For those who could not get to England, he tried his best to arrange for them to go to North and South America, Australia, New Zealand, and even Ceylon.

On June 4, 1938, Freud and company finally boarded the Orient Express. Amazingly, they got through the German heartland unscathed. Passing through France, they finally arrived at Victoria Station in London. At the platform was Jones, with some of Freud's children who had emigrated earlier.

When Freud walked out of the station, the media and public welcomed him with open arms. Jones' eyesight problems, which had prevented him from driving for quite some time, suddenly disappeared and he was able to chauffeur the Freuds around, showing them Buckingham Palace and other attractions. In the coming year, Jones made it his business to ensure the Freud family's stay in London was as comfortable as possible.

On September 1, 1939, less than three months after Freud's escape, the German army moved into Poland, triggering World War II. During that time, Freud had endured two more major operations and his body and mind were already stretched to the limit.

On the day England and France declared war on Germany, Jones wrote a moving letter to Freud, thanking him again for all he had taught him over the past thirty years. He said:

When England last fought Germany, twenty-five years ago, we were on opposite sides of the line, but even then we found a way to communicate our friendship to each other. Now we are near to each other and united in our military sympathies. No one can say if we shall see the end of this war, but in any case it has been a very interesting life and we have both made a contribution to human existence – even if in very different measure. (Freud & Jones, 1993)

Two weeks later, he was called to see Freud for the last time. Reminiscing on this last encounter, Jones later said: "He opened his eyes, recognized me, waved his arms. That waving conveyed his greeting, his saying good-bye and his resignation to all that has happened."

The memorial was short and touching. Jones was asked to give a eulogy in which he said that the occasion reminded him of something his university dean used to say: "He loved life more than anyone else, so he feared death less than anyone else as well." He also said: "It is hard to take leave of him, because we'll never be able to find anyone like him again. We are grateful to him, for how he has lived his life, what he has done during his lifetime, and for his love of us."

WARS RAGING ON, LARGE AND SMALL

For the following decade, Jones faced two devastating wars at the same time. In addition to World War II, he was also constantly in the crossfire between two tenacious and formidable women who hated each other. On the one side, he had Melanie Klein; on the other was Anna Freud. The nature of their academic fights is described in detail in Chapters 7 and 8 and will not be elaborated here. Suffice it to say that it was particularly hard for Jones because he was the one who had made it possible for both to come to England, and each had thus expected and demanded Jones to be on her side.

Caught in such a messy entanglement, Jones tried his best to please both sides, telling Anna that Klein was wrong and telling Klein that he was with her. This tactic only further angered both camps. Jones became so frustrated and discouraged that he hid in his countryside mansion, cutting off contact with both of them.

On top of his son's capture by the Germans soon after the Normandy campaign and the sudden death of his old flame Loe Kann, his difficulties with Melanie Klein and Anna Freud might have been responsible for Jones' unexpected heart attack, which came close to taking his life.

A LIFE FOR A LIFE

Jones dedicated the last nine years of his life to working on the book *The Life and Work of Sigmund Freud* (Jones, 1953, 1955, 1957). Freud's family had always been extremely reluctant to endorse the publication of any biography of

Freud. They also had their reasons to distrust Jones. However, by 1949, there had already been at least three unauthorized biographies. Without the benefit of firsthand observations or original material, these books were done in haste to satisfy the thirst of the public for this mystifying figure whose thoughts had been increasingly exerting impacts on practically all aspects of modern culture. These books were full of inaccuracies, often verging on absurdity.

Attempting to correct such gross deficiencies, some of Freud's most devoted disciples, including Ernst Kris in New York and Siegfried Bernfeld in San Francisco, tried to collect relevant documents and put them together in a coherent narrative. But both of them were already advanced in age, and it was increasingly clear that they would not be able to shoulder such a major task.

After much hesitation, the Freud family decided to ask Jones to take up this responsibility. Excited, Jones readily agreed. His first step was to interview the already frail Mrs. Freud. As he had hoped, Martha provided a great deal of detailed information that helped to make the image of a young Freud more vivid. For example, Martha talked freely with Jones about what happened to her and Freud during their exceptionally long (four years) engagement.

Based on these and other documents, Jones completed his first draft of Freud's early life and gave it to Anna for fact-checking and comments. Anna was relieved by the way Jones portrayed her father, and moved by the tact and respect shown by Jones. She thus decided to make available to Jones the whole collection of more than 4,000 letters between Sigmund and Martha Freud during those years. At the same time, many other letters and documents, including the famous "Fliess letters" that had not been previously published, were also given to Jones. This input greatly energized him in further pursuit of the project.

Jones decided to divide the book into three volumes, each 500 pages long. The first volume, *Young Freud*, originally titled *The Formative Years and Great Discoveries*, was published in 1953. The 10,000 copies of its first printing were sold in less than two weeks, forcing the publishers to search for adequate supplies of paper for reprinting. Jones dedicated the volume to Anna Freud, and in his preface emphasized two major points. First, he said that "It is not a book that would have met with Freud's own approval." In a letter from the twenty-eight-year-old Freud to Martha, Freud said he had destroyed all of his correspondences, diaries, notes, and manuscripts, except his love letters to her. He said: "Let biographers chafe; we won't make it too easy for them. Let each of them believe that he is right in his 'Conception of the Development of the Hero.'"

Jones also said that he needed to confess that his own "hero-worshipping" propensities had been in existence even before he met Freud, and thus he left it to his readers and reviewers to decide whether he was a biographer guiltless of hagiography. And indeed, he was right on this count. In many places in the biography he omitted descriptions of events that might be seen as unfavorable to Freud. Of course, in events that involved himself, he naturally had even more need to be self-righteous, to the extent that his assessments of his collaborators may not have always been exactly fair.

The success of the first volume encouraged Jones to move at full speed towards completion. The second volume, *Years of Maturity, 1901–1919*, appeared in 1955, and the third, *The Last Phase, 1919–1939*, was published in 1957, barely one year before his own death. These two volumes were met with as much enthusiasm from reviewers and the public as the first, and even though Jones' health had rapidly deteriorated in the last few years he rarely let up from his busy schedule of book tours, providing access for various interviews and talking about his exciting years as a pioneer in psychoanalysis.

Jones' son, Mervyn Jones, by then a successful playwright and novelist, read the third volume of the work in one sitting, and wrote to his father immediately: "You've completely mastered the difficulties of writing at one consistent level instead of sometimes focusing on readers who understand psycho-analysis and sometimes for readers who don't." How nice it must have been to receive such praise and admiration from his adult child and to feel that one was able to make major contributions even at such an advanced age.

7

Estranged Brilliance

Melanie Klein's Legacy

I should start this chapter by admitting that, for many years, I harbored a deep-seated prejudice against Melanie Klein. My first encounter with her was during my residency years in Seattle, when I first heard the term "object relations theory." I remember being puzzled and offended by the term "object." Since English is not my mother tongue, I might have missed the subtle nuances of the word, taking it to simply mean something inanimate, passive, and devoid of volition. I didn't understand how such a term could be used to describe the most intimate relationships in our lives.

Then I was exposed to Klein's two most important theoretical constructs: the paranoid-schizoid position and the depressive position. These two terms repelled and confused me even more. Who could believe that, during the first six months of their lives, babies spent so much time fearing being engulfed and mutilated? What kind of tortured mind would propose that all babies sank into deep depression six months after their birth? Klein took away my image of the "happy childhood." No wonder she demanded that every child should undergo "preventive" psychoanalysis! Was she not a *bona fide* lunatic?

Yet, for the next forty years, I kept on being surprised at how often I would see her name and sense her influences in what we do in our daily work. In psychiatric hospitals, numerous patients labeled with "borderline personality disorder" keep us busy and cause us endless headaches and heartaches, because they are good at manipulating the treatment teams, "splitting" the staff into opposite camps, and setting them up against one another, thereby destroying the morale of the workplace. To understand these patients, one has to go back to the concept of "projective identification," a term first coined by Klein.

Furthermore, Klein was also the revered mentor of such seminal thinkers as John Bowlby, the founder of the profoundly influential "attachment theory," and Donald Winnicott (Rodman, 2004), who coined terms including the "transitional object" and the "good enough mother." How can I argue with Bowlby and Winnicott?

Respect is one thing, but really knowing who she was and comprehending what she was all about is something totally different. Such understanding did not happen until recently, when I became interested in the story of Anna Freud and her life-long friend, Dorothy Tiffany Burlingham (Burlingham, 2002). Since the lives and careers of Anna Freud and Melanie Klein were so entwined and since the two of them fought so ferociously for so long, there was no way for me to continue ignoring Klein if I really wanted to get a grip of what Anna Freud was up against. I thus started digging into books about Klein (Grosskurth, 1986; Segal, 1992). To my surprise, I became engrossed with what I read.

A WASTED YOUTH

Melanie Klein was born in Vienna in 1882, to parents of Jewish origin. She was the youngest of four, with two sisters, Emilie (born in 1876) and Sidonie (born in 1878), and a brother, Emmanuel (born in 1877). At the time of her birth, her father, Moriz Reizes, was fifty-three and her mother, Libussa Deutsch, was twenty-nine. Moriz was an internist from Poland who moved to Vienna at the age of forty-seven, where he met the twenty-three-year-old Libussa, who came from Slovakia but was visiting the city. Although Moriz was supposed to be a genius fluent in ten languages, he had not done well in his career. In Vienna, he was not licensed to practice medicine, but was able to work as a dentist, generating only meager income. In order to pay their bills, Libussa was forced to open a small grocery store, which doubled as a flower and pet shop, selling "disgusting" reptiles among other unusual items.

In addition to financial difficulties, the family was greatly affected by illness and death. Melanie's sister, Sidonie, who had been her playmate, died of tuberculosis when Melanie was four. Melanie remembered her shock and sadness, but also her disappointment that her parents didn't shift their attention from Sidonie to her. It seemed like the only member of the family who was nice to her during her childhood was her brother, Emmanuel.

Unfortunately, Emmanuel came down with rheumatic fever when he was twelve, which led to chronic heart trouble, affecting his outlook on life. Although he was smart enough to be accepted by a medical school, he did not believe he was going to live long and started pursuing a bohemian lifestyle, with excessive drinking, narcotic abuse, gambling, and indulgences in carnal pleasures. Hoping to help him change his lifestyle, Libussa borrowed heavily for him to travel in Italy and Greece, but that made it even easier for Emmanuel to live a life of excess and indiscretion.

When Moriz died in 1900, Libussa told Emmanuel to stay away and live out the rest of his life abroad, so as not to bring more shame to the family. Having given up on Emmanuel, Libussa switched her attention to her two daughters, placing all her hope for the family's future on them. Both Melanie and Emilie were beautiful, and many suitors competed for their attention. Emilie was soon married to a dentist who took over her father's practice and did well with it.

Around this time, Melanie met a second cousin of hers, Arthur Klein, and soon became engaged to him. Arthur was at the time studying chemical engineering at a top school in Zurich, with a promising career ahead of him, and was regarded as a good catch. Thus, Melanie put aside her dream of a medical career and focused instead on getting ready to set up a family. However, right after their engagement, Arthur received a scholarship from the USA and set off to the New World for an extended study tour.

Upon Arthur's return in late 1902, while the two of them were busy preparing for their wedding, Emmanuel's health deteriorated precipitously and he died shortly afterward of a morphine overdose at a hotel in Genoa. Arthur rushed there to arrange the funeral and salvaged a box filled to the brim with Emmanuel's unpublished poems and diaries, which were edited by Melanie and published posthumously in 1906. Melanie was immensely grateful for what Arthur had done, but Emmanuel's untimely death started her married life on the wrong foot and continued to be a heavy burden for Klein.

One year later, she gave birth to a daughter, Melitta (Melitta Schmideberg-Klein), who was followed three years later by a son, Hans. As a result, Klein was then stuck at home with two young children. To make things worse, although Arthur did well with his work, the factories at which he worked were all located in the countryside and he was also often on business trips, leaving Klein stranded in strange places, isolated and caring for the children. When not traveling, Arthur needed to entertain visitors and customers. In addition to all the regular childcare and homemaking responsibilities, Klein was also expected to organize one party after another. All this added up to make her feel overwhelmed and suffocated, having no breathing room.

She wrote to Libussa for help. Libussa responded immediately, coming to Klein's rescue, taking over everything with gusto. Klein was grateful for the help, which enabled her to retreat to sanitoria[1] for long stretches of time whenever she wanted. Yet when she was away from home and relieved of her burdens as a young housewife, Klein felt displaced, useless, and worthless. She became increasingly confused about her role in the world. This further eroded Klein's self-confidence, making her even more depressed. Perceiving her mother's spoken and unspoken criticisms, she started to see herself a failure as a wife and as a mother.

---

[1] Sanitoriums in Europe at the time offered rest, fresh air, mineral water baths, and good nutrition for patients suffering from chronic illnesses. Although the original purpose of most of these facilities was the care of patients with tuberculosis, a large proportion of their residents were victims of undiagnosed psychiatric and psychosomatic disorders.

To make matters worse, Libussa always sided with Arthur whenever there were arguments between husband and wife, making Klein feel even more isolated and helpless. The relationship between her and Libussa steadily deteriorated, to the point that they were no longer able to tolerate each other. Sensing she had overstayed her welcome, Libussa moved back to Vienna, claiming her older daughter, Emilie, needed her help more than Klein.

Fortunately, around that time, Arthur was transferred to a post close to Budapest. Klein settled down in the city, finding her way around. She started making friends who were able to provide companionship and emotional support, which helped alleviate her sense of isolation and depression.

This did not last long. In 1913 she was surprised by an unexpected pregnancy, and at the same time heard that Libussa was gravely ill. Four months after Klein gave birth to her second son, Erich, Libussa passed away. Having fought Libussa so hard over so many years, with so much hate and love, Klein did not handle her mother's departure well, and suffered yet another breakdown, leading her straight to the clinic of Sándor Ferenczi.[2]

SERIOUS LEARNING WAS NEVER TOO LATE

Becoming Sándor Ferenczi's patient in 1914 at the age of thirty-two was the most important turning point in Klein's life. Ferenczi was in his early forties at the time, and was energetic, passionate, and engaging. Under his leadership, the Hungarian Psychoanalytical Society prospered.

From Ferenczi, Klein received the kind of nurturance and emotional support she had long been craving. Encouraged by Ferenczi, she studied Freud's writings and decided to use the methods she learned to analyze her younger son, Erich, who was three years old at the time.

She was surprised that there was so much hidden in the young child's mind, submerged in the unconscious domain. Although young children were not good at "free association," their phantasies[3] could readily be elicited when they played.

And what *phantasies* they were! They were not just "benign" images such as seeing breasts in mountains and penises in rocks. The phantasies she unearthed were deeply disturbing, even hellish: Very young children were

---

[2] Ferenczi was a Jewish Hungarian physician who joined Freud in developing and promoting psycho-analysis from the earliest stage of its development and made significant contributions to the movement. In the late 1920s, when his thoughts diverged from those of Freud, he was ostracized by Freud's associates. He exerted major influences on the thoughts and practices of influential thinkers such as Otto Rank, Carl Rogers, and Jaques Lacan.

[3] According to Klein, the term "phantasy" represents unconscious materials and processes, while "fantasy" means daydreams that are at the conscious or preconscious levels.

terrified of being thrown away, eaten up, chopped into pieces, or pushed into a deep hole with no bottom.

Where did these horrors and anxieties come from? Freud provided no answer. According to Freudian theories, the source of children's fear was the Oedipus Complex, which took place between the ages of three and six, when they went through the so-called phallic stage. Experiencing overwhelming desire to possess their mothers, boys started having murderous thoughts against their fathers, which led to a paralyzing fear of being castrated. This fear served as the basis for the development of the superego and the sense of guilt, accomplished through the process of repression. Free floating anxiety emerged when something went wrong during this process. A good example was the case of Little Hans (Freud, 1909), who developed a severe phobia of horses at the age of five. Freud believed this fear originally came from Hans' fear of his father because he had wanted to replace him and was not able to deal with such a prohibited impulse.

Freud's concept of the Oedipus Complex was constructed with clinical materials based on adult patients' recollections. In contrast, with direct observation, Klein realized that children's anxieties started much earlier, during the first year of their lives. She presented this idea as an extension of Freud's thoughts, not a deviation from Freudian orthodoxy. Freud was clearly unhappy and apprehensive about this new development, insisting that guilt and fear were only possible after boys' fear of their fathers' and girls' fear of their mothers' retributions had emerged.

But Klein contended her ideas made more sense. Long before boys started having conflicts with their fathers, they had to deal with their relationships with their mothers. Imagine how shocked and unsettled babies were in the first few months of their lives, when they realized that the all-gratifying breasts were not part of themselves and did not obey their wishes! They must have been so enraged that they inevitably started to fantasize about biting off their mothers' breasts, eating them up, in order to possess them completely. But such violent, murderous phantasies would lead to extreme fear: They would come to the realization that, if they had such impulses, their much more powerful mothers could feel the same and would be even more able to carry out their fantasies. Thus, they were in constant danger of being bitten, eaten, digested and eliminated as feces.

Following this line of argument, babies did not need to wait until the development of the "Oedipus Complex" to be fearful and to have the sense of guilt. Before the Oedipal state, they had already long been ambivalent toward their mothers.

If it were not so, why would there be so many fairytales that focused on themes such as the big bad wolf (pretending to be the grandmother) swallowing Little Red Riding Hood? Why would children be so fascinated with the story of Hansel and Gretel, to be thrown into the witch's cauldron (after eating the gingerbread house)? That the theme is universal is testified by similar children's stories in other cultures, such as the "Grandaunt Tiger" (Yep, 2008), chewing up babies' bones in the middle of the night, so often told to Taiwanese and Chinese children.

Whether these speculations make sense, what was important was that Klein was the first in the history of psychoanalysis to shift the focus of attention from the father (father–son conflicts) to the mother (the baby's relationship with the mother). Looking back, it may be hard for us to believe that in the early Freudian theoretical constructs, the mother was practically absent. To some extent this reflects the male-dominant nature of the roots of Western civilization (also true in most other major cultural traditions). In the Greco-Roman or Hebrew traditions, most of the mythological stories were about men fighting with men. This might be the reason Klein's views were so unique at the time, and why she gained so much attention and attracted so many female followers. The fact that in the coming decades psychotherapy became gradually more feminized speaks volumes about Klein's contributions. For this reason alone, Klein deserves to be honored as one of the mothers, if not *the* mother, of psychoanalysis (Sayers, 1993; Schwartz, 1999).

ON THE WAY TO THE TOP

Encouraged by Ferenczi, Klein wrote a number of papers discussing her ideas and experiences and, in 1919, she was admitted to the Hungarian Psychoanalytical Society as a regular member, which also meant she was recognized as a *bona fide* psychoanalyst.

Regrettably, the political landscape in Hungary was changing swiftly. At the beginning of 1919, the Communist Party in Hungary gained power and established a government hostile to the bourgeoisie. This precipitated international interventions and counterattacks from the radical right, resulting in the establishment of a fascist regime and the "White Terror," with strong anti-Jewish sentiments. Fearing persecution, practically all Jewish analysts left the country and the Hungarian Psychoanalytical Society crumbled.

As part of this exodus, Klein moved to her in-laws' estate in Slovakia, while Arthur went to Sweden by himself for a new job. In 1920, Klein met Karl Abraham at the International Conference of the International Psychoanalytic Association (IPA) at The Hague and managed to convince Abraham to take her on as a trainee, and thus became a member of the prosperous and rapidly expanding Berlin Psychoanalytic Society. There she started a practice of child psychoanalysis, mostly with the children of her colleagues.

The premature death of Abraham in 1925 left Klein stranded, professionally as well as personally. To make the matter worse, she was also deeply hurt in an affair with C. Z. Kloetzel, a married journalist nine years her junior.

Thus, at the end of that year, Klein was again in a bind, needing to find a way to get out of her morass.

Fortunately, several female British psychoanalysts who were in training in Berlin at the time became fascinated with and impressed by Klein's work. Among them the most enthusiastic was Alix Strachey,[4] who mentioned Klein in many of her letters to her husband, James Strachey,[5] as well as to Ernest Jones (see Chapter 6), urging them to invite Klein to visit London.

In the summer of 1925, Klein arrived London to deliver a series of lectures, which were warmly received. This led to Klein's decision to move her family to London in the following year. Jones immediately referred his children and his wife to be her patients, and other analysts followed suit.

What made Klein so successful in England? One thing in her favor was that the makeup of the British analysts at the time was quite different from that of Continental Europe. The Strachey couple, Joan Rivieri, and others, were from the upper social class, not of Jewish backgrounds, and most of them were women. Although some of them had gone to Vienna, Berlin, Budapest, or Zurich to study analysis, the time they spent there was relatively short, and their studies were hampered by language and cultural barriers.

They were therefore happy to have someone like Klein, who grew up in Vienna and had many years of training, both in Budapest with Ferenczi and in Berlin with Abraham. These women analysts were also very interested in Klein's pioneering work on child psychoanalysis and on infant–mother relationships. Many of them quickly became her devoted followers and supporters.

At around the same time, Anna Freud, who had been a primary school teacher, completed her *secret analysis* with her father, and was encouraged by him to develop methods for child psychoanalysis. Anna's ideas and approaches were in sharp contrast to those practiced by Klein. Anna believed that it was not possible to directly apply the approaches used for adults on children as they were not yet mature enough, and also too fragile for the "tough" methods. Anna believed that in order to help the child patient, the analyst should initially allow time to establish positive therapeutic alliances in order to prepare the child to enter therapy.

Faithfully following her father's theories, Anna believed that babies started with a stage of primary narcissism, during which the baby's focus was on seeking the gratification of basic needs. They could not suffer from those horrible mental states and conflicts described by Klein. Klein retorted

---

[4] Alix Strachey was born in the USA but grew up in England. She assisted her husband, James Strachey, in editing the English-language version of the *Complete Works of Sigmund Freud*.

[5] James Strachey was a British psychoanalyst who was most often remembered as the editor-in-chief of the English-language version of the *Complete Works of Sigmund Freud*. He was a brother of the eminent writer Lytton Strachey, and is associated with the Bloomsbury Group, whose members included Virginia Woolf, John Maynard Keynes, and E. M. Foster.

that Anna had no basis for opposing her ideas, as Anna had experiences only with those who were in their "latency period" (six to twelve years).

At first, Freud strived to maintain an appearance of impartiality, but he soon became increasingly agitated by Klein and started to blame Ernest Jones for favoring Klein over Anna, accusing Jones of publishing Klein's contributions quickly but dragging his feet in getting Anna's articles translated and published in the English journal Jones edited.

To placate both sides, Jones suggested that each side (London and Vienna) send a speaker every year to the other's city to lecture, in order to achieve common ground and avoid further escalation of the conflict. This arrangement worked for a time, keeping a semblance of peace between Melanie and Anna.

ENEMIES FROM WITHIN

In addition to fighting with Anna and adjusting to a new working and living environment, Klein found herself assaulted from within – she was confronted with difficulties she had with her own children.

Growing up was not easy for Klein's three children, not only because of the ongoing marital discord between their parents, but also because they were moved around so often. Until the age of fifteen, Klein's daughter Melitta spoke mostly Hungarian, then she was uprooted and moved to Slovakia, where she was required to study and take tests in Slovakian. Even so, she graduated from high school with flying colors and was admitted immediately into the University of Berlin, majoring in medicine.

In Berlin, Melitta often accompanied Klein to events of the Psychoanalytic Society, where she met a handsome, bright, and engaging young man by the name of Walter Schmideberg.[6] They married three years later.

In 1927, after graduating from medical school, Melitta moved back and forth between London and Berlin, receiving training at both psychoanalytic institutes. After Walter straightened up his visa status, the couple moved to

---

[6] Walter Schmideberg came from a prominent Viennese family and received an elitist education allowing him to serve as an officer in the Austro-Hungarian army during World War I, rising to the rank of captain. During that time, he befriended Max Eitingon, an army psychiatrist, who introduced psychoanalysis to him. Serving as a courier between Ferenczi in Budapest and Freud in Vienna, he often delivered care packages to the Freuds, and became a close friend of Freud. In the 1920s he worked with Eitingon to set up Berlin's psychoanalytic training program and also helped to organize international conferences. Walter later developed a serious alcohol problem and, after being divorced from Melitta in the 1930s, he moved to Switzerland to live with American poetess Hilda Doolittle and her lesbian friend Winifred Ellerman Bryher. Bryher was the wealthy daughter of a shipping tycoon who used her money to rescue many Jewish psychoanalysts from Nazi persecution.

London, where both were admitted to the British Psychoanalytical Society and became practicing analysts.

After settling in England, they bought a car together with Klein, taking weekend excursions to the countryside as a family. However, ferocious fights soon ensued, and the dream of harmony evaporated. These fights eventually led to a formal letter from Melitta, demanding to buy Klein out of their jointly owned car. Following this, she wrote an open letter accusing Klein of interfering with her personal life and stealing her ideas. Of all the accusations, the most damaging was Melitta's revelation that most of Klein's earlier case studies were based on "analysis" with her own three children, and that Klein had intentionally hidden this fact.

In addition to being "ambushed" by Melitta, that year was also difficult for Klein because her lover Kloetzel, who had kept in touch and had come to London for occasional visits, decided to move to Palestine, signaling the end of their affair.

In the following year, Klein was hit by an even bigger tidal wave: Hans, her twenty-seven-year-old son, fell off a cliff while hiking in Austria. Melitta regarded this as a suicide, and blamed Klein for the tragedy because of her lifelong neglect and emotional abuse of her children. Klein refused to attend the funeral, saying to one of her friends that she did not want to be sexually harassed by her (then already remarried) ex-husband, who would be present.

THE BIRTH OF THE CONCEPT OF THE "DEPRESSIVE STATE"

It must have been a dark time in Klein's life. The loss of Hans and Kloetzel reawakened Klein's earlier memories of grief over the loss of her brother Emmanuel, and the anger from Melitta mirrored Klein's old wounds caused by conflicts with her mother, Libussa. In addition to these losses and conflicts, Klein was also waging a losing battle against her nemesis and spiritual sibling, Anna Freud, competing for the approval, if not love, of their "father," Sigmund Freud. Anyone could have been crushed by just one of these profound threats and losses. But not Klein. She lifted herself out of the pit of her grief with a new insight on the human condition: the concept of the "depressive position."[7]

According to Klein, the "depressive position" first emerges in our lives when we are between six months and one year old, when we come to the realization that people around us are autonomous, with their own needs and subjectivities. No longer possessing the sense of omnipotent control over the

---

[7] Together with the idea of the "paranoid-schizoid position" that was developed later, the "depressive position" serves as one of the two cornerstones of the Kleinian theoretical constructs. Although both of these "positions" emerge during the first year of the development of babies, they are not termed "stages" or "phases" because they do not fade away after the first year of our lives. Rather, they stay within us and are often reactivated to confront us.

object(s) (others), the child has to deal with and *mourn* such loss. It is a herculean task for the infant to come to terms with its own vulnerability, to give up the primitive sense of "omnipotence" and to accept one's dependence on outside "objects" (others) with their own agency. This process is essential for the development of genuine interpersonal relationships, but it is laden with anxiety and pain. The associated rage often leads to unbearable feelings of sadness, remorse, and guilt.

Through repeated experiences with good-enough parenting, the child is able to integrate internal objects (images) with the external others, thus accomplishing the goals for the initial "depression position." But throughout one's life, new threats of real or imagined losses unavoidably push one into new cycles of similar struggles. Consequently, there is a tension that exists between the *self* and the *objects* throughout one's life, and the management of the "depressive positions" remains a recurrent challenge for all of us at different stages of our lives.

Whether we like the term "depressive position" or not, we now know that "separation anxiety" does not happen in babies until the second half of the first year of their lives. This is when babies begin to suffer from fear of abandonment. Throughout the course of our lives, these issues of attachment remain significant challenges, again and again.

"PARANOID-SCHIZOID POSITION"

In Klein's theoretical system, babies are incapable of entering the "depressive position" in the first few months of their lives because they have not yet developed a sense of "self" that is distinct from the "others." But from where did this sense of "self" emerge, and what could happen if this developmental process does not go well?

Klein's attempts at answering this question led her to the concept of the "paranoid-schizoid position." In this regard, Klein was heavily indebted to the ideas developed by Donald Fairbairn (Sutherland, 1989), a Scottish psychiatrist who was skeptical of Freud's beliefs in the supremacy of the biology-based drives and the "libido" in the development of the human mind. Instead, Fairbairn proposed that, from birth, infants' needs for attachment and relationships are even more essential than the gratification of "basic needs," such as being fed and satisfied with oral needs, labeled "oral sexuality" by Freud.

Fairbairn hypothesized that infants' interactions with "others" (mostly their mothers) facilitated a process of introjection, through which *"external objects"* were gradually transformed into *"internal objects."* Furthermore, he thought that as the newborns were not yet capable of forming the images of a whole person, what were "introjected" initially were *"partial objects"* (such as the breast). These partial objects were associated with experiences and memories, some pleasant, others painful. Together, they slowly filled out the topology of the mind.

But how did the baby stitch together the various introjected "partial objects" into an "integrated whole," which then became the basis of the "self"? Fairbairn thought that this was where the mechanism of "repression" came in, which enabled the baby to trim off some of the incongruent images and to make them appear consistent. However, if something went wrong with this process, often due to incongruent feedback from the mother to the baby, the integration of the self was sabotaged and "splitting" ensued. He postulated that this might be why psychotic patients experienced delusions and hallucinations (e.g., hearing scolding voices that probably represented the internalized voices of parents).

Klein incorporated these ideas into her system and came up with the concept of the "paranoid-schizoid position." She proposed that this was the mental state of babies before they moved into the "depressive position," when they became able to perceive "whole objects." In the more primitive mental state characterized by the "paranoid-schizoid position," babies (and later adult patients) projected images of the self that were "all good" (idealized) or "all bad" (demonized) onto "external objects" (others). Such projections often caused the "objects" (others) to unconsciously identify with the projected images, which then caused a vicious cycle of continual escalation of problems.

The term she coined for such a phenomenon, "projective identification," has become a useful concept for our understanding of borderline personality and narcissistic personality, as well as the dynamics of couple, familial, and group interactions.

In this manner, although the concepts of "depressive position" and "paranoid-schizoid position" may not be familiar to most non-Kleinian mental health clinicians, the influences of these ideas are substantial and enduring.

WAR BETWEEN TWO WOMEN

While busy developing her theories, Klein found herself in a precarious and awkward situation in her relationship with the Freuds. The *detente* between Klein and Anna Freud disappeared soon after the arrival of the Freuds and the Viennese contingent in London, right around the breakout of World War II. At the Society's meetings in London, the new arrivals regarded themselves as the "real" Freudians and called those who had been with Klein the "Kleinians."

The conflicts between the two camps were not obvious in the beginning because, as new arrivals, Anna and her associates made great efforts to restrain themselves. However, when the German air raids and the Blitz started, most

British analysts, including Klein, who had long been naturalized, were able to evacuate from London and hunker down in the countryside, with Klein going all the way to the Scottish Highlands. In contrast, the new arrivals were treated by the British government as "aliens," and were not allowed to leave London. An unexpected consequence of this was that at the Society's subsequent meetings, the Viennese became the majority, and Anna's influence grew exponentially.

Seeing this, Klein lost her fear of the bombing and hurried back to London to rally her followers and organize counterattacks. This resulted in a "war" that lasted for more than a year, while the Germans continued to blanket London and the whole of southern England with devastating bombs.

Hoping to put a lid on the vicious and ugly fights, the leaders of the British Psychoanalytic Society organized four extended meetings euphemistically called "Controversial Discussions." Nothing helped, and the "war" dragged on, with no end in sight. This was so stressful that in the middle of it Ernest Jones, the Society's president, suffered a severe heart attack that almost took his life.

The burden of bringing some semblance of peace fell on Edward Glover,[8] the Society's vice-president, who also became so frustrated and disgusted that he quit the Society completely and distanced himself from all analysts in the country. Even mild-mannered Donald Winnicott lost his patience and kept himself out of the conflict.

In the end, the two camps reluctantly came to *agree to disagree*, which became known as "The Ladies' Agreement." From then on, each camp established its own training program independent of and having nothing to do with the other. Those refusing to take sides formed a third group and called themselves the "Middle Group" (now renamed "the Independent Group"), which provided its own training and allowed its trainees to also participate in the other two programs.

This "women's war" was largely unknown outside of the UK, where Kleinians are seen simply as analysts with a special interest and training in "object relations theory" and are allowed to remain part of the International Psychoanalytic Society.

---

[8] Edward Glover was a British psychoanalyst from Scotland. He went with his older brother, James Glover (1882–1926), to Berlin to study with Abraham in the early 1920s, and succeeded his brother to serve as Ernest Jones' second-in-command when James died in an accident. He was originally friendly with Klein, but became hostile to her in the 1930s, leading eventually to his withdrawing his membership from the British Psychoanalytical Society, to become an individual member of the International Psychoanalytic Association so that he could continue to function as an analyst and at the same time develop his reputation as an expert criminologist. He was well known for his tender care of his daughter, who suffered from Down's syndrome.

BATTLING TO THE LAST MINUTE

In the last fifteen years of her life, Klein continued to be popular and influential, with more and more British students seeking her guidance. However, many professionals were repulsed by her intensity, flippancy, and egotism. Intolerant of people who might disagree with her on even minor details, she managed to alienate many seminal thinkers, including John Bowlby and Donald Winnicott. Even R. D. Laing, the famous existential psychiatrist, said he was glad that when he was a student Klein was too busy to pay attention to him and then commented: "I am lucky that she was not my mother."

In the spring of 1960, Klein started to often feel unusually tired and was told she had anemia. She decided that the best way to get rid of fatigue and to reinvigorate herself was to have a vacation at the top of the mountain peaks of Switzerland. Setting off by herself for the trip, she reached the famed resort town of Villas-Sur-Ollon to enjoy fantastic views of Mt. Blanc, as well as the Rhone River Valley.

One day, hearing that Klein was very sick, her student Esther Bick hurried there to find Klein close to dying. She was immediately transported back to England. Upon arrival at the London airport, she was rushed by ambulance directly to hospital, where doctors found she had been suffering from advanced colon cancer. An emergency operation was performed, with the complete removal of the tumor. However, right after the surgery, when she was recuperating in her hospital bed, she got into an altercation with her attending nurse and drove her out of the room. That night she fell and fractured a femur head. Complications ensued, which ended her colorful life. Klein was seventy-eight years old.

Although Klein's daughter, Melitta, had emigrated to the USA and stopped communicating with her, she continued to hold grudges and seized upon any opportunity to malign her mother. On the day of Klein's funeral, Melitta happened to be in London to deliver a speech. She refused to attend the funeral and was seen in high spirits, flaunting flamboyant red boots in public. However, Klein's son, Erich, her first "patient," had managed to maintain an amiable relationship with her to the end. During Klein's last years she insisted on coming regularly to Erich's house to have lunch and to spend time with her grandchildren. When her daughter-in-law suggested that she come only when invited, Klein acted as if she had not heard her, and continued to show up every Sunday, rain or shine.

She seemed to have a particularly close relationship with her eldest grandson, Michael, who once told her that when he grew up he wanted to be a psychoanalyst, just like grandma. Klein looked at him sternly and told him that he had too many major issues he needed to work on and thus he was not suited to becoming a psychoanalyst, but he would make an excellent scientist. Michael indeed grew up to become a well-known nuclear physicist, receiving many awards throughout his life. At Klein's funeral, Michael and his siblings were the ones who were most stricken. Judging from their reactions to her passing away, Klein proved to be a very successful child psychoanalyst after all, at least in her grandchildren's eyes!

8

When Freud Met Tiffany

Anna Freud and the Origin of Child Psychoanalysis

In 1972, after starting my training at the Department of Neuropsychiatry at the National Taiwan University Hospital, my alma mater, I came across countless volumes on child psychoanalysis, many written by Anna Freud (Young-Bruehl, 1988), neatly stacked away in the basement of the department's building, gathering dust. These were part of the collections of Tsung-yi Lin, the founding chair of the department who had been away for years, serving as the director of mental health at the World Health Organization (WHO). As there were hundreds of other psychiatric classics that were also stored in the same room, my attention soon drifted away, and so ended my first encounter with Anna Freud.

Then, several years ago, while working on a biography of Erik Erikson (Friedman, 1999), I was surprised to find out that Anna was Erikson's mentor as well as his analyst. That was when I realized that she was not "just" Freud's daughter, but had independently made significant contributions to the field as well.

If she were not a Freud, would I have taken her more seriously when I first saw her writings? I do not know. But the fact remains that her connection with Freud the Master biased my initial perception of her, which I assume could have happened for many others as well. While there was no doubt that her career benefited greatly from being Freud's favorite child, it was also true that her brilliance and contributions were too easily overshadowed by her special relationship with "the Maestro."

This notwithstanding, as I examined Anna's life story more closely, I started to see that she really was an extraordinary woman who struggled all her life to achieve a balance between her sense of duty to her father and her need to develop her own thoughts and advance her own career. Anna did not have an easy life; she was not born with a silver spoon in her mouth. She paid an inordinately large price for the privilege of being Freud's devoted daughter and defender.

THE METAMORPHOSIS OF AN UGLY DUCKLING

Born in 1895, Anna was the youngest of Freud's six children, with two sisters and three brothers. That year, Freud turned forty. With the publication of his book *On Hysteria*, he finally started to gain a reputation as a promising psychotherapist.

For reasons still subject to debate, it was also around this time that Freud's relationship with his wife, Martha, changed significantly. Although they almost never fought, they had somehow grown emotionally distant from each other, and were rarely intimate. Anna's arrival seemed to be a surprise, not particularly welcomed by either Freud or his wife. Immediately after Anna's birth, Martha developed severe post-partum depression and went traveling by herself for two months, leaving Anna's care to a nanny.

Of the Freuds' three daughters, Anna was the only one who never attracted much attention from her mother. Her eldest sister, Mathilde, was adept at domestic activities, such as cooking and embroidering, and was thus close to Martha. Sophie, her second elder sister, was very pretty and attracted attention wherever she went.

Anna grew up overshadowed by both of them, seeing herself as an ugly duckling. In order to catch people's attention, she acted out often, which made her even more isolated. Jealous of her beautiful sister Sophie, Anna picked fights with her often, but these fights caused her even more trouble.

Not getting comfort at home from the womenfolk, Anna shifted her focus to her father. She soon figured out that the best way to catch Freud's attention was to read his books and show him she understood his ideas. This worked and Freud started to let her tag along, attending various meetings. He often also kept her around when visitors came calling. Because of these contacts, Anna was exposed to different languages from early on in her life.

But this strategy stopped working once she reached adolescence. She was overwhelmed by her strong sexual urges and was not able to refrain from frequent masturbation. This was made worse by her imaginative mind, which constantly bombarded her with elaborate sexual fantasies. In one of these fantasies, she was transformed into a handsome young man, who was locked up in a dungeon by a middle-aged knight who tortured him with unthinkably humiliating methods, but also loved and cared for him.

Not being able to deal with these fantasies and impulses, she sank into a severe depression and became anorexic, losing so much weight that her menstrual cycle stopped (Davis, 1999; Young-Bruehl, 1988). Hoping that a change of scenery might improve her mood, and also to keep her and Sophie apart, her parents sent her away to Italy to stay with one of her uncles.

Unexpectedly, Sophie got married while Anna was still "vacationing." Worried that Anna might not be able to deal with her jealousy and would act out during Sophie's wedding, Anna's parents "ordered" her to extend her "vacation" instead of returning home. While in "exile," Anna started to write long letters to her father, detailing her sexual fantasies and her problems with masturbation. She also expressed her passion for psychoanalysis and her yearning to become a part of her father's world.

When Anna finally returned home after being away for half a year, it was a totally different place. Both of her older sisters had been married and all three of her brothers had either started college or been drafted into military service and came home only occasionally, on weekends.

In the household, Anna was left with three "elderly," her parents and her aunt Minna Bernays.[1] Without Sophie as her competitor, and with the two older women either emotionally withdrawn or burdened with physical ailments, Anna became the one to take care of Freud's daily needs.

Freud was well aware of this deepening mutual dependence between the two of them. He was also worried about Anna's lack of interest in boys, suspecting that she might be homosexual. Many times, he expressed his fear that, unless something was done, her fate could parallel Antigone[2] in the great Greek tragedy, or Cordelia in Shakespeare's *King Lear*.

Misgivings notwithstanding, Freud did not make it easy for Anna to leave him. Even though she was shy and awkward, and did not pay attention to fashion and appearance, Anna was pretty enough to attract attention and she did not lack male suitors. People who expressed interest included her American cousin Edward Bernays,[3] her brother Martin's classmate Hans Lampl,[4] the psychoanalyst Siegfried Bernfeld,[5] and the adolescence expert

---

[1] Four years younger than Martha, Minna Bernays' personality was totally different. She was outgoing, gregarious, and direct in expressing her opinions. She was engaged to Ignaz Schönberg, a good friend of Freud and an expert on Sanskrit, who went to Cambridge University for a research position after completing his PhD at the University of Vienna. Unfortunately, just before he was ready to take Minna to England to get married, he was diagnosed with a severe case of tuberculosis. After withdrawing from their engagement, he died the following year. Minna never showed interest in marriage thereafter and was only able to hold down temporary jobs in the following years. She moved in with the Freuds in 1896 to help Martha run the household, and to assist Freud with editorial and clerical chores. Gradually she became Freud's bridge partner, and often accompanied him during his travels. Although it has been rumored that they might have had a short-term affair, this has never been convincingly proven.

[2] Antigone was King Oedipus' daughter. After Oedipus found out that he had committed incest by unknowingly marrying his own mother, he blinded himself with pins and exiled himself from his kingdom. His daughter, Antigone, stayed with him and took care of him for the rest of his life.

[3] Edward Bernays was the son of Martha's brother and Freud's sister (also named Anna). The whole family immigrated to the USA when Edward was one year old. He later became an expert on public relations and political propaganda and is regarded as the father of the field of public relations.

[4] Hans Lampl received financial support from Freud for his medical education. After graduation from the University of Vienna, he became a medical researcher. He later received training in psychoanalysis in Berlin and was married to Dutch analyst Jeanne de Groot. They then moved to the Netherlands and he became the founder of the field in that country.

[5] Siegfried Bernfeld came from Eastern Europe and received a PhD in sociology from the University of Vienna in 1915. While undergoing psychoanalytic training, he was also active in social reform and the

August Aichhorn.[6] Also included among her admirers was Ernest Jones, Freud's spokesperson in the English-speaking world. Their romantic overtures were all discouraged by Freud, whether he expressed such disagreements verbally or otherwise.

WHAT'S WRONG WITH BECOMING MRS. ERNEST JONES?

The case of Ernest Jones was particularly illuminating. In 1914, on the eve of World War I, the eighteen-year-old Anna had just passed her qualification examination for elementary school teaching. For this achievement, she was rewarded with a vacation to southwest England, and a visit to her half-uncles[7] in Manchester.

At the seaport she was surprised to see Ernest Jones standing by the dock with a large bouquet of fresh flowers in his hand. Apparently, at a moment's notice, the thirty-five-year-old Jones had dropped his patients and other obligations in order to spent two whole weeks with Anna, giving her a personal guided tour of the whole of England!

When the news reached Freud, he was shocked, and immediately jumped into action. He wrote separately to both Jones and Anna, warning them against any romantic entanglements. He also asked Loe Kann, Jones' mistress for the past seven years, who had just started her analysis with Freud, to rush to England to "protect" Anna from Jones' machinations.

Shortly thereafter, World War I broke out and the Austro-Hungarian Empire declared war against France and England. Severed were not only diplomatic relationships, but any form of communication across the English Channel. Freud was at his wits' end, not knowing how to get his daughter back safely.

Fortunately, Anna was able to catch the last ship leaving England, chartered by the Austrian embassy to bring its employees back home. Slowly drifting along the Atlantic coast, the ship made many stops, including

---

promotion of education for the general population while attempting to integrate psychoanalysis and Marxism. He later emigrated to the USA and settled down in San Francisco.

[6] August Aichhorn came from a family with limited means and was originally a schoolteacher. He was later given the mission of setting up educational systems for problem children. This assignment enabled him to have extensive contact with adolescents from diverse social class backgrounds. His unique ability to quickly grasp their patterns of speech, customs, and behavioral patterns made it easy for him to be accepted by his students. His book *Wayward Youth*, published in 1925, is still an important reference book in this field. Anna often went with him to ghettos to gain firsthand experience of problem children and adolescents' living environments. With Anna's encouragement, he later became a member of the Viennese Psychoanalytic Society and served as the training analyst of Heinz Kohut, founder of self-psychology. Not being Jewish, he was able to continue his practice in Austria and provide training for psychiatrists during World War II, and he played a crucial role in the rebuilding of the Viennese Psychoanalytic Society after the war.

[7] Both Emanuel Freud and Philipp Freud, Freud's half-brothers, and their families lived in Manchester.

Gibraltar, finally landing at Genoa. From there the party was allowed to take the land route to Vienna and Anna was delivered home in one piece. Freud was relieved. He did not know that the thought of becoming Mrs. Jones had never crossed Anna's mind. What she really enjoyed was Loe's companionship for the entire trip home.

THE MAKING OF A MODERN-DAY ANTIGONE

For five years, from 1915 to 1920, Anna worked as an elementary school teacher. She was a hardworking and strict but caring teacher, and was liked and respected by her superiors and her students. But her father's work remained her passion. She worked tirelessly in her spare time to edit his writings and translate his and his followers' writings, mostly from German to English, but occasionally also from English to German. She was always present at the Wednesday meetings as well as other meetings and lectures organized by the Viennese Psychoanalytic Society.

Being so close to Freud, she was able to find answers to any questions on psychoanalysis from her father, literally day and night. Consequently, even though she was not a physician, and did not even have a university degree, she was able to gain so much insight on psychoanalysis that she gradually became an expert on its theories and practices.

But Anna wanted to be a *bona fide* psychoanalyst and Freud wanted to make her a psychoanalyst. What did they need to do to make it happen? At the time, the psychoanalytic movement was still in its infancy and the requirements for such a title were simple: the candidate had to be "formally" analyzed and had to have presented at least one paper at one of the Society's conferences.

But who would dare to analyze the Master's daughter? How could Freud allow any of his followers to dig into the depth of Anna's heart and soul, thereby becoming intimately familiar with the most private details of Freud's household? This must have been why Freud decided to become Anna's analyst himself. Lasting more than four years, the analysis was conducted in total secrecy.

Was it successful? It might have been too successful. At the beginning of the analysis, Anna was consumed by intense jealousy and fought an uphill battle with her depression and anorexia. Four years later, she emerged as a stable, calm, determined, and confident young woman. What was the secret of her transformation? She said that it was her decision to pursue the goal of "altruistic surrender."

But what did this mean? To whom and for what was she surrendering? It turned out she was surrendering to her father and to the cause of his movement. Despite his foreboding and misgivings, Freud succeeded in molding his daughter into a modern-day Antigone, making her his Cordelia. This was

exactly what he had been worried about all along. However, was it not also
what he had been hoping for, not even completely unconsciously?

A few years later, Freud's oral cancer and endless surgeries further
deepened his dependence on Anna, which finally sealed the deal and tied
the two of them together for the rest of their lives. For the next sixteen years,
Anna was constantly by his side, working tirelessly as his nurse and caregiver,
without rancor or complaint.

In 1924, when Freud's condition worsened to the point that his days
seemed numbered, Otto Rank (Lieberman, 2010), the secretary for the
Society for twenty years, started to distance himself and eventually left
Vienna. The responsibility of running the Society fell upon Anna. Her calm
and competent leadership averted the crisis.

From then on, she became indispensable to Freud, privately and publicly.
Their symbiosis was complete and unbreakable. Oedipus had his Antigone,
King Lear had his Cordelia, and Freud had his Anna. They were all lucky men,
but they were lucky at the expense of their daughters. Was this justifiable?
Was it worth it? Nobody could answer such profound questions. What we do
know is that life was not easy for Antigone or for Cordelia. We suspect that
this might have been the case for Anna as well.

A PRINCESS WITHOUT PRINCE CHARMING

Anna remained single all her life. In fact, as far as we know, she never dated.
Was this because her affection and devotion toward Freud was so all-
consuming that she simply did not have any time or energy for anyone else?
Or could there be other explanations?

Because of her reticence, we know little about her emotional life. What we
do know is that throughout her life she did develop intense friendships with
many of her female friends. As already mentioned, during her trip to England,
she preferred the company of Jones' mistress, Loe Kann, to that of Jones.
Another example is Lou Andreas-Salome.[8] Although in terms of personality,
lifestyles, and life experiences, Anna could not be any more different from
Andreas-Salome, they nevertheless remained close friends with deep mutual
admiration for close to thirty years.

And then there was Eva Rosenfeld,[9] who was regarded by Anna as her
alter ego for eight years (1924–1932). The nature of their relationship was such

---

[8] Lou Andreas-Salome was a German-Russian born in St. Petersburg. She was a prolific writer and was
also known for her affairs with many writers and philosophers, including Friedrich Wilhelm
Nietzsche and Rainer Maria Rilke, and was well known and influential in artistic and literary circles
in Europe. She went to Vienna and stayed there for a year (1912–1913) to be trained by Freud for
psychoanalysis, and then moved to Munich to start her own practice. Freud valued her friendship
and asked her to be Anna's mentor.

[9] Eva Rosenfeld was originally the owner of a facility for the care of foster children that provided
lodging for some of Anna's child patients. Recommended by Anna, Eva was accepted by Freud as

that Anna once told Eva in a letter, "*You are me; I am you. We are one.*" But if we have to choose one who might qualify as her "partner for life," that would have to be Dorothy Tiffany Burlingham (Burlingham, 2002).

THE LAST TIFFANY

As the youngest daughter of Lois Comfort Tiffany, the world-renowned jeweler and master of the art of stained glass, Dorothy was an heiress to the Tiffany fortune.

The affluence of the family notwithstanding, Dorothy's childhood was nothing but misery. When she was six months old, her three-year-old sister succumbed to scarlet fever, pushing her mother into a state of chronic depression. To make the matter worse, the nanny taking care of her compared her constantly with her deceased sister, making her feel that she was the ugly duckling of the family, in addition to feeling vaguely guilty for being somehow responsible for her sister's death.

When she was thirteen, her mother died of colon cancer and her father started drinking heavily. The virtually "orphaned" Dorothy was sent to boarding school and largely forgotten. But toward the end of twelfth grade, her father yanked her out of the school because he was lonely and needed company. For the next four years, Dorothy was trapped inside her family's immense and luxuriously furnished mansion. She felt like she was in prison and constantly yearned for someone to come to her rescue.

One day, her Prince Charming materialized in the person of Robert Burlingham, a handsome medical student three years her senior, also from a family of means. Going against her father's wish, she continued to date him, and married him in the following year.

Unfortunately, her Prince Charming did not give her a fairytale life. Even before they were married, Burlingham had already showed signs of emotional instability. Dorothy brushed these worrisome signals aside, assuming that his erratic behavior was caused by his frustration over the delays to their union, and that they were signs of his affection for her. Imagine how puzzled and shocked she was when their marriage did not take care of his problems. Burlingham continued to suffer from severe mood swings. These attacks came and went without warning, catching everybody by surprise. They ruined Dorothy's dream of "living happily ever after."

To make the matter even worse, Burlingham's mother found Dorothy an easy scapegoat for her son's ailment, accusing her of not taking good care of him. Since "mother knew best," whenever he got sick she would come over to

---

a patient. When Anna decided to start an experimental school for her patients, Eva provided her the facility for the project, and worked with Anna and Dorothy Tiffany Burlingham to run the school. However, after moving to England, Eva went through another analysis with Melanie Klein and was rejected by Anna as a traitor.

take him away. But as soon as Burlingham was back on his feet, he would escape from his parents' house and return to Dorothy. Dorothy had counted on Burlingham to rescue her from her impossible family entanglement, not knowing that she had jumped from the frying pan into the fire.

The arrival of her four children, in quick succession, further complicated the situation. They were often sickly, making her attempts at mothering even more challenging. But there may be an upside to her children's health needs. They provided her with excuses to escape from her mother-in-law's meddling and accusations. For example, the severe asthma of her oldest son gave her a reason to take the whole family to Arizona for the fresh air and mild weather. The real truth, though, was that being far away from the oppressive New England, Dorothy was also able to breathe easier.

But even Arizona was not far enough. No matter where she was, she continued to feel trapped and overwhelmed by the responsibility of taking care of her four children, in addition to keeping her volatile and unpredictable husband at bay and fending off criticism and accusations from her in-laws. She was drowning and at her wits' end, and she needed to escape from it all. But where?

That was when she learned about Anna Freud's new venture into child psychoanalysis from one of her cousins who was getting ready to move to Budapest to study psychoanalysis with Sándor Ferenczi. Following in their footsteps, Dorothy took her four children with her to cross the Atlantic Ocean, without letting anyone know where they were going.

Dorothy's first stop was Switzerland, to place her children in an English-speaking boarding school. Then she left for Vienna by herself to visit Anna, hoping that child psychoanalysis would cure her eldest child's asthma and behavioral problems, which included lying and stealing.

She could not have chosen a better time. After having searched for her own path for ten years, Anna had just made up her mind that she was going to completely devote herself to her father and to psychoanalysis. In order to be able to do so, she had also decided to forego marriage and children. Dorothy's four children gave her an opportunity to satisfy her mothering needs. All four of them soon became Anna's patients, and Anna expended a great deal of energy and attention on them. This arrangement was also immensely comforting to Dorothy, who no longer felt helpless and completely trapped.

They soon became the best of friends and then practically like a family. Every weekend, Dorothy would use her brand-new Ford Model T to drive Anna and the Professor (Freud) to the countryside, along with her four children, for sightseeing, and picking strawberries when in season. Soon it was summer, and Freud's family went to the picturesque Semmering for their long vacation, as they had been doing for years. Dorothy and her four children tagged along. There, Anna spent a great deal of time teaching them to swim, play chess, and pick mushrooms. At night, she told stories that mesmerized all of them. Dorothy was relieved and was able to finally relax, able to enjoy "real family life."

In order to experience psychoanalysis at a personal level, Dorothy started her own analysis. Although, at the beginning, she was analyzed by Theodor Reik,[10] she was soon able to switch to Freud, thanks to Anna's intercession. Dorothy's analysis went on for a total of twelve years, ending only with Freud's death. Considering the fact that Dorothy barely received any loving attention from her parents during childhood, this should not have been too much of a surprise.

To make it easier for herself and all four of her children to attend therapeutic sessions, she bought and remodeled the fourth and fifth floors of the Berggasse 19 building, sharing Freud's address. She also installed an elevator to take her and her children to the second floor, where they could go directly to Anna's and Freud's therapy rooms without having to leave the building. Using the elevator, they could also visit Freud's family, located on the second floor as well, with minimal hassle.

In 1930, the relationship between Dorothy and Anna moved up to an even more intimate level. With Freud's oral cancer in remission, the two of them were able to take a long trip just by themselves, going as far as Switzerland and Italy, with Dorothy driving a new luxury Daimler.

After the trip, Dorothy decided to buy a four-acre farm about a forty-five minute drive from Vienna. There, she and Anna spent their time raising chickens and cows, gardening, planting all sorts of vegetables and flowers, all by themselves. They were not only self-sufficient in terms of food, but also clothing, which they tailored and sewed themselves.

At this point, the Freud and Burlingham households were practically fused, inseparable. Seeing this, Freud finally resigned to the fact that the two families had joined in a state of symbiosis, destined to be together forever.

LEAVING ONE'S HOMELAND IS HARD TO DO

Taking leave of any place was easy for Confucius. He simply scooped up his half-cooked rice and was on his way. But not when he had to flee his home country. He lingered and lingered, kept on murmuring, "Go slow, go slow."

(Mencius, 372–289 BC)

After Adolf Hitler rose to power in Germany in 1933, there was little doubt that Austria was soon to be annexed. Seeing the writing on the wall, most psycho-analysts and intellectuals attempted to leave not only Vienna, but Continental

---

[10] Theodor Reik started studying psychoanalysis under Freud in 1912, after completing his PhD in psychology at the University of Vienna. He escaped from the Nazis to the Netherlands in 1934 and was able to immigrate to the USA in 1938. He has written many important books addressing issues related to literature, religion, criminology, and the techniques of psychotherapy. His most influential books include *Listening with the Third Ear* (1948) and *A Psychologist Looks at Love* (1944).

Europe. That is, everyone except Freud, who kept insisting that his destiny was to live and die in Vienna. He said he was not afraid of Hitler and that the cultured Austrians would not submit to his rule. He also joked that Austrian Nazis were just as incompetent as other Austrians. They would not have what it took to govern the country.

He underestimated the will of Hitler. Proving his prediction wrong, the Germans marched into Austria in 1938, without a shot fired. In spite of this, Freud would not budge. Although Dorothy was suffering from a serious relapse of tuberculosis at the time, she immediately sprang into action. She took it upon herself to contact Ernest Jones in England and Princess Marie Bonaparte[11] in France. She also contacted the American Embassy to request protection for the Freuds.

Several days later, the Nazis invaded the psychoanalytic publishing house and arrested Anna's brother, Martin Freud. At the same time, they also broke into Freud's residence and confiscated their cash and valuables. One week later, the Gestapo came to arrest Anna. Anna took along a large amount of hypnotic, determined to kill herself if the situation became dire. Fortunately, she was not tortured, and was released the following day. Throughout all of this, the Nazis did not touch Freud, probably because a car flying the American flag was parked prominently next to the house.

After all these incidents, Freud finally reluctantly agreed to emigrate to London. It was of course a very dangerous undertaking, made possible only because of the intervention of Ernest Jones, Princess Marie Bonaparte, and William Bullitt,[12] the American ambassador. But the one who orchestrated and coordinated the whole rescue mission was Dorothy, who monitored the situation around the clock, despite the fact that she was still hospitalized and critically ill.

Driven out of Austria, Dorothy moved to neighboring Switzerland and continued to work on the documents necessary for the departure of the Freuds. At one point, Dorothy even risked her own personal safety to return to Vienna "illegally" to bring Minna, Anna's aunt, out of the country. Dorothy was so preoccupied by the whole process that she was not even able to attend

---

[11] Princess Marie Bonaparte was Napoleon Bonaparte's great-great-grandniece and was married to Prince George of Greece and Denmark. Her grandfather was one of the founders of the Monaco casino business. From a very young age she had been intensely interested in trying to understand the phenomena of female orgasm and frigidity. The results of her studies, using a pseudonym, were published in 1924. The following year, she started her study with Freud and worked as a psychoanalyst for the rest of her life. She was also an expert on Edgar Allan Poe, the first translator of Freud's publications into French, and a founder of the French Psychoanalytic Society.

[12] Bullitt became a life-long friend of Freud after his analysis with him in the 1920s. They co-authored a psychobiography of Woodrow Wilson, the twenty-eighth president of the USA. The book received mostly negative reviews and was seen as superficial and biased, and clearly reflected Bullitt's hostility toward Wilson for their past conflicts. People also were puzzled at the willingness of Freud to endorse such a controversial book, which was seen as an indication of the depth of their relationship.

her daughter's wedding, held in London. When she was finally able to relax at the beginning of June, with the whole Freud party (including his housekeeper, physician, and dentist) safely in England, she was surprised to find that her life-threatening tuberculosis was no longer there.

After settling down in England, Freud received calls from many artists, including Virginia Woolf and Salvador Dali. He was also invited by the Royal Society of London to become a member. Freud was very pleased with these warm receptions and joked that he was almost ready to yell "Heil Hitler!"

Soon after their arrival, Anna bought a manor at 20 Maresfield in Hampstead, an upscale neighborhood in north London. Remodeled by Anna's brother' Ernst Freud, an established architect, the layout of the house was identical to the one they lived in, back in Vienna, with all the furniture and antiques placed in exactly the same locations. There, Freud lived out the final year of his life, surviving several more surgeries.

With the steady progression of his illness, the pain caused by the cancer and the surgeries became excruciating. Freud stubbornly refused to take any narcotics because he needed to keep his mind clear in order to see his patients and complete his last book, *Moses and Monotheism*. One year later, in September 1939, Freud decided that he had finally reached the end point. With Anna's approval, he asked his personal physician to inject a large dose of morphine, which helped him to depart from this world in peace.

WHO WAS THE REAL PRINCESS?

While the final chapter for Freud had ended, a new chapter for Anna was just beginning to unfold. She needed to restart her practice in a totally new environment, using a new language. As a newcomer, she also needed to develop relationships with fellow British psychoanalysts and to reestablish her role as a leader in the field. Although Ernest Jones, the president of the British Psychoanalytic Society, did all he could to make sure the Freuds safely escaped from the Nazis, his loyalty was to Freud and he did not see Anna as a heavyweight worthy of his full support. He also still held a grudge against her for rejecting his advances more than twenty years earlier.

But the one who gave Anna the most headaches was Melanie Klein, whose move to London had preceded Anna's by more than a decade, and who already had a large following in England. Klein was self-centered, dogmatic, and uncompromising. At the same time, she was charismatic and persuasive. Although her theories and practices diverged significantly from Freud's original ideas, she never questioned that she was the real Freudian, the one who understood what psychoanalysis was all about.

In other words, she, not Anna, was the real inheritor of Freud's legacy. *She was the real princess.* This, of course, did not sit well with Anna. How could a usurper like Klein make such a ridiculous claim? Legacy and theoretical divergence aside, she also disagreed with Klein on many clinical issues. For example, she believed that therapy should not focus exclusively on the mother–child dyad. In addition to working with mothers, clinicians should also pay attention to the influence of the environment (school, other family members, culture, and society) on the development of the child.

The situation became explosive when they started to work on the training programs for child analysis. Klein insisted that only those who had completed their adult analysis could be included in the training in child analysis. Anna disagreed, arguing that such a long process of training would make therapists further removed from children's worlds. Instead, her plan was to recruit college graduates and train them to become child therapists.

Not willing to take sides, and unable to defuse the feud, Ernest Jones disappeared to his country retreat. The fights ended up in a stalemate, leading to the partitioning of the British Psychoanalytic Society into three groups, with the Middle Group in addition to those siding with either Anna or Klein.

Paralleling this protracted "war between two women," World War II raged on. Relentless bombing of London led to numerous children losing their homes and their parents. In response to this crisis, Anna and Dorothy set up the Hampstead War Nursery to provide care and treatment for these children and also to conduct research on their plight and their response to interventions.

At the end of World War II, they established the Bulldogs Bank Home to house orphans arriving from Continental Europe, who had survived the concentration/extermination camps. Anna's and Dorothy's detailed, long-term observations of these children became sources for their voluminous reports and publications. Together, they documented the devastating effects of war trauma – physical and psychological – in these children, who grew up constantly in the shadow of fear and loss, retarding their development and diminishing their ability to adjust and cope with new challenges.

Their data showed that those lucky enough to have long-term, stable caretakers were most likely to live healthier lives with better emotional balance. But what happened to those who did not even have such minimal adult nurturance? It turned out that if these children were grouped together in such a way that they were able to provide support to one another, they still had a fighting chance of survival compared to those who were deprived of such connections. These observations became the foundation for later developments of the *attachment theory* by John Bowlby.

Given how different Anna and Klein were, and how much they looked down upon each other, what is truly remarkable is that they shared the same focus on the mother in understanding the development of the child. This is an important advance relative to Freud's father-centered theories. And this must have been the reason why contemporary scholars often put them together and call them the "Mothers of Psychoanalysis" (Sayers, 1993).

LOVING YOU TO DEATH

Shortly before the Christmas of 1937, Dorothy's husband suddenly decided to go to Vienna to convince Dorothy to leave a Europe that was marching toward war and total destruction. Dorothy was alarmed. She sent her oldest son, "Bobbie" Robert Burlingham Jr., and daughter, and daughteram, "Mabbie" Mary Tiffany Burlingham-Schmiderer, to Paris to head him off. The mission failed and Burlingham soon arrived in Vienna.

For the next three months, he stayed at a hotel close by, showing up at Berggasse 19 every morning, bombarding Dorothy and their children with his demands. In March the following year, they finally reached a compromise: Their youngest son, Michael Burlingham, was to accompany Burlingham back to the USA and then to enroll at the Massachusetts Institute of Technology (MIT).

Burlingham had hoped to rescue the "damsel in distress," believing that it would lead to the reunion of the family. Returning to New York empty-handed, he fell into another bout of deep depression and was not even able to attend his daughter's wedding in London that May. A few weeks later, he jumped from his posh apartment on the fourteenth floor and ended his life.

From the perspective of contemporary psychiatry, there is little doubt that Burlingham's affliction was bipolar disorder, which seemed to run in his family. His sister, five years older, was withdrawn and isolated all her life, and was hospitalized for psychosis at the age of fifty-four. One of his aunts was also unable to function all her life. His grandfather, De Wit Lawrence, was an alcoholic and was diagnosed by the great neurologist Jean-Martin Charcot as suffering from melancholia. Six months after the death of his first wife, he impulsively married a French widow with a dubious reputation, and squandered the family's estate in a short period of time.

All these point to a heavy loading of genes associated with mood disorder in Burlingham's family. But it is important to note here that this was not a family line only laden with misfortune and illness. In fact, for several hundred years, numerous members of the clan had excelled in business, politics, and the arts. The family had been one of the wealthiest and most successful in the New World.

Such a family history reminds us of recent research findings showing a strong relationship between bipolar disorder and creativity (Andreasen, 1987; Jamison, 1993, 1995). Relatives of bipolar patients often possess abundant energy, passion, and optimism, and are more likely to succeed in their work lives. Many bipolar patients also live enriched lives and make major contributions to society, provided that they do not suffer from relapses too frequently, or only suffer from hypomania, a milder form of mania that may not cause too much disruption in their life's trajectory.

But psychiatric patients impose heavy, at times unbearable, burdens on their family members. Even for families as resource-rich as the Burlinghams and the Tiffanys, chronic stresses and conflicts associated with the care of psychiatric patients still could lead to disastrous outcomes. Knowing this, it becomes easier for us to understand why Dorothy needed to "escape" to Europe, and why she and her children needed the support and nurturance of Anna and of psychoanalysis.

But such nurturance is a double-edged sword. It carries the risk of fostering dependence, leading to other serious problems. This may be why Dorothy's children, with the exception of the youngest, had not been able to do well in their lives. Bobbie, the oldest, grew up to become a drifter and a playboy, unable to hold on to a stable job. Although asthma continued to be a serious problem in his life, he nonetheless became a heavy smoker. Later in life, he also started to suffer from frequent episodes of mania and depression, further complicated by alcohol abuse. Spiraling downward, he became progressively less self-confident, which further deepened his dependence on Anna. At the age of fifty-four, still undergoing psychoanalytical therapy with Anna, he suddenly died of an asthma-induced heart attack.

Mabbie, the second born, was trapped in a similar bind, retreating to London and the safety of Anna's tender care whenever she ran into difficulties in life. Four years after the death of Bobbie, fleeing her marital difficulties, she again went into hiding at Anna and Dorothy's house. Several months later, vacillating between euphoria and despair, she found her escape by overdosing on sleeping pills.

One might ask whether it was good or bad for them to have run into Anna when they were little. Were they helped by the 40 years of psychoanalysis? Or, on the other hand, if they had not been "trained" to become so totally dependent on Anna, would they have been more likely to develop their own problem-solving capabilities?

After having conducted extensive interviews with Dorothy in her old age, Michael Burlingham, one of her grandsons, did hold some grudges against Anna. Summarizing the three generations of the entangled relationship between the Burlinghams and the Freuds, he said: "Anna lived for her father and for psychoanalysis. Dorothy lived for Anna, and Dorothy's children were stuck with psychoanalysis that never ended, in order to secure maternal love from Dorothy and Anna."

Of course, hindsight is 20/20. But going over the history, we could see clearly where Anna might have erred. She was an extremely serious, hardworking person, devoting all her life to changing her child patients' behaviors and to "improving" their mental health. Having invested so much of herself in Dorothy's four children, who were her very first "patients," she needed them to be her "model patients." The more problems they had, the harder she tried to heal them. But the harder she tried, the more dependent they became.

We cannot say for sure that Bobbie and Mabbie would have fared better if Anna were able to uphold her boundaries and refer them out for other therapists. But in such a scenario, they might at least have a fighting chance to benefit from new advances in psychopharmacology. It was right around that time that a number of effective medications for bipolar disorder, including lithium, had been discovered.

But, as the saying goes, "lookers-on see most of the game." This was so for Freud in regard to Anna, and it was also true for Anna in her relationship with the Burlinghams. Their "blunders" need not be held against them. Nevertheless, these tragedies could serve as cautionary tales for us, reminding us how easily things could go wrong in these intricate enterprises called psychotherapy and psychoanalysis.

FREUD FOREVER

Dorothy moved into 20 Maresfield Gardens after Martha Freud passed away in 1951. From then on, she shared the same roof with Anna for close to thirty years, living, working, and traveling together, never out of each other's sight. In addition, they also shared the ownership of two seaside vacation homes, one in eastern England (Walberswick in Suffolk) and the other in Ireland.

Although belittled and harassed by the Kleinians in England, Anna's reputation and popularity grew steadily in other corners of the world, especially in North America. Measured and practical, her views on a large array of issues, including child psychology, parent–child relationships, children's custody, and the care of orphans, were widely appreciated and accepted.

Not having had any college diploma, she was thrilled to accept honorary professorships at renowned academic institutions, including Harvard, Columbia, and the University of Frankfurt. After many years of hesitation, Anna finally also overcame her love–hate relationship with Austria and went back to accept an honorary doctoral degree from the University of Vienna.

Dorothy had also been busy. In addition to helping Anna with correspondence, filing and other managerial details, she co-authored some of Anna's publications and conducted her own research projects, focusing on the psychological problems of twins and the development of children with vision problems.

Anna's and Dorothy's reputations and contributions aside, perhaps what is most admirable is that, from the time they met, they had stayed with each other, supported each other, and cared for each other, for more than half a century.

During the last few years of their lives, a young psychoanalyst happened to drive past their scenic vacation home in Ireland. She had to stop all of a sudden because a white Mini Cooper was parked right in the center of the narrow country road. The young woman thought the car had broken down and went over to offer help. She was surprised to see Anna in front of the car, smiling brilliantly, saying, "We are alright. We are just two old women who love to drive around, having fun. We take turns, one drives, the other takes in the view." This might be why Dorothy said, "I am really a very lucky person," when summarizing her life for one of her grandchildren.

9

Phoenix Forever

Viktor Frankl and the Origin of Logotherapy

Viktor Frankl's *Man's Search for Meaning* (Frankl, 1959) was one of the very few books that moved me deeply during my college years. Thanks to Frankl's candid and vivid descriptions, I was able to have some grasp of the unimaginable cruelties of events that took place in the Nazi concentration/extermination camps, while at the same time deeply shocked by the extent of evil that can be part of human nature.

More importantly, Frankl's message was a message of hope. He demonstrated that even in times and places a thousand times worse than Dante's purgatory, Hieronymus Bosch's hell or the *narakas* described in Buddhist sutras, it was still possible for some to defy defeat and find meaning in one's existence. According to Frankl, objectively, the probability of one getting through the concentration/extermination camp was negligible, if not close to nonexistent. But at the end, the few who did eventually survive were those who stubbornly refused to accept such an "objective" assessment of the situation.

Frankl also made it clear that, in an environment where the entrapped were regarded as "non-entities," what made the difference in terms of survival was one's ability to hold on to a sense of dignity, retaining the ability to care for others, not letting go of one's capacity for "being human." By discarding dignity and humanity, one might gain some advantages in the short-term, but the price to pay was enormous in the long run.

As someone who had been through it all, Frankl was persuasive, and his messages were astonishingly uplifting. Focusing on hope and agency does not mean that we minimize the profundity of the nightmares of the Holocaust. Symptoms of posttraumatic stress disorder (PTSD) are persistent and incapacitating, reverberating throughout the sufferers' lives, not infrequently leading to suicide (Alvarez, 1974; Styron, 1979, 1990). Frankl was in no way immune to PTSD symptoms. What was truly remarkable was that, despite all the nightmares, obtrusive thoughts and images, emotional numbing, chronic insomnia, and recurrent depression, Frankl continued to live his life to the fullest for more than half a century. His concentration/

extermination camp experiences not only enriched his life but became foun-
tainheads of his inspirations and the foundation of his therapeutic
approaches.

For all these reasons, it's important that we take a closer look at Frankl as
a person, to gain a better understanding of where he had come from and how
he became the person he was (Frankl, 1996).

AN EXCEPTIONAL BEGINNING

Frankl's parents were both Jewish. Although his mother came from
a prominent lineage, his father was a villager from the countryside who
migrated to Vienna at a very young age, initially hoping to enter the medical
school. Due to financial restrictions, he was unable to finish his studies, and
instead entered the public services system, eventually rising to the position of
the director of the city's Department of Social Welfare.

Born in 1905, Frankl was the middle child, with a brother two and a half
years older and a sister four years younger. Of the three children, Frankl was
the smartest. At the age of three he declared that he wanted to become
a doctor, making his father very happy.

He was an exceptionally articulate and energetic little boy who often came
up with surprising ideas, with a penchant for playing pranks and tricks, not
only on his playmates, but on adults as well. When he was seven, he declared
himself an expert in performing tonsillectomies, and one incident in particular stayed in people's minds for many years and became family lore: Poking
a pair of scissors into his younger sister's mouth and hiding a small red-
painted stone in his other hand, he claimed that he had cut out his sister's
tonsil and demanded to be paid accordingly.

Frankl was far from just a "hyperactive" child; he also studied hard and
did well at school. Entering middle school, he got good grades in regular
classes and found time to read extensively in philosophy, theology, and
psychology.

It was through his voracious reading that, at the age of fifteen he encountered Freud's writings. By sharing Freud's exciting theories on dreams and
sex, he became popular among his classmates. The success of these "lectures"
emboldened him to write a review summarizing what he had learned from
reading Freud's articles and books, which he mailed to Freud. To his surprise,
Freud responded warmly, and even published his paper in one of the psychoanalytic journals, without much editing. This encouraged him to write to
Freud regularly and the Master responded to each of his letters with courteous, if brief, notes.

Thus encouraged, Frankl wrote to Freud immediately after entering the
medical school at the University of Vienna, requesting to be formally
admitted to the Viennese Psychoanalytic Society and to start attending the

famous Wednesday night seminars. He was stunned by the rejection. Paul Federn, who interviewed him for his request, told him that even though members of the society had high regard for him, he was not eligible for membership until his graduation from medical school, as well as completing several additional years of intensive analytical training.[1]

This enraged the cocky Frankl. He did not want to be "brainwashed," and decided to look for a different mentor. He found such a person in Alfred Adler, who had left Freud in 1912 to establish his own school of "individual psychology" and had been busy setting up child guidance clinics in Vienna and beyond.

The famous *Café Siller*, where Adler held court almost every night, was conveniently located at the center of the city, next door to the building where Frankl had been born. Frankl quickly became a key member of the Adlerian movement and published his second professional article in its journal the following year. When the Adlerian circle had its First International Conference at Dusseldorf in 1926, the twenty-one-year-old Frankl was already so highly regarded that he was given the task of delivering the keynote speech!

At the conference, Frankl stressed that "symptoms," such as depression and social withdrawal, were not necessarily pathological or maladaptive, and should not be automatically equated with mental illness. In fact, they might well be manifestations of people's struggle for meaning in life and were therefore part and parcel of their search for a more meaningful and fulfilling future. He also emphasized that human nature was intricate and may not be simply explained by concepts such as the inferiority complex and the need to compensate and excel, concepts central to Adler's teaching (Adler, 1931).

Although Frankl's speech was well received by the audience, Adler was not pleased. Frankl assumed that, this notwithstanding, he and Adler were still on good terms. Yet when he showed up at Café Siller when the conference was over, he was stunned by his rejection by the person he regarded as his mentor. He became a nobody, a stranger, someone undeserving of even a nod.

He nevertheless managed to see a silver lining in his being rejected by the two Masters: Now he was able to devote his time and energy to medical studies. However, for someone with his drive, medical practice alone was not enough. He soon found a new cause to "make a difference" in the world.

---

[1] Paul Federn was an Austrian psychologist who joined Freud's circle in 1904 and became one of Freud's most important supporters and followers at the time, along with Alfred Adler and Wilhelm Stekel. He escaped from Vienna in 1938 and resettled in New York, where he was not well received by the analytical communities and denied the status of a training analyst until 1946. He committed suicide in 1950, mistakenly convinced that he was suffering from terminal cancer. He made substantive contributions in the development of ego psychology and in the psychoanalytic study of psychosis.

A PIONEER OF ADOLESCENT SUICIDE PREVENTION

His new mission had to do with the adolescents in Vienna. Drawing from his own personal experiences and his observations of others at close range, he knew how difficult it was for the youth to cope with the stresses confronting them at this stage of their lives. Such difficulties were made worse for the Viennese for at least two major reasons. One of them had to do with the extremely high expectations for academic achievement. To do well in the brutally competitive system, they had to pass regular tests, one after another, culminating in the final examinations at the *gymnasiums* (roughly equivalent to high schools in the American system), the results of which sealed one's fate in terms of graduation and entrance into higher education.

On top of this, they had to deal with the severe sexual repression that was typical of the "Victorian Age," where sex was a taboo, misconceptions and prejudices were rampant, and transgressions were mercilessly punished. Yet, side by side with the restrictions, temptations were everywhere, and there seemed to be no escape from the curse of the still ill-understood venereal diseases.

Many of Frankl's fellow students were not able to deal with such stresses and developed severe anxiety and depression. Quite a few ended up committing suicide. Responding to this "crisis," Frankl initiated and organized a suicide-prevention network for adolescents. He persuaded a number of psychiatrists, general practitioners, psychologists, priests, and clergy to provide free counseling and crisis intervention in real time. The program was such a success that for a whole year, there was no completed suicide among the adolescents in the greater Vienna area.

After graduation from medical school in 1930, Frankl continued to pursue training in neurology and psychiatry and became chief of neurology at Vienna's Rothschild Hospital in 1938. Around the same time, he also opened a clinic located in the center of the city. With his already considerable reputation, passion, and experience, he soon became a recognized specialist in neurology and psychiatry, and was much sought after.

This period did not last long. In 1938, Austria was invaded by the Germans, and the systematic persecution of the Jews started in earnest. Antisemitic demonstrations were held daily and brutal attacks on Jews made it impossible for them to even venture into the street. Like his fellow Jews, Frankl was forced to wear the yellow Star of David on his clothes and was allowed to treat only Jewish patients.

As with many Austrian Jews and intellectuals, Frankl applied for immigration to the USA and received a visa that could have gotten him out of the grips of the Nazis in time; however, at the last minute, unable to abandon his aging parents, he decided not to leave.

Although Frankl was short and in no way considered handsome, he had never lacked female attention because he was so exceptionally smart, funny, and considerate. But for many years he seemed more intent on new conquests, instead of finding a meaningful relationship. Now, with the world turning upside down, Frankl felt an urgent need to settle down, and was lucky to soon find his love of a lifetime in a young nurse by the name of Tilly Grosser. On December 31, 1941, they put on formal wedding clothing, replete with the required Star of David. Since there was a decree prohibiting Jews riding in taxis or street cars, they walked all the way from their home to City Hall to apply for a marriage license. It was the last day that this could be done, as a new law prohibiting Jews from marrying one another was scheduled to take effect when the new year came, the next morning.

THE UNTHINKABLE HAPPENED

Soon afterwards, all Jews were removed from Vienna and herded into the Theresienstadt Ghetto. Similar to the much more infamous Warsaw Ghetto, Theresienstadt was in reality a waystation for Jews to be sent to concentration/extermination camps such as Auschwitz.

As no one knew when one's turn would come to be transported out of the ghetto, the sense of perpetual suspense was unbearable and drove many to suicide. Here, Frankl's extensive experiences in suicide prevention again were useful. He was such an effective speaker that, despite hunger and malnutrition killing the residents on a daily basis, Frankl's lectures drew huge crowds. His topics were wide-ranging, including "The body and the soul," "Sleep and sleep disorders," "How to improve the health of the nervous system," and "The psychology of rock climbing."

The topic of rock climbing deserves a brief explanation. Short and poorly coordinated, Frankl was never good at sports. But rock climbing, which relies less on physical strength and demands a high level of concentration, was a different matter. As explained by Frankl, rock climbing was intoxicating because it often led to the merging of the mind and the body. This in turn resulted in a state of bliss, as the *self* fused with the rock and the rock became part of the self. In any case, this was his explanation on why he was so "addicted" to this special sport, so much so that he was still doing it into his eighties, claiming that he became an even better climber as he aged, since experience and mindset more than compensated for dwindling body strength.

In October 1944, all hell broke loose: It was Frankl's turn to be transported to Auschwitz. Against his vigorous protest, Tilly insisted on accompanying him to the death camp in order to stay by his side, come what may. Unfortunately, this did not work, as males and females were separated on their arrival at the gate to Auschwitz. They were never to see each other again.

Many years passed before Frankl was able to ascertain that Tilly was one among the more than one million people who perished in that camp. Along with Tilly, practically all of Frankl's family members and relatives, with the exception of his younger sister who had emigrated to Australia, also disappeared without a trace.

How did Frankl escape a similar fate? He said that he had been assigned to the line for the gas chamber but managed to switch to the other line while the guard was not watching. Having narrowly escaped death, the "lucky ones" were pushed into a boxcar of a train, packed like cattle. The train went south through Czechoslovakia, ironically passing through the city center of Vienna, without stopping. It then turned west and eventually reached Dachau, the other equally infamous concentration/extermination camp.

THE INITIAL ARRIVAL STAGE

At Dachau, Frankl was no longer a doctor or someone respected for his intellectual prowess and academic standing. He was stripped of everything and became a number, a non-entity to those having power over him. How does one weather the shock and the depredation in such a situation, in order to persevere? Frankl described in vivid detail his life during this phase of his concentration/extermination camp experience, which he called the "Initial Arrival Stage."

Soon after arrival, Frankl found a new set of skills that would mean life or death for his stay there. He discovered how to preserve energy the best he could; to evade being noticed and targeted by the guards or *kapos* (fellow prisoners chosen to control others in the camps), so as not to be beaten up too often; to use whatever tools were available to shave one's beard clean, and to slap one's face regularly, in order to make it look ruddy and healthy, and therefore still capable of hard labor.

He also tried his best to ingratiate himself with the cook and those in charge of dispensing the rationed food, so that they might dip the ladle deeper and hopefully put some tiny pieces of bacon crumbs or chunks of vegetables in his bowl. Each of these tiny efforts were critical for his survival on a day-to-day basis.

THE APATHY STAGE

But no matter how hard one tried to adapt in such an impossible situation, there came a point at which all efforts started to appear pointless and nothing mattered any more. The mind that had been stretched and crushed so constantly needed ways to get itself insulated, to protect itself from the relentless onslaught that came day in and day out. Reaching this stage, prisoners stopped paying attention to what was going on around them; they became numb and oblivious to the cruelties. Frankl called this second stage of life in the concentration/extermination camps the "Apathy Stage."

The apathy served as a double-edged sword. It created a thick crust of protective scars, but the resulting coldness of heart also made it hard for the person to retain a sense of meaning for their existence, and to maintain the vitality crucial for his or her survival. Frankl reported many relatively healthy people who all of a sudden stopped trying, refusing to do what was necessary to get them through the day. Instead, they might magically produce one last cigarette out of thin air, lying in bed and having the last smoke with great abandon, before taking leave of the world with no further struggle.

THE LIBERATION-RECOVERY STAGE

The very few who were lucky to survive the ordeal and were rescued at the end of the war entered the deceptively promising phase Frankl termed the "Liberation-Recovery Stage."

For survivors, "liberation" meant that the most difficult phase of their lives was just beginning. "Liberated" Holocaust survivors moved around like ghosts. Extremely emaciated, completely exhausted, afflicted with illnesses of all kinds, they were not prepared to deal with the "freedom" they had been dreaming of, day and night. Having lost their spouses, children, parents, siblings, relatives, and most if not all of their friends, they found themselves utterly alone. There was nothing awaiting them; their communities and neighborhoods had been completely wiped out.

When in the concentration/extermination camps, their goals were clear-cut, explicit, concrete. They just needed to survive, no matter what. Without even that goal to hold on to now, they were at a total loss. It seems paradoxical, but in truth most refugees, including Frankl, developed severe depression and even became suicidal after their rescue, when their lives were objectively much safer, less prone to random violence and threat of annihilation.

Ironically, leaving the concentration/extermination camp in Bavaria, Frankl had nowhere to go. The country called Austria had been engulfed by the Third Reich and was not restored after the war, partly because it was occupied by the four "Allied forces" that were deeply suspicious of one another. Eventually repatriated to the "Western" side of Vienna, Frankl was unable to obtain permission to travel to his old neighborhood, which was located on the Russian side. Finally finding a way to cross the dividing line, he couldn't find his apartment. The whole area had been so thoroughly bombarded that nothing was left standing.

THE LONG ROAD BACK TO LIFE

Frankl would not have survived if he had not found a job at the City Hospital. Being able to work again helped him to feel somewhat anchored. But what saved him was his writing.

Encouraged by some of his colleagues who had known him before the war, he started working on his first book, which was eventually published as *The Doctor and the Soul*. He had been working on his first draft of this book while still in the Theresienstadt Ghetto. In 1944, prior to leaving for Auschwitz, he had sewn the draft into the clothing he was wearing. On arrival at the camp, he was ordered to take off all of his clothes so as to be hosed down, like an animal. When he came out of the communal "shower" facility, all of his clothes were gone. Instead, he was given what was left from someone who had just been sent to the gas chamber. In a matter of minutes, what he had been working on for years was completely wiped out.

Nevertheless, Frankl continued to be obsessed with the book. When everything was gone, almost nothing still under his control, putting his thoughts into writing, with the faint hope of eventually passing on his ideas to others, became the sole meaning of his life and the only reason for him to continue living. At Dachau, the hope of somehow rescuing his book and completing it became an obsession. He managed to find scraps of paper and a pencil and started to reconstruct the outlines of his lost book. After being released from the camp, the completion and publication of this book prevented him from acting upon his suicidal impulses.

He had hoped that working on the book would have a cleansing function, enabling him to leave the nightmares behind, making it possible for him to start a new life. On the contrary, the writing led to the opening of a floodgate: Memories and thoughts kept tumbling out, threatening to destroy whatever semblance of sanity and order he was just barely able to maintain in his post-Holocaust life. In desperation, he spent nine days and nine nights completing another book, which he initially titled *Say "Yes" to Life*, later translated into English and titled *Man's Search for Meaning*.

The book was published anonymously because he wanted to be able to write without constraints and to be as truthful and honest as he could. Unexpectedly, it became an instant best-seller. When it came time to publish the second edition, in order to show his willingness to take responsibility for the content of the book, Frankl very reluctantly agreed to reveal himself as the author.

LOVE RETURNED

As someone who was sharper and more quick-witted than most, Frankl tended to be impatient and intimidating when dealing with people. Tormented by the unspeakable losses and traumas associated with the Holocaust, he became even more impatient and abrasive. As a result, in the hospital, he built a reputation as someone to keep at a distance. This further aggravated his sense of isolation and loneliness.

Surprisingly, this impasse was broken by a young surgical nurse named Elly (Eleonore Katharina Schwindt), who was able to see through his façade of aloofness and was not intimidated by him. One day she was taking care of a patient who had just come out of an emergency operation and needed a bed for recovery, but the only vacancy in the hospital was in the neurology ward. Since no one dared to speak to the formidable and abrasive Frankl, Elly volunteered. This encounter was "fatal" to Frankl. He was stunned by her innocent beauty and moved by her good-heartedness. He found himself obsessed with her, and started asking around: Who was that girl with such clear sparkling eyes?

It did not matter that Elly was Catholic and Frankl was still a practicing Jew. He found in Elly the stability and structure he needed. With Elly, he rediscovered his passion for life, and was able to return to this "live" world that was not only filled with sorrow and grief, but also joy, hope, and forward momentum. They became partners for life.

WHAT MAKES LIFE MEANINGFUL?

Long before the war, Frankl's view on human nature had already diverged from those of both Freudians and Adlerians. He disagreed with their "deterministic" orientation, objected to the idea that men were driven either by "sexuality" or by the will to power and trapped in their struggles. Instead, he believed that what really mattered was that human beings wanted to be free and to live a meaningful life.

Paradoxically, Frankl's concentration/extermination camp experiences, where freedom was hard to imagine, where dignity and meaning were purposefully and systematically deprived, further strengthened his beliefs in the necessity and possibility of freedom and meaning in life. These experiences and beliefs became the foundation of his "logotherapy," which has inspired the development of various schools of "existential analysis" and the existential-humanistic movement in the next few decades.

Similar to other existential philosophers and therapists, Frankl emphasized that meaning was not an abstract concept but evolved from "ordinary people's daily lives".[2] Meaning does not exist unless we define it and look for it (thus, *Man's Search for Meaning*).

But, where do we find meaning in life? Frankl proposed three major paths: (1) working and creativity; (2) communion with nature and with others ("love"); and (3) facing suffering head-on when adversity and even catastrophe cannot be avoided (transcendental meaning).

---

[2] Reminiscent of a famous saying by Wang Gen: "Tao is what works for ordinary people in everyday lives." Wang Gen was a Ming Dynasty philosopher.

The first path, meaning through work and creativity, is perhaps the most straightforward and easiest to grasp. To pursue this path, one does not need to be an accomplished artist, a scholar, or a successful industrialist. Auto-mechanics or plumbers who have mastered their trades are more likely to derive satisfaction and find meaning in their work than bankers or medical doctors who are burned out and alienated from aspects of their professions that are creative and generative.

The importance of a sense of communion with nature as a source of meaning is also easy to grasp. Many of us share the experience of awe when witnessing the beauty and majesty of natural scenery. Along with the awe, there comes a sense of communion, of somehow being one with something bigger than us. Such experiences might appear mystical, but they are direct and powerful, providing us with a feeling of purpose and connectedness, convincing us that there is meaning in our lives, even if it cannot be easily delineated.

The concept of "love," Frankl admitted as being trickier. We all crave love, but what is "love?" Frankl regarded the common Freudian interpretation equating love with "sublimated" sexual drives as naive and misleading. He also disagreed with Theodor Reik (1944), who proposed that love was the result of the projection of one's "ego ideal." Instead, Frankl insisted that "love" was part and parcel of one's being human. Love is in this sense a priori. Existing before our logical thinking, it could not, and need not, be explained by rational reasoning. This force of "love" enables one to see and to appreciate the essence and particular uniqueness of the person one loves, as well as the qualities and potentialities that might still be dormant inside that person, not yet apparent even to the person himself/herself. This is why one's love of another person makes that person unfold and grow. In this sense, love is inherently liberating, enabling its "object" to search and find that part of the hidden self, leading to self-realization. Concurrently, loving someone is also liberating and enriching to the one who has "fallen in love," making him or her see that part of the self that they have not been in touch with before.

THE MEANING OF SUFFERING

But, is it possible to find meaning in life when one is deprived of meaning from work, love, and everything else, when the only thing left is suffering?

Having lived through his Holocaust experiences, Frankl was firmly convinced that the answer to this question is an unqualified "yes." In saying this, he always emphasized that what he meant by "suffering" was not suffering that could be resolved or avoided. Meaning in suffering is no excuse for not taking action when there are ways to eliminate or minimize suffering. Otherwise, it is just plain masochism.

But, when there is no escape, when there is no apparent way to change one's fate, there is still one last thing in one's possession: the freedom to choose one's attitude, one's stance. One could choose despair, or choose to stare at the cataclysm, facing it with courage, not giving in to "fate" (or absurdity, as Camus [1955] called it). This has got to be the most uplifting message one could get in facing life's adversities!

Frankl said that most prisoners incarcerated in the concentration/extermination camps felt hopeless because the chance of surviving the camp was very slim. Facing this reality, he himself made a conscious decision to convince himself that if he was not able to face his suffering, he would not be able to face his life even if he were lucky enough to escape the camp. "What am I if I could not find meaning in the suffering that I am part of at this time, and instead had to depend on events that were out of my control (such as if I could by chance escape the camp) to gain meaning in life?"

Although it has been almost seventy years since Hitler's demise, Frankl's tragedy and insights remain relevant. Catastrophes, natural and man-made, occur regularly. Massacres and genocides continue to erupt from all corners of the world. For millions of today's refugees struggling constantly for survival on all fronts, Frankl's ideas remain extremely practical and useful.

But the relevance of Frankl's ideas does not stop at those who are facing disasters as usually defined. Every one of us, eventually, has to face our own "disasters." Cancer, infections, kidney failures, accidents, and myriad of life's "undertows" lurk all around. Eventually, aging and death happen to every one of us. Confronted with these, one could take the position that life is futile. Or one could decide to face adversity with dignity.

We might not be as "brave" as Frankl, but ultimately it does not matter how we compare to him or other exceptional role models we might try to emulate. As Frankl said, what mattered was not the ending; what mattered was that, irrespective of how minuscule the chances were, the potentialities were always infinite.

The Diving Bell and the Butterfly (Bauby, 1997) represents a more recent example showing how catastrophe can lead to an unexpected new departure and outlook in life. It was written by Jean-Dominique Bauby, the editor-in-chief of *Elle*, the most popular fashion magazine in France. He had led a life of leisure, fame, and class until he suddenly suffered a stroke at the age of forty-three. Emerging from a deep coma that lasted for more than twenty days, he was confronted with the so-called "locked-in syndrome," with total paralysis of all of the muscles except his left eyelid. It was as if his body was submerged in deep water and he could survive only because there was a diving bell,[3] providing some air, at least for a while.

---

[3] Ancient Greeks invented the method of sinking huge bronze bell jars into deep water to supply air for the divers, hence the name diving bells.

Yet, in contrast to the immobility of his body, his mind was like a butterfly, completely free to roam around at lightning speed. One moment it reached back to obscure corners of his past, in the next moment, in his imagination, it flew to the distant future and to all corners of the earth.

Bauby was extremely lucky in that he came across a speech therapist who was able to decode the meaning of his blinking. Using the blinking, he developed a system to convey his thoughts one alphabet letter at a time, by laboriously going through the whole list of letters, one by one, to reach the one he wanted. Through this extremely long and tedious process, Bauby eventually completed a unique book filled with thought-provoking reflections, humor, and an irrepressible sense of vitality and passion.

Published just days before his passing away, the book became an instant best-seller. It was soon adapted into a movie, which also became a popular hit. Both showed that, even with so many limitations in the physical sense, the mind was still free.

One could argue that without the stroke and the locked-in syndrome, Bauby would not have been able to experience such an elevated level of awareness. Looking at it this way, who could say that there was not a blessing in disguise in Bauby's suffering and demise?

THE EXISTENTIAL VACUUM OF MODERN MAN

Frankl and Bauby's stories demonstrate that even in the most devastating situations, it is still possible to find meaning in existence and reasons for affirming life. In contrast, in modern societies, suffering is too often neatly packaged, hidden, and denied. Life is supposed to be easy and carefree. Meaning and purpose in life are expected to effortlessly reveal themselves, not requiring active searching. Paradoxically, such a sense of entitlement leads people to what Frankl called an "existential vacuum." No longer guided by cultural traditions, some youngsters may lose themselves in superficial gratifications that serve to push them further away from the richness and solemnity of life, making it difficult for them to sustain passion in life. They drift and float, unable to find an anchor or direction. They are thus trapped in their personal purgatory, desperately craving meaning, but not knowing which way to turn, which direction to take. This may be part of the reason for the increase in the prevalence of various psychiatric and substance-use problems in modern societies (Hidaka, 2012), and why such trends seem to be so relentless and persistent despite the wealth and resources available for people fortunate enough to live in such a "privileged" world.

THE MERGING OF WESTERN AND EASTERN PHILOSOPHIES

Over the years, Asian scholars (Fu, 1983; Wong, 2012) have noticed remarkable resemblances between Frankl's ideas on suffering and thoughts central to Buddhism and other Eastern philosophical traditions. "Everything [*sankhara*] is impermanent [*anitya*]; everyone [*sasrava*] suffers [*duhkha*]," one of the three most foundational Buddhist tenets, reflects Frankl's personal experiences at the concentration/extermination camp. However, when introduced to the West, these concepts of suffering have typically been misconceived as negative and misinterpreted as evidence of a passive acceptance of fate, and thus "escapism." Coming from an unrelated intellectual tradition, Frankl argued effectively that suffering does not have to be meaningless and the acceptance of suffering is not passivity. On the contrary, confronting limitations and suffering is indispensable in engendering meaning in life.

Frankl's thoughts also echoed another basic tenet of Buddhism, *Anatman*, the illusiveness of the Self (*Atman*). In many of Frankl's articles, he argued forcefully that the best, if not the only, way to achieve what one desires is not to actively pursue it. In other words, the way to get what one wants is to get rid of the "I" that is often in the way. That which is desired happens only when one puts one's *self* aside, losing one's awareness of *self* by being absorbed in what one is doing or experiencing.

At a practical and concrete level, we often see examples of how self-awareness gets in the way of our achieving what we want to achieve. For example, there is no way we can force ourselves to fall asleep, to have an erection, or to have an orgasm. The harder we try, the more difficult it gets. Based on such an understanding, Frankl invented (or discovered) the treatment method termed "paradoxical intention," which is often used by behavioral therapists to treat sleep and sexual function disorders.

What is thought-provoking here is that even though overlaps between Frankl's thoughts and Eastern philosophical traditions are so apparent, there is no evidence that he had ever been exposed to or was influenced by Eastern philosophical writings. Therefore, such remarkable convergences serve to further highlight the originality and suppleness of Frankl's mind. At the same time, they also demonstrate that, cultural diversities notwithstanding, human minds follow similar patterns and often come to surprisingly similar conclusions, even if they emerge from very separate traditions.

PART II

FROM SEA TO SHINING SEA

10

Rose Garden Revisited

Miracles of Frieda Fromm-Reichmann and Joanne Greenberg

One of the best things that happened in 2008, when I was at Stanford, was the chance encounter with a book by Gail A. Hornstein, titled, *To Redeem One Person Is to Redeem the World: The Life of Frieda Fromm-Reichmann* (Hornstein, 2005). Before reading the book, all I had known about Frieda Fromm-Reichmann was that she was the model for the therapist depicted in the best-seller *I Never Promised You a Rose Garden* (Greenberg, 1964), which was translated into Chinese and published in Taiwan by my dear friend Sunhoo Foo[1] more than forty years ago, when we were both in training. It was a book written by someone who called herself Hannah Green. No one knew at the time who she was, a well-kept secret not revealed until recently. Hannah Green turned out to be a famed and prolific writer by the name of Joanne Greenberg, and Frieda Fromm-Reichmann was indeed her therapist for many years.

When I read the book for the first time, I was still a neophyte to the field of psychiatry and knew little about schizophrenia. Greenberg's book, with vivid and candid descriptions of her own personal experiences, became an important sourcebook for my working with patients whom I was struggling to understand and care for. In describing her horrifying and confusing years of being burdened by a devastating illness, she did not spare us the details, nor did she dangle hope for an easy cure. Consequently, as much as I appreciated her talent in being able to write such a book, I had assumed that she would not have fared well eventually, as was the case of most of the patients under my care at the time, whose lives had been so dishearteningly ground to a standstill.

This was why I was so surprised by the real story of Greenberg. It was true that, even after leaving Fromm-Reichmann's hospital, she continued to be weighed down by severe psychotic symptoms and needed to stay in outpatient treatment for many more years. Regardless, she was eventually able to complete her schooling, fall in love, get married, and raise a family.

---

[1] https://nyulangone.org/doctors/1720048259/sun-hoo-foo, retrieved September 12, 2018.

Not only that, she also became a successful writer and published more than twenty widely read and acclaimed novels and prose collections. In addition, she taught creative writing and anthropology at universities, served as a lecturer on Hebrew and the Torah at synagogues, and volunteered as a firefighter and a medic in her local community. All these accomplishments are astounding, considering how ill she had been and how long she had been so disturbed.

Psychotic symptoms afflicted her when she was only ten years old. That was when she started hearing voices and seeing things that were not supposed to be there. Living in a made-up world detached from reality and frightened constantly by bizarre experiences, she became withdrawn and suicidal. After years of trying valiantly to hide these horrifying experiences, she finally collapsed and broke down at the age of sixteen, leading to her hospitalization at the Chestnut Lodge, one of the most well-known premier psychiatric facilities at the time.

There, she ran into Frieda. Frieda Fromm-Reichmann has been regarded as "the Master" of psychoanalysis as applied in the treatment of schizophrenia. Her *Principles of Intensive Psychotherapy* (Fromm-Reichmann, 1960) has remained the classic of this specialized field ever since its publication. At different stages of my career, I have made half-hearted attempts to crack the secret of the book, but it was not easy to get through more than a few pages at a time.

I Never Promised You a Rose Garden is different. It is firsthand, jargon free, and reader-friendly. It describes the author's experiences at the hospital in detail, without hyperbole or sentimentality. Greenberg does not spare us the gory details, nor the sense of despair over relapses. She does not paint an idealized picture of Frieda either. In the book, the therapist was just a friendly and approachable middle-aged woman who did not try to impress her with profound insights or personal charisma.

There is no high drama or climatic breakthroughs. What the book does clearly show is the empathy, perceptiveness, and patience emanating from Frieda. Even though Frieda was already a world-famous expert at this point, she did not put herself on a pedestal, but was right there with her patient, sharing her anguish and despair.

Although Frieda never gave up hope for the patient's recovery, or at least some improvement, she also did not offer easy answers or minimize the difficulties and uncertainties that were very much part of her patient's future. That was exactly what she meant when she told Greenberg, "I never promised you a rose garden."

Yet the author of *Rose Garden* did recover. She not only recovered, but for all appearances became even healthier and more functional than most people who have not suffered from schizophrenia. This is not to say that the process of the recovery was easy – it was the opposite of easy.

She stayed at the Chestnut Lodge for more than two years and then continued to receive outpatient therapy for an additional five years. It was a long, torturous process. Nevertheless, day by day, step by step, she slowly climbed out of the abyss, started learning to live by herself, entered college, dated, fell in love, married, and began her writing career.

Even for Fromm-Reichmann and her colleagues at the Chestnut Lodge, Greenberg's recovery was a miracle beyond what they had dared to expect. It was a miracle because it was so unusual, so infrequently seen, it became the focus of Frieda's intense scrutiny, extensively explored in her later publications and discussed in her lectures. Frieda even proposed to Greenberg that they work together to explore how and why their therapy had worked so well. Unfortunately, the plan was aborted by Frieda's unexpected heart attack that took her life. Nevertheless, this idea planted the seed that eventually grew and blossomed into Greenberg's *Rose Garden*.

While the book does not provide clear-cut clues on how to recover from schizophrenia, the author's well-described recovery helps to shed light on some of the long-debated questions in psychiatry, such as "Can schizophrenic patients completely recover?" and "Can psychotherapy, and more specifically, psychoanalysis, be effective in the treatment of schizophrenia?"

CAN SCHIZOPHRENIA BE COMPLETELY CURED?

For a whole century, Emil Kraepelin and Sigmund Freud competed for the honor of being called "Father of Psychiatry." Both happened to be Frieda's teachers. Interestingly and unfortunately, for completely different reasons, both of these "Fathers" of ours came to the conclusion that schizophrenia was "incurable."

With limited exposure to schizophrenic or other psychotic patients, Freud's assertion was more theoretical. He believed that schizophrenia represented an extreme form of regression so pervasive that recovery may not be possible.

Kraepelin, on the other hand, spent his lifetime observing psychotic patients incarcerated in asylums, documenting their symptoms and charting the progress of their illnesses over years and decades. The voluminous data collected and analyzed allowed him to distinguish two types of chronically psychotic patients. On the one hand, there were a large number of patients whose psychotic symptoms, no matter how bizarre and disturbing, appeared to be episodic, interspersed with periods of relative lucidity. Further, these episodes correlated closely with their moods, which could be extremely high or alarmingly low. Kraepelin labeled such a condition "manic-depressive psychosis." In contrast, the rest of the "lunatics" warehoused in asylums continued to manifest severe psychotic symptoms, often with progressive and pervasive deterioration of their functioning. He gave this latter group the ominous name of "dementia praecox," which was later replaced by the term "schizophrenia," coined by Eugen Bleuler.

But whether we call it dementia praecox or schizophrenia, these terms reflected the beliefs of Kraepelin and the majority of those working in the asylums that this condition was caused by a neurodegenerative process that was hereditary and irreversible. The influence of Kraepelin was so profound that, for the next 100 years, most psychiatric clinicians held firm to the belief: "Once a schizophrenic, always a schizophrenic." Such a belief led to the neglect and isolation of these patients, who were typically incarcerated in institutions far removed from "civilization" – mental hospitals constructed in the late nineteenth century were typically built more than a day's stagecoach ride from major metropolises.

"Institutionalization" further diminished patients' daily functioning and intensified their sense of alienation, driving them further and further away from "normal" society. In turn, their alienation and "degeneration" served to reinforce the hospital staff's pessimistic outlook on their prognosis.

It was ironic that, in the several decades following the publication of *Rose Garden*, "neo-Kraepelinians" gradually regained dominance in psychiatry. While this movement resulted in the refinement of the diagnostic criteria for psychiatric disorders, schizophrenia is still defined as a chronic, severe, and deteriorating condition. Based on such a definition, schizophrenic patients are not supposed to fully recover. It is therefore no wonder that contemporary psychiatrists, as well as the general public, continue to hold pessimistic views about schizophrenia.

But there is reason to suspect that such a conviction has been based on biases in our observations. Unlike the author of *Rose Garden*, the overwhelming majority of schizophrenic patients (and in fact most psychiatric patients) who have recovered from their problems are reluctant to reveal their histories for fear of stigma and discrimination. They become invisible. At the same time, most patients who continue to require psychiatric care are those who have had more difficulties. Since these are the patients most visible to clinicians, versus those who have improved and left the system, mental health professionals gain the impression that their patients do not get better over the years.

Clinicians are often surprised when confronted with community-based longitudinal follow-up studies, which show that 5–10 years after the onset of schizophrenia, about one-third of them improved to the extent that they were able to return to the community to live a more or less normal life. Even at the Chestnut Lodge (McGlashan, 1986), which was often the "last resort" for patients who had failed treatment at other facilities, retrospective reviews of the courses of their patients over several decades showed that one-third of them eventually achieved significant improvement. Out of these, one-third (i.e., one-ninth of all patients) approached total recovery.

CAN PSYCHOTHERAPY, AND MORE SPECIFICALLY, PSYCHOANALYSIS, BE EFFECTIVE IN THE TREATMENT OF SCHIZOPHRENIA?

Although our understanding is still limited on why some schizophrenic patients recover or improve while many others are unable to do so, what we do know is that, regardless of how severe patients' illnesses are, and how distorted and detached from reality their minds are, their lives do not just come to a standstill.

No doubt their trajectories in life and their daily routines have been turned upside down by their illness. But they still *exist* and they exist in a social context, interacting with different sets of "people." Whether those they interact with are "real" (such as their parents, siblings, friends, doctors, mental health workers, fellow patients) or imaginary (objects of hallucinations and delusions), such interactions constitute the elements for their efforts to reconstruct new orders in life. In this sense, patients' environments, especially social environments, are crucial in determining what happens to them next.

Reflecting this line of reasoning, patients "warehoused" in traditional asylums, receiving minimal attention and care, are much less likely to escape persistent deterioration. Conversely, those fortunate enough to receive care in an enriching environment should have a much better chance of reestablishing some sort of equilibrium, which in turn enhances the possibility of their improvement, if not recovery. This is exactly where modern-day psychiatry and clinical psychology have made the most remarkable contributions in the care of schizophrenic patients. Ideally, we provide not only medications and human contact, but also activities, individual and group therapies, therapeutic community meetings, family meetings, and psychoeducation. Together, they provide our patients with a better fighting chance, and are psychotherapy in a broad sense, whose efficacy and effectiveness are beyond doubt.

Still being debated is whether specific types of psychotherapy, especially those focusing on the exploration of patients' "inner world," such as psycho-analysis, have a role in the care of schizophrenic patients. Part of the difficulties in such debates have to do with challenges in the evaluation of the effectiveness of psychotherapy. Obstacles for this kind of research include selection biases of candidates for therapy, favoring those with financial means and motivations, making it difficult for many schizophrenic patients to be engaged in therapy.

But even if we put these debates aside and assume that, at least for a small number of patients, psychoanalysis could be lifesaving, we would still be confronted by questions in the realm of "cost-effectiveness." After all, psychoanalysis is time-consuming and inordinately expensive. Is it fair for it to be only available to those who can afford it? Is it possible for society to deploy tens of thousands of well-trained therapists to spend thousands of hours with every single patient, working intensively with them for months, if not years? The fact that elite private psychiatric hospitals offering psychoanalysis to their schizophrenic patients, such as the Chestnut Lodge, have not been able to stand the test of time and have been closed or restructured, says volumes.

Yet who can come up with the price tag for any individual's life? Can the value of personal salvation be judged simply with money and time spent? This is exactly why Gail Hornstein, the author of Frieda's biography, titled her book *To Redeem One Person Is to Redeem the World*.

FRIEDA FROMM-REICHMANN AS A "WOUNDED HEALER"

Joanne Greenberg was lucky. She was admitted to Chestnut Lodge in 1948, when the hospital was at the height of its fame and Frieda was widely regarded as one of the most talented psychoanalysts, still full of energy and vitality. Although it would be reasonable to suspect that *I Never Promised You a Rose Garden* might have idealized her as a therapist, the book did clearly convey Frieda's agility, gracefulness, and patience.

What made the treatment of this case so successful? In the last few years of her life, Frieda became increasingly preoccupied with the question. In many of her lectures and publications, she attempted to identify technical issues that might have led to the favorable outcome. But the message she was most eager to convey was that, to be successful in treatment, a therapist has to be able to experience, empathize, and accept the patient's profound sense of fear, anxiety, despair, and loneliness. Equipped with intuition, training, and experience, most professionals do possess such ability, to varying degrees. But what made Frieda stand out in this regard? Was this simply because she was a genius?

We have reason to believe that Frieda's exceptional capacity for empathy is rooted, at least in part, in her personal life experiences. Under the veneer of her glorious professional success, her life had been inundated with loneliness and disappointments. Coming from a traditional Jewish family, as the first of ten siblings, she spent her childhood playing the role of mediator (and therefore therapist) between her dominant mother and ineffectual father. Growing up under the shadow of the Nazis, her adolescence was full of fear and insecurity. Raped in broad daylight during her teens, she received blame instead of sympathy. Her mother's reaction was anger, hostility, and rejection.

Shy, reserved, and picky, she had never dated, let alone fallen in love, until she reached the age of thirty-six. Then she was caught unaware, suddenly swept off her feet by the twenty-five-year-old Erich Fromm,[2] a charismatic

---

[2] Erich Fromm would go on to become a prolific writer and social critic, most famous for the book *Escape from Freedom*. Along with Harry Stack Sullivan (see Chapter 11) and Karen Horney, he was instrumental in shaping the interpersonal psychotherapy (neo-Freudianism) movement.

genius who was also narcissistic, arrogant, and emotionally needy and dependent. Starting as his therapist, Frieda was soon mesmerized by him, caring for and indulging him as if he were her own son.

Together, they set up a psychiatric hospital providing treatment based on existentialism and Jewish mysticism. Two years later, it ended in bankruptcy, leaving her with a large debt. When Erich developed tuberculosis, Frieda sent him to a sanitorium in the Swiss Alps for recuperation, the cost of which further worsened her financial situation.

Then, Erich started an affair with Karen Horney,[3] who was five years older than Frieda (thus, fifteen years older than Erich). After being deserted by Erich, Frieda had no other intimate relationships. Instead, she focused her energy completely on her work. Living in the hospital grounds, she did not have much of a social life and did not seem to have close friends either. Although she never admitted it, one could only imagine how lonely and bleak her personal life must have been. One could also further speculate that this personal experience of loneliness and desolation enabled her to more easily enter schizophrenic patients' inner worlds.

Seeing it this way, Frieda is indeed a good example of a wounded healer. "Wounded healer" sounds like a self-contradictory concept: How could someone who is burdened with pathology solve others' problems? But, as shown throughout this book, most famous therapists struggled with significant medical, psychological, or behavioral problems in their lives. Their own traumatic experiences enabled these "wounded healers" to be more perceptive and more able to empathize with those who have been similarly "wounded." This ability to connect and enter the patients' world is the most crucial ingredient for therapy to be effective.

The author of *I Never Promised You a Rose Garden* "graduated" from Fromm-Reichmann's clinic in 1955, fell in love, and got married in the same year. After honeymooning in Europe, she moved from the East Coast to Colorado, and started her exceptionally productive life that lasted many decades, and is still going strong.

In that same year, Frieda was invited to be a senior fellow at the Center for Advanced Study in the Behavioral Sciences at Stanford University (CASBS), where she finally had a whole year to focus on writing. Remarkably, her last manuscript was titled "Loneliness." Uncharacteristically, she had great difficulty completing the task. After a number of revisions, she was still not able to

---

[3] Karen Horney was a German psychoanalyst who, together with Harry Stack Sullivan, Erik Erikson, and Erich Fromm, promoted the movement of interpersonal psychoanalysis (part of the neo-Freudianism), emphasizing cultural and social factors in human development instead of focusing on biologically driven instinctual theories that are the basis of classic Freudianism. She was one of the first to rebel against Freud's doctrine of "penis envy" as the basis of understanding female psychology. She also made significant contributions to the study and treatment of neurotic conditions.

bring it to a form satisfactory to her. One might say that she died struggling with "loneliness," symbolically and figuratively.

Frieda's loneliness might have contributed to a "good life" for the author of *I Never Promised You a Rose Garden*. Is it a fair trade? She might have salvaged many suffering individuals, but was she able to salvage herself? And was she able to redeem the world?

11

The "Queer" Genius Who Shaped American Psychiatry

Who Is Harry Stack Sullivan?

[A] witty Irishman, who has a facade of facetiousness which it is a bit difficult to penetrate ... [There is] a considerable discontent that might perhaps express itself in alliances with other discontented spirits.

(William Alanson White, in Ozarin [1999] and Perry [1982])[1]

Sullivan was loved and hated with equal intensity ... [N]o one knew all of Sullivan ... [H]e was the closest thing to a genius I've ever seen.

(Dexter Bullard, second superintendent of the Chestnut Lodge, in Cornett, 2008)

Sullivan was like a Zen master, totally present to the patient.

(Gail A. Hornstein, in Hornstein, 2005)

Largely forgotten now, Harry Stack Sullivan once played a significant role in the development of American psychiatry in the early twentieth century (Perry, 1982; Silver, 2002), whose influence is easily comparable to that of the Menninger brothers (Karl[2] and William Menninger[3]). During the twenty-odd years of his relatively short academic career, he established a comprehensive psychiatric examination system that is still in use today (Sullivan, 1954); promoted the practice of detailed clinical charting and

---

[1] White was Sullivan's boss at St. Elizabeth's Hospital in Washington, DC; this quote is from 1923, in a letter of recommendation written by White for Sullivan. White was one of the most influential leaders of American psychiatry at the beginning of the twentieth century and a key person in the introduction of psychoanalytic theories into American settings. From 1903 to 1937, the year of his death, he was in charge of the Government Hospital of the Insane (later renamed St. Elisabeth's Hospital), which was transformed from a supersized national asylum into a first-rate research and teaching hospital, playing a crucial role in the establishment of the National Institute of Mental Health (NIMH).

[2] Karl Menninger was the older of the two Menninger brothers, who along with their father, Charles Menninger, started the famous Menninger Clinic in Topeka, Kansas, that for most of the twentieth century was regarded as the "mecca" of American psychiatric training. Karl was a prolific writer whose books, including *Man Against Himself*, *The Vital Balance*, and *Theory of Psychoanalytic Technique*, popularized Freudian theories and practices in the USA.

[3] Younger of the Menninger brothers, William Menninger worked effectively with the American government during and after World War II to promote services and training programs nationwide.

clinical case conferences; and created models for the inpatient treatment of acute schizophrenic patients where he organized therapeutic teams to build milieus to promote patients' recovery. He worked closely with Frieda Fromm-Reichmann to promote the use of active psychotherapy in treating schizophrenic patients, which was widely practiced in elite American psychiatric institutions for several decades.

Sullivan's most important contribution came from his efforts to revise classical Freudian theories and practices. Contrary to traditional psychoanalysis, he believed that the most challenging issues confronting individuals' development was not sex or libido, but the pursuit of security. Concurrently, throughout people's lives, the biggest tasks are not overcoming intra-psychic conflicts, but the establishment and maintenance of intimate and sustained interpersonal relationships. He also proposed that alienation, isolation, and loneliness, especially during childhood and adolescence, play a crucial role in the pathogenesis of psychiatric disorders.

Due to the efforts of Sullivan and other like-minded innovators of his time, we now see these ideas as common sense. However, during his lifetime they were regarded by "mainstream" psychoanalysts as deviant and subversive. Along with Karen Horney and Erich Fromm, his ideas led to the development of attachment theory and the establishment of the school of "interpersonal psychoanalysis."[4]

But Sullivan has gradually faded away in psychiatry's collective memory since his death in 1949. We might blame his abstruse writing styles and the relative sparseness of his publications for the rapid decline of his visibility, but even more importantly it was also due to his aloofness and eccentricity, which made people around him uneasy.

The oddity in his behavior had deep roots. Although it has not been proven, there were rumors of his having alcohol and gambling problems. In his young adulthood, he was hospitalized several times with schizophrenia as a possible diagnosis. But even more importantly, he was in all likelihood a closet homosexual who was conflicted about his own sexual orientation. Together, all these pointed to the fact that he was someone who struggled with his own identity throughout his life. He often found himself at odds with social norms and needed to strive heroically to maintain a semblance of balance in life (Wake, 2006). His life-long struggles enabled him to empathize with the fear and loneliness of his patients. His tragedy was that, although he was a genius in "healing" others, he was unable to heal himself.

---

[4] Bingham Dai, the world's first psychoanalyst of Chinese descent, was trained by Sullivan in the 1930s. Dai was active at the Peking Union Medical College Hospital from 1935 to 1939, making impressive contributions in promoting psychotherapy with Chinese patients. He believed that he was able to achieve such success because he focused on interpersonal relationships rather than intra-psychic conflicts, which is much more congruent with Chinese culture (Dai, 1984).

DESOLATE CHILDHOOD

Sullivan's difficulties had deep roots. Although his parents were both Catholic Irish immigrants, they somehow ended up settling down in the deep protestant country in rural New England. Going against the common stereotypes of the Irish and Irish Americans, Sullivan was a single child, and his parents were emotionally distant, reserved, and non-demonstrative. This might be because they were struggling with their own mental health problems, as his mother was hospitalized several times in her life in psychiatric hospitals, although the diagnosis is unknown.

Growing up in such settings, Sullivan was a lonely child, isolated, marginalized, and deprived of playmates. Entering adolescence, it got even worse. His classmates formed cliques that excluded him. He had no friends and felt he did not belonged to any groups.

As a smart child with good grades, Sullivan had no trouble being admitted to the esteemed Cornell University. Yet, one year later, he was expelled from the school for unclear reasons. Leaving Cornell, he disappeared for the next two years, likely spending some of the time in a psychiatric hospital (Wake, 2006). Resurfacing in 1911, he continued to receive psychotherapy, but was well enough to enroll at the Chicago College of Medicine and Surgery, a new and yet-to-be-accredited medical school.

Earning a medical degree did not make life easier for him. From 1916 to 1919, he changed jobs at least five times, from the coast guard to a pharmaceutical company, then an insurance company, then back to the government at the Department of Defense, finally ending at a Veterans Administration (VA) hospital. To all appearances, he was a lost soul with no sense of direction in his life.

A TURNING POINT IN LIFE

Sullivan's lucky break came in 1919, when he was assigned to St. Elizabeth's Hospital to coordinate the care of veteran patients. Somehow, his talent for establishing empathetic relationships with patients was noticed and appreciated by William Alanson White, who introduced him to Adolf Meyer (Lamb, 2014), chairman of the Department of Psychiatry at the nearby Johns Hopkins University. Under the tutelage of these two heavyweights in American psychiatry, Sullivan gradually built up a reputation as a talented expert on schizophrenia. As a result, when Ross Chapman, another student of White, was appointed as the director of Sheppard-Pratt, an elite private psychiatric hospital, Sullivan was invited to serve as the director of clinical research. The two worked well together, implementing a series of innovations aimed at applying White and Meyer's progressive agenda in the care of severely mentally ill patients.

Although White was sympathetic to Freudian theories, he was by no means a typical Freudian, taking particular issue with the pessimistic attitudes of psychoanalysts regarding the prognosis of schizophrenic patients. On the contrary, he believed that it was the mission of psychiatrists to understand the pathogenesis of this ubiquitous and devastating condition and to search for effective therapeutic approaches.

ADOLF MEYER, PSYCHOBIOLOGY, AND LIFE CHART

Meyer came from Switzerland, with deep ties to the Burghölzli Hospital, the main psychiatric teaching hospital for the University of Zurich. Although having lived in the USA for many years, Meyer still communicated regularly with psychiatric leaders in Europe, including Emil Kraepelin, Eugen Bleuler, and Sigmund Freud, and closely followed the evolution of their ideas and activities. He was a great synthesizer, never hesitating to accept whatever made sense to him and to weave ideas together into his own thinking.

In his view, a good psychiatrist, and in fact any good physician, should always strive for a comprehensive and in-depth understanding of patients' lives, by closely examining events and circumstances important at different stages of their lives, and finding out how they dealt with challenges associated with life events.

Meyer emphasized the importance of assuming a "holistic" approach, simultaneously taking biological, psychological, and social factors into consideration. For such a purpose, he coined the term "psychobiology," which is still widely in use today. Unfortunately, the meaning of the term has gradually shifted, with increasing emphasis on the biological aspect of human development at the expense of the social and psychological dimensions.

Fortunately, some of his students, especially George Engel and John Romano, were able to carry his torch and proposed the biopsychosocial model that has become a catchword in contemporary psychiatry.

Another important contribution of Meyer, the concept of the "life chart" (Ghaemi, 2007), unfortunately now largely forgotten, is a useful tool in reminding us that a patient is not just a collection of symptoms and signs manifested cross-sectionally, but has a long life history populated by influential people and enriched with meaningful events.

Similia Similibus Curantur

One of Sullivan's earlier contributions was the systematic application of Meyer's ideas on the treatment of schizophrenia. Based on his own experiences and data collected at Sheppard-Pratt over a number of years, Sullivan found that pre-adolescence was a crucial stage in life for the development of schizophrenia. He argued that during this time period it was crucial for a person to have a *chum* his own age so that he would be able to develop a healthy sense of belongingness and form a solid identity. Without such experiences, it would be difficult for the person to grow up knowing who he was, resulting in identity confusion, increasing the risk for developing schizophrenia in later years.

Following this line of thought, he proposed that the way to correct such a deficit was to provide patients with a second chance to remedy the missing process. In order to do so, he established a special ward at the hospital for first-break young male patients. Adopting the principle of *similia similibus curantur* ("like cures like"), he personally selected and trained a group of young men matching their patients in terms of age and personality. In doing this, he deliberately excluded professionals (psychiatrists, nurses, and other therapists) from the ward because of his belief that professional training distanced them from their patients.

In addition, since he believed that most schizophrenic patients struggled with confusion about their sexual orientation, he also deliberately chose those with similar tendencies to work with these patients. In so doing, he expected staff members to serve as role models, to help patients reduce their self-doubt and anxiety, and to enhance their sense of self-worth and self-acceptance.

At a time when almost all experts believed that schizophrenia was incurable, his patients' "remission rate" reached 62 percent. What a pleasant surprise! Over the decades, such remarkable achievements have been repeatedly questioned by experts in the field. Many have suggested that Sullivan's definition of remission was too loose. Others pointed out that since Sullivan's patients were highly selective, many of them would have recovered by themselves, even without intervention. These reservations notwithstanding, the results were still quite remarkable, suggesting that the sense of being understood and accepted did play a crucial role in patients' improvement. It is reasonable to expect patients in such a supportive milieu to feel safe enough to express their deeply buried thoughts, impulses, and experiences, to share them with someone they trust, without fear of being criticized, accused, and abandoned. Relieved from the burden of needing to be on the defensive, to be always on guard, they would be much more likely to improve.

SULLIVAN'S LIFE-LONG STRUGGLES WITH HIS OWN SEXUAL ORIENTATION PROBLEMS

With wider attention, rumors started to circulate regarding inappropriate physical or sexual contacts between staff and patients in Sullivan's ward. This was in a way expected, since almost all of them were young men supposedly with homosexual tendencies (or at least were sympathetic toward such inclinations). In the process of exploring their own homosexual desires and fantasies, it would not be a surprise if some of the staff members at times lost control of their impulses and acted improperly.

What happened in Sullivan's ward raised important questions that the mental health field are still struggling with, more than half a century later: How do we define professional boundaries and how can they be enforced? What kind of "nonverbal" (i.e., physical) communications are within bounds? Is embracing or kissing acceptable? When are such contacts therapeutic and not just excuses for staff members to exploit the vulnerable patients under their power? Was it possible that Sullivan was not aware of such possibilities?

Sullivan's involvement with the special ward is clearly reflected in the hospital's records and the reports of those who worked there. His management was hands-on, providing detailed instructions covering all aspects of the operation of the ward. Living inside the hospital's campus, he encouraged staff to drop in at any time to discuss a patient's condition and responses to interventions. William Elliot, one of the staff members working there at the time, said, "Sullivan was just like a boxing coach. He was everywhere. You jumped when he told you to jump, and you stopped the minute he told you to stop."

Yet, in all of his publications and lectures, he never dealt with the topic of boundary violations. This perhaps was a reflection of his own ambivalence, leading him to consciously or unconsciously avoid talking about it.

Regarding his own sexual orientation, Sullivan was vague and cryptic. Throughout his life, he vacillated between revealing and concealing. In 1927, Jimmie Inscoe, a fifteen-year-old boy at the time, suddenly appeared in his household. For the next twenty-two years, Jimmie lived with him, functioning as his housekeeper and secretary. Sullivan publicly acknowledged him as an adopted son and even changed his last name to Sullivan.

At the same time, Sullivan often boasted of being a "playboy," implying that he had affairs with many of his female colleagues, including his analyst, Clara Thompson.[5] Was any of this true, or were they all smokescreens? Was he bisexual or was this boasting for the purpose of deflecting people's suspicions? Such contradictions and inconsistencies would seem puzzling if we did not put them in the context of the ethos of the time. Although homosexuality has been widely discriminated against and marginalized in most societies since antiquity, the phenomenon was further stigmatized and demonized toward the end of the nineteenth century and the twentieth century. This probably was due to two of the major trends that became

---

[5] Entering the St. Elizabeth's training program just a little later than Sullivan, Thompson soon became a close friend of his. In 1927 they went together to attend Sándor Ferenczi's lecture and were both deeply moved by him. Since Sullivan could not afford to go to Budapest for long-term analysis, he suggested that Thompson did so on his behalf. Thomson agreed and went to Hungary on two occasions, staying there for a number of years. After returning from Hungary, she became Sullivan's analyst.

prominent in Western civilization. One was the so-called eugenics movement that gained momentum with the widespread misunderstanding and misapplication of evolutionary theories. The other was the accelerating trend in what anthropologist Francis Hsu (1983) called "rugged individualism."

As the concept of evolution was distorted and simplified into the slogan of "survival of the fittest," homosexuality became not just an issue of morality or even religious abomination, but a threat to collective existence. It came to be regarded as "unnatural," a sign of degeneration that had to be eradicated in order to not threaten the propagation and survival of the social or racial group to which the individuals belonged.

At the same time, the rise of *rugged individualism* conferred upon individuals an unprecedented degree of freedom and room for maneuver. Yet along with the freedom came increasing pressure for a person to define his or her own role and identity. A boy no longer just grew into the roles assigned by society, but needed to behave in a "manly" fashion to demonstrate that he indeed was becoming a man. The fear of oneself becoming a "sissy" – turning into a homosexual – made young men sensitive to others' "abnormal" identities, which threatened their own sense of identity and security. This might be one of the reasons why homosexuality seemed to be least tolerated in the USA, the most individualistically oriented society in the twentieth century (Hsu, 1983). Ironically, the emphasis on individual freedom resulted in making people less tolerant of social deviation.

Reflecting these developments, homosexuality had been regarded by psychiatrists as abnormal and blamed for predisposing people to many psychiatric disorders, especially paranoid schizophrenia. Until the 1970s, psychiatric residents who were openly gay or were suspected to have homosexual tendencies were widely discriminated against. Even in the most progressive university programs, the policy was often: "You can be a quiet homosexual, or you can be a flamboyant heterosexual, but if you are a flamboyant homosexual, you have to go" (Scasta, 2003).

Even after 1986, when "homosexuality" was finally removed from the official psychiatric diagnostic system, many psychiatrists continued to be uneasy about revealing their own sexual orientation. This is why so many well-known academic leaders were unable to "come out of the closet" until they were in their seventies or eighties, after decades of "failed therapies."

Considering the risks and complications of "coming out" in Sullivan's time, his hesitancy and evasiveness becomes more understandable. In his day and age, it was already exceptionally brave for him just to set up a special ward to focus on patients' difficulties with sexual orientation and to publicly discuss the relationship between patients' confusion about their sexual orientation and the development of psychiatric disorders.

Looking at Sullivan's life, we might feel sorry for his inability to live openly as a homosexual. But in his time, to be able to live with the one he loved was already a monumental achievement. Even today, there is still a great deal of resistance to homosexuals' fight for the right to marry their beloved. The fact that "gay marriage" still looms large in American presidential campaigns serves to remind us how deep-rooted and widespread anti-gay sentiments still are in our supposedly "post-modern" societies.

THE SUFFERINGS AND REWARDS OF BEING A "MARGINAL MAN"

Just as noted by White, Sullivan remained a prototypical *marginal man* throughout his whole life. His homosexuality, his "minority status" (as a lone Irish Catholic surrounded by Protestants when growing up), his lonely childhood, and the "breakdowns" and hospitalizations during his early adulthood converged to make it hard for him to be part of the "mainstream." This profound sense of "marginality" and his endless struggle between denying and accepting his "self" represented an inordinately heavy burden for him throughout his whole life. At the same time, his ambiguous homosexual tendencies also caused a great deal of anxiety in those around him, who were often at a loss as to how to behave in his presence.

But the profound sense of marginality also enabled him to enter the inner worlds of schizophrenic patients. His experiences of being marginal made it possible for him to understand patients' loneliness, confusion, alienation, and desolation. His suffering enabled him to get close enough to patients that he was almost able to hear their breathing and sense their body heat. Such direct, genuine, nonverbal "contact" is conducive to the treatment and recovery of most psychiatric patients. This is exactly why Sullivan said: "Those who have never been hurt would not be able to really sense others' pain: Only those who have been wounded time and again are able to have an overall view of how people got hurt, and how they could be helped to recover."

But the price of living a life as a "marginal man" was high. Sullivan died unexpectedly when he was at the relatively young age of fifty-seven, alone in a small hotel in Paris. When his body was discovered, he had already been dead for quite some time. Scattered around the room were many different kinds of pills that would have killed anybody. The coroner's report listed subdural hemorrhage as the cause of death instead of suicide. Since he had a long history of heart problems, further compounded by a damaged liver and impaired kidney functions, natural death was not unexpected. But even so, dying alone in a dingy hotel room in a foreign country is not something to which anybody would aspire.

12

Anthropologists in a Daughter's Eye

*The Amazing Coming Together of Margaret Mead
and Gregory Bateson*

When most people think about cultural anthropology in the twentieth century, the first name that comes to mind is Margaret Mead. Born in 1901, she published her famed *Coming of Age in Samoa* (Mead, 1928) at the young age of twenty-seven. In the next half-century, her research findings and insights not only dominated the development of the field of anthropology, but also left deep imprints on many related fields, including sociology, psychology, and psychiatry. Through her numerous lectures, magazine articles, newspaper commentaries, and appearances on radio and television programs, her thoughts also influenced the behaviors and lifestyles of the general public, reverberating even to this day.

What was the source of Mead's creativity and charisma? Who was the real Mead behind the glamorous appearance? Who was Mead in private, and what was her personal life like? We had few answers to these questions until the publication of the memoir of her daughter, Mary Catherine Bateson' a well-established anthropologist herself (Bateson, 1994). Combining this with the autobiography (Mead, 1972) Mead wrote toward the end of her life focusing only on her younger years, it became possible for us to reconstruct the outline of her as a person and to gain insight into her third husband, Gregory Bateson, whose career was arguably as remarkable as that of her's, if less glamorous.

SWEET MAIDEN IN SAMOA

Both of Mead's parents came from "blue-blooded" New England lineages. Her father was an economics professor at the University of Pennsylvania. Her mother devoted her life to promoting feminism and the rights of immigrants. As the oldest of five siblings, Mead became the "head of the household" from an early age, assuming responsibilities and making decisions that should have been her parents', and discharging such duties with flourish and gusto.

She was also known to be good at keeping secrets, clearly shown in events surrounding her first marriage. Although she started dating the brother of her math teacher in high school (Luther Cressman, who later became a well-known archeologist), and they became engaged to each other, she kept this secret until the eve of their marriage, just prior to her graduation from college.

It was during the last year of college that another momentous event took place. To fulfill a requirement for graduation, she randomly chose a class in anthropology as one of her electives, not knowing that it would lead her to a glorious career to which she would dedicate her whole life.

She could not have entered the field at a better time: This was when cultural anthropology was going through a rapid transformation, during which "cultural evolution" was gradually replaced by "cultural relativism" as the guiding principle. Whereas previously, scholars had been more interested in the construction of theories and speculation based on secondary data, the new trend emphasized "fieldwork" and "first-person" observations, relying on copious and detailed field notes to describe and interpret the behaviors and thought processes of people of different cultures. In order to achieve such goals, cultural anthropologists needed to immerse themselves in the local culture, live the local life, wear the local clothes, eat what the locals eat, and participate in their religious and recreational activities. As much as possible, the researcher strived to become an "insider," so as to understand the rationale and function of cultural phenomena that might appear "bizarre" to outsiders.

In order to gain access for observation and documentation, researchers use themselves as the tool, actively participating in "indigenous" lives. Is it possible? Does it work? Participation and observation seem contradictory. Participation interferes with observation; but without participation, observations are superficial. How does one balance the two? How does one solve the paradox?

Actions have to be taken even if these puzzles remain to be solved. Researchers at the time were worried that "primitive" cultures were rapidly disappearing due to their contacts with Western civilizations. Accordingly, there was a sense of urgency in studying them before they were "contaminated" and evaporated. The young Mead understood the urgency and was excited by the challenges. She not only wanted to go to a "primitive" tribe, but it had to be the tribe that was most remote and least documented.

Where would this place be? After careful consideration, she decided it had to be the most far-flung, inaccessible island, deep in a corner of the immense Pacific Ocean. This decision made, she went to see Franz Boas, the revered professor at Columbia University, widely regarded as the father of American cultural anthropology. There, she ran into Boas' assistant, Ruth Benedict, the future author of a number of groundbreaking books, including *The Chrysanthemum and the Sword*, the book that convinced the American military to keep the Japanese Emperor in place as an inducement for the surrender of the Japanese armies toward the end of World War II. Mead and Benedict soon became best friends.

Surprisingly, in 1925, the ordinarily strict and cautious Boas agreed to let the twenty-four-year-old Mead go to a small island in American Samoa by herself, to live in a village for close to a year, in order to experience in person the intricate details of the islanders' lives. This was highly unusual, especially considering that Mead had not yet had any field research experience at the time.

The mission Boas imparted on Mead was for her to observe and document the adolescence of young Samoan women. In contemporary "Western" societies, adolescence was a particularly painful stage of human development, suffused with uncertainties, struggles, and angst. Boas hoped that cross-cultural comparisons could shed light on why growing up during this stage was so difficult: How much of this might be determined by nature, and thus universal, and how much was secondary to nurture, caused by cultural upbringing and injunctions?

In order to reach American Samoa, Mead had to go to California and Hawaii first, before eventually arriving at Pago Pago, the territory's capital. There she waited for three more weeks for a supply ship to take her to the island of Manu'a, her final destination.

Settling down at a makeshift workstation attached to the only clinic in the village, she shed her American attire in exchange for the native straw skirts, became used to walking around barefoot, taking baths in the streams, learning to weave rattan mats, and eating fish and taro instead of meat and bread. Watching sunrise and sunset with the villagers, going to their dances at night, she quickly learned the local language and customs.

Villagers gradually warmed to her. Many of her initial visitors were prepubescent and adolescent girls. Since Mead was just a few years older, she was able to relate to them and gained their confidence. As their conversations expanded in scope, she was dumbfounded to find that these young girls were extraordinarily familiar with the details of sex and lovemaking. Although still unmarried, they already had experiences in all sorts of sexual activities and were unabashed in talking about them. Writing down verbatim the things these young women related to her, she was elated. What they said proved her mentor, Boas, and her good friend, Benedict, right: *The Sorrows of Young Werther* really was the product of Western civilization!

With her talents in language and literature, she was able to quickly finish a manuscript reporting these exciting new findings, which was published in 1928 as *Growing Up in Samoa*. The book immediately became a best-seller, and subsequently went through countless reprints and was translated into many languages. It is still in print even now, almost a century later.

Why is the book so successful and popular? Of course, first and foremost, it is a reflection of Mead's talents in research and writing. Equally importantly, it also came out at the right time, when Americans needed new perspectives to support their emerging optimism and individualism. The book persuasively convinced its readers that our lives are not preordained and predetermined, whether by God's will or by heredity. Instead, we are in charge of our lives, we are the masters of our own fates, capable of shaping and reshaping ourselves, adopting different lifestyles, and modifying our behavioral patterns.

Contrasting our society with that of the Samoans, it seemed clear that the pain and suffering of our youngsters were caused by the pressures and burdens of our culture's often conflicting demands on them. So, given such insights, we should reexamine these social norms and consider ways to modify them, so that the next generation of our citizens would not need to be hampered by unnecessary restrictions and would be able to enjoy a greater degree of freedom to pursue what was really important for them.

From such a cross-cultural angle, Mead became a forceful critic of contemporary American society and culture, and a powerful spokesperson for a whole new generation of Westerners searching for a new direction.

She happily assumed such a role, wrote countless articles and commentaries for newspapers and magazines, eagerly participated in radio interviews, and became an eloquent and forceful public speaker. In so doing, she also popularized cultural anthropology, transforming it from a quaint academic pursuit into a field wielding considerable power in influencing public opinion.

FALLING IN LOVE WHILE CROSSING STORMY OCEANS

Success notwithstanding, physically and psychologically, Mead's return from her remote South Pacific island "paradise" back to the "civilized world" was not an easy one. From Samoa, she reached Australia first, from where she boarded a ship that ambled hesitantly across the Pacific and Indian Oceans, braving one storm after another, each more capricious than the previous one.

She was also exceedingly lonely, and homesick for the exotic land she had just left behind. This sense of loneliness was further deepened because she could not find anyone to share all the exciting observations and ideas swirling in her head. It was finally made better when Reo Fortune (Dobrin & Bashkow, 2010) came on board at Sydney, a young New Zealander psychologist on his way to Cambridge, UK, to study anthropology.

During the long trip circumnavigating Australia, passing Ceylon, Yemen, Sicily, then eventually reaching Marseille, they stayed together day and night. Talking constantly and passionately, they readily falling in love. They were not only lovers, they became soulmates.

The sight of Mead's husband, Cressman, at the Marseille dockside interrupted this feverish love affair, but only for a short while. As planned, Mead and Cressman had an extended tour of Paris before returning to the USA, but all the oceans that had separated them for the past year got in the way, and the gulf was too wide and too deep to cross. Eventually, they parted ways amicably, clearing the path for Mead to be reunited with Fortune.

But after Samoa, what was there still to be excited about? Was there any place on Earth that could be even more remote and thus more entrancing? Mead and Fortune agreed that, if there was to be such a place, it had to be New Guinea. Although Branislav Malinovski, the formidable Polish-British anthropologist, had already published the famous classic, *Argonauts of the Western Pacific* (Malinovski, 1922), its focus was on the Trobriand Islands that were off the coast. The huge inland New Guinea remained largely unexplored and mysterious because it was so mountainous, with villages scattered in hidden valleys that were difficult to reach. Tribes across the island were isolated from one another and developed languages and cultures that were unique and distinct. The only thing uniting the whole island seemed to be the practice of headhunting.

After Fortune received his PhD from Columbia University in 1931, the two departed for the New Guinea highland, venturing deep inside rugged mountain ranges and dark rainforests. They were well funded and equipped, with more than six months of food supplies. However, all of their porters disappeared before they reached their destination, either because the trip was too strenuous, or the porters were worried about losing their heads to the unpredictable headhunters deep in the mountains.

Stuck where they were, Mead and Fortune settled into a small village not of their choosing. Frustrated, they started blaming each other. Bickering constantly, they became increasing aware of the differences in their personalities, upbringings, and value systems. From Mead's point of view, Fortune was incredibly selfish and intensely (almost insanely) competitive, verging on paranoia and cruelty. She was right, most people found Fortune difficult to deal with.

It took them several months to find their a way back to the coast, where, replenished and refreshed, they started their expedition again and immediately ran into Gregory Bateson.

FALLING IN LOVE UNDER THE WATCHFUL EYES OF HEADHUNTERS

Bateson was the third son of the world-famous British geneticist William Bateson, who rediscovered the law of Mendelian inheritance,[1] and coined the term "genetics." As a serious scientist, William Bateson had extremely high expectations for all three of his sons.

Unfortunately, Gregory's eldest brother, John, was killed in battle in 1918, right before the end of World War I. After John's death, William shifted his

---

[1] Originally discovered by the Augustinian friar Gregor Mendel.

attention to his second son, Martin, forcing him to study biology even though his goal in life was to become a poet and a playwright. Two years later, the continuing tug of war between father and son led to a tragic end. On John's birthday, Martin committed suicide directly under the statue of Anteros[2] at Piccadilly Circus, the busiest and most public place in London.

This left Gregory as the only son to carry on his father's legacy. Although Gregory's interest was also in literature and the humanities, he felt obliged to fulfill his parents' wishes, and did his best to become a biologist. In this process, he by chance discovered the field of anthropology, which he thought straddled science and the humanities. He decided to take it up as a compromise between his parents' wishes and his own. It was the study of anthropology that took him to New Guinea.

That the mild, absent-minded, and often clueless Bateson was even able to survive living among the warlike headhunters was already a miracle, his imposing height of six feet five inches notwithstanding. Whatever the real reason was, he managed to keep his head intact, and also survived repeated attacks of malaria, dysentery, and other tropical diseases. However, if Mead and Fortune had not shown up when they did, it is doubtful he would have survived his own loneliness.

Bateson had been in despair for quite some time, blaming himself not only for achieving nothing after several years in New Guinea, but even more so for not having been able to find direction for himself. Indeed, Mead and Fortune provided him with new purpose and focus, in addition to companionship.

Bateson immediately directed all his tender attention toward Mead, doing his best to make her life comfortable. He also instantly became good friends with Fortune, and opened his heart to him, without hesitation or reservation.

Mead's American-style optimism was infectious, which revitalized Bateson's passion and confidence. Coming from totally different worlds, they attracted each other and stimulated the creative drive innate to each of them.

This triangle persisted for some time, bringing them much joy despite the undercurrents of jealousy and competition (King, 2014). Of course, such arrangements cannot be sustained indefinitely. Mead and Bateson became more and more drawn to each other, at the expense of Fortune, who gradually faded away and eventually left.

Mead's encouragement and support enabled Bateson to complete his analysis and synthesis of the data he had collected over several years in New Guinea, resulting in the publication of his first book, *Naven* (Bateson, 1936), just in time to be presented to Mead as a gift for their wedding. The 375-page

---

[2] In Greek mythology, Anteros ("anti-Eros" – Eros' counterpart) is the younger brother of Eros and the avenger of unrequited love.

book described in detail the customs, belief systems, social structure, music, art, and wedding and funeral ceremonies of the Iatmul, a group famous not only for their practices of headhunting and cannibalism, but even more so for the extraordinary artistry of their sculpture.

Perhaps the most surprising aspect of the book is the theme of *Naven*, the most important festival of the Iatmul. This event was characterized by the performance of *transvestism* and ritual, simulated homosexual acts. Naven was an integral and central part of tribal lives, organized not only to celebrate the acquisition of new heads, but also for other less dramatic achievements, such as successful hunting or fishing trips, or even for a good crop of sago.[3] During the festival, uncles of the "heroes" would put on the women's best straw skirts and try to outdo one another with their charms. At the same time, their aunts would dress as warriors, wielding staves and spears in a manly fashion.

What might be the meaning of Naven? The villagers were unable or unwilling to explain. They simply stated that these were the right things to do. Bateson exhausted himself searching for answers, going back to antiquity, and ended up feeling defeated. In contrast, Mead's explanation was simple and common sense: These rituals served to highlight differences in gender roles and to strengthen the need to maintain such differentiations in their daily lives.

Mead was remarkably productive during these years as well. Of the many books she published, *Sex and Temperament* (Mead, 1935) was perhaps the most influential. The book describes in detail the gender roles, relationships, and divisions of labor between men and women in three tribes. The first one she described was most familiar to us, with men enjoying a higher status and wielding more power than women. The second one was characterized by equality across gender lines, where men and women shared all works equally. What was most surprising, though, was that the third society she described was one in which women held most of the power, with men playing sub-missive roles.

Sex and Temperament was received by feminists with great enthusiasm; they regarded it as proof that "maternal love" was but an excuse for society to chain them to domestic care. At the other end of the spectrum, conservatives were angered, seeing the book and its author as a threat to conventional morality.

What is much more important than such divergence in responses was that the book heralded a shift away from the belief in biological (meaning genetic) determinism (even Freud said, "anatomy is destiny") to "environ-mental" or "cultural" determinism. This new trend led to the belief that newborn babies were "blank canvases" waiting to be shaped by social and

---

[3] Sago is edible starch obtained from a palm, and is a staple food in parts of the tropics.

cultural forces as mediated through their parents, relatives, teachers, and friends. Such cultural forces not only determine individuals' ideas and behaviors, but also their temperaments and characters.

Such a "socialization" process of is ongoing, persisting throughout one's whole lifespan, but there is no doubt that infancy and childhood are the most important stages of such developments. Thinking along these lines, it was only natural for researchers and opinion leaders to assume that our psychological and behavioral problems are rooted in the parent–child relationship. Thus, in order to improve mental health and prevent psychiatric disorders, we need to systematically investigate and understand the way infants and children are raised in modern societies. This led to the establishment of guidelines and models for healthy parent–child (though of course at the time people naturally assumed that this meant mother–child) interactions.

This development also confirmed Mead's belief that cultural anthropology had an extremely important role to play in molding child-rearing practices, and that results from field studies could provide important contributions to fostering the development of healthier adults.

HOW EXPERIENCES IN SOUTH PACIFIC OCEANIA SHAPED MODERN CHILD-REARING PRACTICES

That was exactly what Mead did. It so happened that, not long after her return to New York, she bumped into Benjamin Spock, a physician who had recently graduated from medical school and was in the middle of his pediatric training at Columbia. They soon became fast friends. From Mead and Bateson, Spock learned that child-rearing practices diverged remarkably across cultures, each with its strengths and weaknesses. These cross-cultural facts significantly influenced his views on child development, which were reflected in his subsequent writings. His *Dr. Spock's Baby and Child Care*, first published in 1946, immediately became a best-seller, and was translated into more than forty nine languages. With regular updates, it remained the "Bible" for childcare, benefiting generations of children growing up in developed and developing countries.

Mead's friendship with Spock came in handy for herself when, in 1939, after years of grudgingly accepting her fate of being infertile, she was surprised by her own pregnancy. Facing this surprising new challenge, Mead was ecstatic. What a godsend! What a perfect collaborative project for her and Spock!

The first thing she asked of Spock was that he accompany her into the maternity ward at delivery, so that the baby would have the world's best pediatrician to attend the minute it started its life. She also arranged for the whole delivery process to be filmed, and insisted she nurse the baby herself.

Just in case she could not produce enough milk, she also engaged a wet nurse on standby, who could step in if necessary.

Under duress, Spock reluctantly agreed with her, for her to not feed the baby with a fixed schedule, but to do it according to the baby's needs and demands. It turned out that Mead did have enough milk and was able to nurse the baby "on demand." This might be hard to believe since Mead was already a world-famous scholar with a busy schedule, including frequent international travel. How did she do it? Much later, her daughter Catherine said something like: "Mom of course was a firm believer of her own theory, and she did feed me whenever I was hungry. But the definition of hunger was determined by her. Whenever she was busy, I was much less likely to be hungry. It goes to show what an accommodating and considerate child I was!"

Honed by twenty years of experience in field research, Mead fully utilized her innate skills to observe, document, and analyze all aspects of Catherine's life, right from the beginning. Catherine's childhood became a shared project for Mead and Bateson, but Bateson rarely showed up in their recordings, as he mostly hid behind cameras and video recorders. Nobody knows how many baby pictures were taken of Catherine – they were just too numerous to count. But for her parents, they were far from enough. Mead often expressed her regret at not having installed bright lamps throughout the house, in order to capture interesting pictures at a moment's notice. "Catherine" was a serious academic research project.

Many years later, when the adult Catherine wanted to throw away some of her childhood drawings, Mead informed her with complete sincerity that none of the materials related to her childhood were her personal property. After all, these were part of the most well-documented childhood in human history, and could become important sources for future scholars studying human development!

Mead and Bateson never had a house that belonged just to the two of them. At Catherine's birth, World War II had just started. Bateson rushed back to England, intending to join the army. When rejected because of his age, he went directly from there to Burma, serving as an intelligence officer and consequently becoming an absentee parent. At the same time, in addition to many other travel engagements, Mead was also often called to Washington, DC for consultations. Such trips became even more frequent after the Pearl Harbor attack. As a result, Catherine was often placed under the care of their close friend, Lawrence K. Frank.

Frank and his wife took her in as a daughter. Since one of their own sons was Catherine's age, such an arrangement also afforded her with a playmate. In addition to a British nanny and a housekeeper hired by Mead, there were also many other adults and teenagers in the household, who indulged her and took care of her. This arrangement reflected Mead's belief that the American "nuclear family" was unhealthy for the development of children. Instead, it was the traditional "extended families" that were the right environment for children. Of course, such arrangements also made it easier for Mead to come and go as needed.

In Catherine's memoir, written decades later, she did her best to rationalize her parents' frequent and abrupt disappearances – it was wartime. Most children's fathers were far away, fighting the enemies, and mothers were needed to do the jobs left by their husbands to keep the economy going. Regardless, her sense of confusion and regret is still clearly visible if the memoir is read closely.

All things considered, Catherine was lucky to have an "extended family" to rely on, since her "nuclear family" would soon crumble. Even though Bateson eventually returned to New York, he continued to live in his own world most of the time, oblivious of others' existence or responses. Also, as Mead's fame grew, the gap between the two of them widened.

It is fair to say that Bateson spent the first half of his life trying to escape from the confines and control of his parents. Similarly, we might speculate that he spent the second half of his life fighting against being engulfed by Mead. Contained in her barely five-feet tall frame, Mead had boundless energy. She was quick-minded, sharp-tongued, passionate, and ever ready to jump in to make decisions for her friends and colleagues, whenever she felt she could be of help. In contrast, the six feet five Bateson appeared forever lost, often not even able to decide where he should place his big hands and feet.

What he was good at was engaging in deep thoughts. By nature, he was skeptical of simple or quick answers and was hesitant to abide by professional boundaries. The war gave him a chance to escape from his regular world and from himself. At the end of the war, he became even more lost, not knowing who he was and in which direction he was heading. Was he a Briton or an American? Was he just Mead's husband and cameraman? Mead sent him to see a famous Jungian analyst, and the analysis lasted several years. The treatment made Bateson an ardent Jungian, but it was unable to solve his problems.

As they never set up a permanent household, it is hard to know when Bateson finally left Mead. Somehow Catherine gradually realized that she had two homes. Her mother's home was part of that noisy, lively, huge compound where people came and went. Her father's was initially a small, disorderly apartment in New York, which became even more chaotic when he moved to northern California's Bay Area.

These changes notwithstanding, Catherine never doubted her parents' love for her. Any time Mead was in town, she would spend twenty minutes in the morning doing Catherine's braids, which gave them time to chat and bond. On the west coast, Bateson took her camping, where they observed and discussed the habitat and behaviors of various animals, trying to figure out how they communicated and interacted.

Bateson was particularly fascinated by octopuses, and often took Catherine on expeditions to the seaside to capture these creatures and bring them home, where he kept them in a big fish tank. While Bateson was busy studying their nervous systems, speculating on whether they had the ability to hold thoughts, Catherine was fascinated by the way they swam, overawed by the graciousness of their movements, even when they were fighting.

Later, when Bateson received a research grant from the National Institute of Mental Health and established a project at Stanford University to study the interpersonal interactions of schizophrenic patients, the main focus of Catherine and Bateson's activities shifted to watching videotapes of patients' interactions with their family members. It might be fair to say that father and daughter talked about anything and everything, with the exception of the mundane "trivia" of everyday life.

Love notwithstanding, it was not easy for Catherine to grow up with an absent-minded father and a mother forever on the move. Before adolescence, Catherine coped well by being considerate, observant, and well-behaved, and was amply rewarded by the love and attention of those around her.

However, growing up in New York proved far more complicated than doing so in Samoa. Mead the "expert on adolescents" tried her best to shield Catherine from being affected by "unhealthy" societal pressure, such as the stereotypical definition of gender roles. However, the adolescent Catherine's need was to abide by social norms, to be treated just like other ordinary adolescents. Mead knew well, of course, that all adolescents needed to fight against authorities in their lives in order to define their own "selves." What she did not expect was that the authority her daughter needed to fight against was Mead herself.

Catherine needed to get away from Mead, the authority in her life that was often not present yet also forever present. In eleventh grade, she finally saw her chance when she went with Mead to Israel. Once there, the over-whelmed Mead asked a group of young Israelis to take care of her. After touring a number of kibbutzim, Catherine returned to Jerusalem but refused to see Mead again. Instead, she left a message at Mead's hotel indicating that she wanted to stay in Israel to study Hebrew and Jewish culture.

Mead was beside herself. How could she leave her beloved only daughter in one of the most dangerous places in the world, where there had been perpetual unrest, especially at that time, with another Arab–Israeli conflict lurking on the horizon? But Catherine would not back down. Amazingly, the strong-willed Mead eventually gave in and they reached a compromise: Catherine would stay in Palestine for one year, at the end of which they would reassess the situation.

Catherine was not Jewish, so why did she choose Israel when there were so many other places in the world she could have gone? In her memoir, Catherine said that her not being Jewish (more exactly, her mother not being

Jewish) was exactly the point. At the time, she felt that wherever she went, she would not be able to escape Mead's influence as she had friends all over the world. The region of the world where Mead seemed to have the fewest connections was the Middle East.

This decision was significant for Catherine for another important reason. It led to her meeting her future husband, who was of Armenian origin and was able to facilitate her taking up the study of Middle Eastern languages as her profession. Language being closely tied to culture, she was gradually drawn back to the field of cultural anthropology, becoming her parents' colleague, with accomplishments that made her parents proud.

FAME AND CONTROVERSIES

In contrast to Mead, Bateson was largely ignored by the academic world and the public until toward the end of his life. His disdain for disciplinary boundaries made it difficult for experts in any field to comprehend his views. At the same time, he usually was so self-absorbed and clueless that he was at a loss as to what others were after. He was thus regarded as aloof and odd, and so avoided and ignored.

After moving to the west coast, he had a golden opportunity to use his skills in anthropology to conduct qualitative research on schizophrenic patients. He and his students made significant contributions exploring the interpersonal communication patterns of these patients, focusing particularly on their interactions with family members, as well as their dialogues with therapists. Such pioneering works eventually led to important contributions to the field's understanding of the nature of psychotic problems, as well as the process of psychotherapy.

However, as profound and complex as these issues were, they failed to maintain his interests and attention, which soon drifted to other creatures of the whole biological world. Instead of focusing on psychiatric patients, he became increasingly fascinated by the behaviors of octopuses, seals, sea otters, and even whales. Venturing into ecology,[4] cybernetics,[5] and chaos theory (and the butterfly effect[6]), Bateson was decades ahead of his time.

Bateson was also decades ahead of his time in asserting that the human mind was not just the product of the activities of the individual's central

---

[4] In any ecological system, different species compete and at the same time depend on each other, just as patients' symptoms are often manifestations of overt and covert conflicts among other members of their families.

[5] All complex systems, including the individual's mind, society, ecological systems, computers, and artificial intelligence, are only sustainable because of the existence of multiple and layered feedback systems, which are involved in mutual regulations crucial for the stability and functioning of the whole system.

[6] The fluttering of a single butterfly in South America may trigger a series of chain reactions, eventually leading to the formation of a typhoon in Southeast Asia.

nervous system, but is contingent upon the interactions among individuals. In other words, the emergence of the mind and the "self" is dependent on social contacts and is therefore more cultural than biological. At the time, these ideas were regarded as flimsy and unjustifiable, if not outright bizarre. However, much of what he proposed has in recent years become the consensus of contemporary neuroscientists (Brothers, 1997). Unfortunately, such confirmation came too late for him, and during his lifetime he was a prophet with few followers.

Disappointed with his colleagues in psychiatry and neuroscience, he self-exiled to Hawaii and the Caribbean, finding comfort in the company of seals and other sea creatures. What he did not know was that, in his absence, a young generation of psychotherapists were inspired by his theories on interpersonal interactions and communications. Together, they developed new approaches in family and marital therapies that revolutionized the field (see Chapter 14).

Coming into the 1960s, young leaders of the anti-war movements "discovered" Bateson. For those worried about the looming threats of nuclear proliferation and the destruction of the natural world, who were disappointed with capitalism, communism, and traditional religions, Bateson's reflections on ecology and the nature of the mind became the basis of their search for new directions. People were fascinated by his ideas even though they were often obscure, convoluted, and unsystematic. He suddenly became a popular speaker and was in high demand at various retreats and gatherings of New Age movements. Unexpectedly, he found himself becoming a guru.

His newfound status as a guru paved the way for him to become a permanent faculty member of the Esalen Institute, the famous center for self-actualization and integrative health in Big Sur, California. He stayed there until the last days of his life.

While there, when he was diagnosed with late-stage lung cancer, many of the other Esalen "residents" who were shamans, spiritual media, or psychic healers enthusiastically offered him myriad "miracle cures." As an "incurable" skeptic, he nevertheless gladly submitted himself to their ministrations because he wanted to be open-minded.

At the same time, capitalizing on his fame, he used himself as an example to show that illnesses and death were but part of the process of living, and were essential for maintaining the ecological system. This being the case, he saw no reason to defy nature by artificially prolonging his life. In this way, his cancer became his teaching tool with which he tried to change the attitudes of physicians and other health professionals, as well as public opinion leaders to achieve a more balanced view of "end-of-life" care. His students in this regard included Jerry Brown, then the governor of California.

As if competing with Bateson, Mead soon developed pancreatic cancer with metastasis to the lung. Although in theory she agreed with Bateson regarding the need for accepting death as part of life, she was not about to leave the world without putting up a good fight. Whether useful or not, she insisted on being hospitalized, having all the tests done, and trying out any available therapies.

During that short period of time, numerous friends and colleagues rushed from all over the world to pay their respects and provide support. Even though already very sick, she never refused to see them and gave them as much attention as possible. Instead of focusing on herself, she tried to comfort them and continued to give them advice concerning their professional and personal lives. Her daughter, Catherine, later said that Mead was indeed a totally committed performer who never gave up her stage, maintaining her presence with dignity and graciousness until the last minute of her life.

Although Mead left this world in 1978, she remains alive in many people's minds today. The ideas she proposed almost a century ago continue to stir up heated debates. As the pendulum has swung back and forth between the emphasis on nature and nurture in the field of behavioral sciences, people holding opposite views have been eager to use her as a proxy in their fights.

A prominent example was Derek Freeman, a New Zealander anthropologist who published a book five years after the death of Mead, with scathing and unrelenting criticisms. Having lived in Samoa for many years, he believed he was more qualified than Mead to understand Samoan culture. He argued that since Mead had stayed on the island for less than a year, she was not likely to have mastered the Samoan language and might have easily misunderstood what she heard from the young island girls. He further insinuated that Mead might have been biased in her observations, and even "falsified" data to support her mentors' theories (Freeman, 1983).

The book received a great deal of attention, both in the professional field and from the general public. Overnight, Freeman became world famous and his book was widely quoted by those who believed that nature was more powerful than nurture in shaping human behavior. However, many other scholars questioned Freeman's motivations and criticized him for not daring to publish his book while Mead was still alive, suspecting that he had something to hide.

In response to such criticisms, Freeman visited the village where Mead had stayed and found an old woman who was one of Mead's main informants. According to Freeman, the old woman said that most of what she and her friends told Mead were jokes and made-up stories, aimed at impressing and shocking her. However, this was more than sixty years later – during this long timespan the islanders had drastically changed their lifestyles and adopted Christian religious beliefs and attitudes. So, it was possible that the old woman had forgotten how things used to be when she was young.

What is the truth then? Mead's daughter, Catherine, summed it up well. She said that anthropological research depended primarily on participant observation, where the researchers needed to immerse themselves in the culture to "see" things as locals did. They were like lenses through which hidden views were revealed. But lenses differ in their colors, opacities, and angles of reflection, which determine what is perceived. Thus, to be successful, the anthropological researcher's main challenge is not just the accurate reporting of what they observe, but the ability to be cognizant of their own limitations and blind spots.

But is this true only for the field of anthropology? Using the analogy of lenses, it was exactly the reliability of the lenses in the telescopes used by Galileo Galilei in his astronomical research that was at the center of the debates that raged for decades during his lifetime, leading to his reluctant relinquishing of his theories on heliocentrism in order to appease his colleagues and escape Church persecution.

The dilemma faced by anthropological researchers has even closer parallels to the challenges faced by clinicians, who can never be distant and fully "objective." They always have to see things through their own eyes, keeping in mind that they can never be completely objective. It is in this sense that "knowing oneself" becomes such an important issue for all clinicians and therapists. Epistemological questions are never abstract, for they permeate all aspects of our lives.

"WHO EXACTLY ARE YOU, MOTHER?"

Mead did hide herself well, behind highly filtered screens. During her lifetime, no one knew or ever suspected her of being a lesbian or bisexual. Her friendship with Benedict was widely known, which was amply reflected in her own autobiography. Although Benedict was more than a decade older than Mead and their personalities and temperaments were completely the opposite (Benedict was sensitive, introverted, and chronically depressed), they were as close as twin sisters, talking to each other all the time and writing constantly to each other when apart. Mead revered Benedict, treasured all of her papers and books, and wrote a moving biography of her after she passed away. Until Mead's own death, no one suspected that they were lovers. It came as a surprise when, after Mead's funeral, Catherine found out the nature of their relationship while going through Mead's personal belongings.

Catherine was furious. She felt deceived. She was most angry that Mead never let her in on this. As an expert on gender research and an ardent advocate of feminism, why did Mead need to hide her bisexuality? What role did this have in her repeated marital "failures?" Did Mead really love Bateson? Was Catherine the product of a union based on love? These questions troubled Catherine for a long time.

Thinking back, Catherine started to see the signs whose meaning she had neglected for so long. She finally understood why, not long after Benedict's passing away, Mead started living in the same house with Rhoda Metraux. Although they maintained the appearance of occupying separate floors of the building, they actually lived together! Metraux was also an accomplished anthropologist, and was also shy, introverted, and had a temperament not dissimilar to Benedict's.

Catherine eventually found a way to forgive her mother. Mead was a public figure, a celebrity who needed to protect her image. This was not only crucial for her own career but, even more importantly, for the development of the academic field as a whole, as well as for the success of her mission in changing society's views on feminism and child-rearing practices. Mead made choices that might not have been fair to those close to her, but, in the process, she sacrificed a great deal as well.

Were these worthwhile sacrifices? Who could tell? What was clear was that this "dark side" of her life played a role in deepening her understanding of the complexity of human nature and contributed to her amazing ability to delve into the motivations and emotional lives of those who on the surface could not be any more different from her in terms of their beliefs, customs, and aspirations. In this sense her "weakness" became her strength, enabling her to see through the surface and understand how people think and feel, despite the divergence in their backgrounds.

BALI FOREVER

Catherine eventually overcame her shock and disappointment and came to terms with the loving, if idiosyncratic, relationship between Mead and Bateson. She believed that in their own ways, they did love each other deeply. Such love and affection certainly evolved and morphed over time, but it runs throughout Catherine's memoir, Mead's autobiography, and Bateson's often obscure and complicated writings.

Directly or indirectly, Mead continued to pay close attention to and take care of Bateson until the ends of their lives. At the last conference they both attended, Mead noticed and reminded Bateson that he had forgotten to put on his socks. Who could say whether this was love or just "pathological entanglement?"

It might well be that the two years they spent on the magical island of Bali were their happiest. Day after day, they were both fully immersed in the daily lives of the Balinese, busy documenting the islanders' joys and sorrows, achievements and limitations. They left us with 25,000 pictures, 22,000 feet of film, and a mountainous pile of notebooks. Looking at the images and recordings of so many festivals and religious rites that they witnessed together, we cannot help but be drawn into that rich and colorful world. It would not be too difficult to imagine that these were not just the recordings of the amazingly rich Balinese culture; they were also reflections of the rich and nuanced relationship between these two geniuses and their joy of being with each other.

13

Gandhi Is Gandhi: Luther Is Luther[1]

How Did Erik the Vagabond Become Erikson the Guru?

Erikson may be regarded as the most widely known psychoanalyst after Freud and Jung. His "Eight Life Stages" theory (the psychosocial developmental model) is something with which most college students should be very familiar. "Identity crisis," originally coined by him, has become a household term worldwide. It is thus surprising that, despite his fame, most people know very little of Erikson the person and even less about what might have been the source of his inspiration and creativity.

Therefore, readers are likely to be surprised by recent books such as Lawrence J. Friedman's biography on Erikson, *Identity's Architect: A Biography of Erik H. Erikson* (Friedman, 1999), and the memoir by his daughter, Sue Erikson Bloland, titled *In the Shadow of Fame* (Bloland, 2005).

It turned out Erikson's insights and theories were very much tied to his own life stories. His personal background and early life experiences were full of twists and turns, at times almost beyond imagination. Throughout his life, he was repeatedly forced to face and cope with issues related to his own origin and his own identity. The daunting process of sorting out these issues enabled him to find his own life's purposes, which in turn enriched our understanding of how we define ourselves and how we perceive the world. In Erikson, we see how sometimes a deeply wounded person could turn disadvantages around and make himself into an exceptionally intuitive and talented healer, as well as a brilliant thinker.

WHO AM I?

Erikson never knew who his father was. His mother, Karla Abrahamsen, came from a well-to-do Jewish Danish merchant family that had been in

[1] The title of this chapter was inspired by the following quotation from *The Collected Songs of Cold Mountain*: "Cold Mountain (Hanshan) Is Cold Mountain, Foundling (Shide) Is Foundling." Cold Mountain and Foundling were two legendary wandering monks whose poems were highly revered, with many translated English versions (e.g., Red Pine, 2000.)

Copenhagen for centuries, well integrated into mainstream society. Pampered by her doting father and four older brothers, she lived a fairytale life growing up. Unfortunately, Karla's mother passed away when she was sixteen, depriving her of crucial guidance about entering society and finding her Prince Charming. It was a relief for the family when, at twenty-one, she found Valdemar Salomonsen, a successful stockbroker six years her senior, and they soon got married. As is apparent from his last name, he also came from a "pedigreed," acculturated, Jewish Danish family.

What followed the wedding ceremony was a shock and remained a puzzle to everyone. On the first night of their honeymoon trip, just after they had arrived in Rome, Salomonsen abandoned Karla and ran away, leaving her stranded in a foreign city before they even had a chance to consummate their marriage. Karla's eldest brother came to her rescue and escorted her safely back to Copenhagen.

Salomonsen was never seen again. Rumor had it that he drifted to the USA and Mexico and eventually died there a number of years later, of an unknown cause. All this notwithstanding, Karla insisted on continuing to use Salomonsen as her last name.

Two years later, Karla found out she was six months pregnant. In a hurry, the family spirited her away to Frankfurt, where she gave birth to Erik, who took Salomonsen as his last name. The two of them settled down in Buehl, a small German town several miles away from the famed Black Forest and the Baden-Baden hot springs neighboring the French border. Buehl was an artists' colony, which fitted well with Karla's interests in the arts, literature, and philosophy. As a swarthy and handsome young woman with shiny long black hair, she attracted the attention of the town's residents and made friends easily among the artistically inclined.

Her popularity notwithstanding, people were puzzled by her baby having blue eyes, blonde hair, and pinkish pale skin. There was no way Erik could be the son of the vanished Salomonsen, who had been out of the picture since long before Erik's life started. So, who was Erik's real father? This remained a secret, which Karla kept all her life.

Judging from Erik's appearance, people assumed his biological father was not of Jewish extraction. Rumors abound, with speculation that the man was a non-Jewish Dane. Did Karla keep the secret purely out of a sense of shame? Was the father an artist who had seduced Karla with his talents, but was not able to marry her because of gaps in their families' religious and social backgrounds? Or was it because the father came from a noble lineage whose identity could not be exposed? These rumors stayed with Karla and continued to haunt Erik for decades to come.

However, lack of a father might not have been a completely negative situation for Erik. Although Karla was a single mother, she was a single mother with means. She did not need to worry about feeding or clothing herself and her son, and she spent most of her time and energy doting on Erik.

Regrettably for Erik, the monopoly on his mother's time and attention was abruptly "stolen" by an "invader" when Erik was two years old. This invader was a middle-aged pediatrician by the name of Theodor Homburger, a successful doctor with an extremely busy practice in Karlsruhe, a bustling industrial metropolis midway between Frankfurt and the idyllic Buehl. In fact, Homburger was in such a high demand as a physician that he could hardly spare any time to date and he had long resigned to the prospect of becoming a confirmed bachelor.

By chance, Karla heard about his skills as a pediatrician and asked him to look into Erik's chronic problems with bloating and indigestion. Homburger lived up to his reputation. He altered Erik's dietary formula, and the problems were gone in no time – Karla was impressed! Theodor and Karla shortly fell in love and marriage followed. It could be said that Erik was their matchmaker.

This was a very pleasant surprise for the Abrahamsens as they no longer needed to cover up what people saw as Karla's past indiscretions. They were particularly pleased not only with Homburger's profession, but also with his family background. He came from a rich Jewish family with several genera-tions of accumulated wealth, and he himself was a leader within that community.

At the same time, the marriage came as a great relief to the Homburgers as well. They were particularly pleased at the beauty and worldliness of Karla, and were relieved that they finally didn't need to continue to prod or nag Theodor to settle down.

The only loser in this new development was Erik – the invader stole a great deal of his mother's time and attention. Homburger claimed to be his birth father,[2] but as Erik grew older he became more and more skeptical of this claim. Homburger was short and dark-skinned, with a full head of curly black hair and even a goatee! Not only that, this new father of his was formal and boring, certainly no match to Karla's artist friends in Buehl.

Growing up in such a confused state, Erik found life even more difficult when he started school. Most of his classmates were Gentiles, and were often hostile and rude to him because he was a Jew. At the same time, the Jewish boys in his neighborhood saw him as an unredeemable *goy*[3] because of his blue eyes, blonde hair, and fair skin.

To further complicate the matter, Karla took him to visit Copenhagen often and insisted in talking to him only in Danish. All of this resulted in difficulties for him to decide whether he was a Jew, a Dane, or a German. He

---

[2] It took Theodor quite a few years to complete the adoption of Erik, who subsequently changed his name to Erik Homburger.

[3] A Jewish term for a non-Jew.

dutifully followed the customs and rules of the Jewish congregation, but this did not provide him with a clear sense of belonging. He then tried to become a devoted member of a pan-Germanic nationalist group, but his Jewish background got in the way.

The more his stepfather tried to force him to study hard at school in order to enter a medical school and follow his own footsteps, the more he resisted, who often contemplated dropping out of school completely. He finally graduated from the gymnasium but refused to go to college.

Instead, he started wandering the countryside, aimlessly, for seven long years. Drifting further and further afield, he disappeared from his family's radar for months at a time. At one point he enrolled in a small art school, learning to do sketches and woodprint engraving, but soon he was on the move again. He did manage to stay put in Munich for close to two years, trying in vain to establish himself as an artist.

Finally, he reached Florence, Italy. There, he feasted on the numerous masterpieces of art accumulated over the centuries. But this enriching experience convinced him that he was never going to become an accomplished artist. Giving up the hope of an artistic career, his roaming became completely aimless, devoid of any clear direction or destination. Occasionally, he was able to exchange his sketches for a meal here or lodging there, but he remained alive mostly because whenever he returned to Karlsruhe, Karla would give him funds behind Theodor's back.

The more he wandered, the more he realized he was going nowhere. No longer knowing what he was looking for, he sank into deeper and deeper depression, mixed with violent mood swings. He lost a great deal of weight, becoming gaunt; he let go of his personal hygiene and stopped caring about his grooming and clothing. Toward the end, he was not even able to talk coherently.

Many years later, thinking about his seven years of wandering, he was sure that he was spiraling rapidly downward, on the verge of psychosis, and might well have ended up killing himself.

FINDING ONESELF IN VIENNA

It was just his luck that, at such a critical juncture, Erik received an invitation from Peter Blos,[4] a good friend of his from his gymnasium days, to move to Vienna and teach at a new school there. Blos' family background was similar to Erik's. His mother was a painter of Jewish descent and his father was a progressive, "eclectic" Christian physician who believed in the importance of preventive medicine and prided himself on his holistic approaches in his

---

[4] Peter Blos immigrated to the USA as well, and later completed his training and became an eminent child psychoanalyst.

practice. He was also interested in spiritual traditions, including Buddhism and Hinduism.

Blos grew up aspiring to become a bohemian, but one with purpose and direction. Instead of becoming a vagabond, he attended the University of Heidelberg. Majoring in education, he attained the required credentials to become a primary school teacher. He then transferred to the University of Vienna to study biology, and eventually obtained a PhD.

While in Vienna, he became a private tutor to the four children of Dorothy Tiffany Burlingham, the American heiress to the Tiffany fortune (Burlingham, 2002; see Chapter 8). Burlingham had just escaped with her four children from New York the previous year, leaving her husband, Robert Burlingham, a neurosurgeon incapacitated by recurrent manic-depressive episodes for more than a decade. For the treatment of recalcitrant asthma and behavioral problems of her oldest son, Robert Jr. (Bobbie), she contacted Anna Freud. Soon, all four of the Burlingham children were under Anna Freud's care and Burlingham herself entered psychoanalysis with Sigmund Freud.

Like Burlingham, a number of other well-heeled American women were in town pursuing psychoanalysis with their children in tow. Thus, Burlingham and Anna came up with the idea of establishing a new school guided by psychoanalytic principles. It started with 15–20 students of various ages, with Blos in charge. At that time Blos was but a twenty-something with little previous experiences in pedagogy and felt the need for a confidante and confederate to share his responsibilities. He immediately thought of Erik. He also thought that such a move would be good for Erik, and would offer him the opportunity to be exposed to psychoanalysis.

What no one had expected was that Erik would turn out to be an excellent teacher. His many years of wandering fostered in him an uncanny level of perception, and allowed him to be in tune with his students' emotions and motivations. His "maladjustments" made it easier for him to be on the same wavelength as these "poor rich" American kids who were lonely in their new environment, struggling with a totally different culture and language. His skills in drawing and woodcut printing also served to attract his students' attention, and they were fascinated to watch him work.

At the same time, these successful experiences in his very first regular job also boosted Erik's ego and encouraged him to become more active in pursuing this line of work. In order to enhance his teaching abilities, he enrolled himself in a Montessori training class and obtained a certificate. He also audited various classes at the university and accumulated more than enough credits for a bachelor's degree. Only his lack of focus and indecision on settling on a major prevented him from reaching that goal.

A LIFE SCULPTED BY THREE WOMEN

We could say that Erik's life was shaped by three women. The first was, of course, his mother, Karla. However, in Vienna, Karla was soon to be supplanted by two formidable competitors. One of them was Anna Freud, who insisted on becoming his analyst. The other was a Canadian by the name of Sarah Serson, who changed her first name to Joan around the time she met Erik.

Joan was an exceptionally energetic, strong-willed young woman one year Erik's junior. After obtaining a master's degree from Columbia University, she entered its doctoral program in dancing and completed all the required courses. She then went to Europe to learn modern dance and to do field research for her dissertation. After staying in Berlin for a short while, she heard that Isadora Duncan was in Vienna and rushed to the city, hoping to become Duncan's student, only to learn that Duncan had just died in a car accident in France. Stranded in Vienna, Joan found a job at Blos' new school, teaching dancing and English.

Soon after, she met Erik at a masquerade dance party and immediately fell in love with him. Moving into the living quarters Erik shared with Blos, she crowded Blos out in no time, and soon became pregnant and gave birth to their first son, Kai.[5] As his friends and relatives started to pressure him to get married, Erik became morose and belligerent. However, after being reminded of the pain he had experienced as a fatherless child, he stopped resisting and warmed to the idea.

And they married three times! As a joke, they picked April Fools' Day for their civil ceremony. This was followed by a religious event at the Jewish temple to placate Erik's Jewish mother and stepfather. Then they decided they might as well have another one at the Anglican-Episcopalian church, as Joan was a daughter of an Episcopalian minister. It did not matter that Erik was late and forgot to bring his wedding ring. Their marriage lasted more than sixty years and they became each other's best friends and partners in the fullest sense.

Erik's relationship with Anna Freud was characterized by a similar degree of hesitation and indecisiveness on Erik's part. Anna appreciated Erik's talent despite his lack of education and experiences, and wanted him to become her student and "patient." Although Anna was only seven years Erik's senior, she was more than qualified to play such a role. At the time, she was already the secretary of the Viennese Psychiatric Society. As her gravely ill father's constant companion, nurse, and caretaker, Anna had started to regard herself as

---

[5] Kai Theodor Erikson grew up to become a prominent sociologist who made major contributions to our understanding of the social consequences of disasters. He was the seventy-sixth president of the American Sociological Society.

the heir and guardian of the psychoanalytic movement. Along with Burlingham and a number of other female analysts, she also pioneered the new and promising field of child psychoanalysis.

As an inducement, Anna offered to only charge Erik $7 per month for his analysis six days a week. In addition, Anna would provide extensive supervision and consultation, amounting to several more hours each day.

What could be more generous than these terms? Yet, for weeks, Erik kept stalling, saying that he was an artist, even though he had already accepted the fact that he did not have the talent to break into the art scene and make a name for himself. It was more likely that he was resisting the chance of exposing himself and becoming dependent on Anna, who might have been regarded as a controlling mother figure, threatening to corral him, if not engulf him. Anna finally told Erik that she had asked her father and the Master had said Erik should accept the challenge. This effectively ended his indecision.

For a long time, he continued to question the wisdom of such a decision. He had thought that psychoanalysis was too language-based and too abstract for a visual artist like himself. But several months into his analysis, all of a sudden, he realized that language also has structure and shapes and thus represents a natural extension of training and experiences in the arts.

His mastery of the skills in drawing and carving actually became his strength. Watching children playing with toys, he was able to quickly grasp their intra-psychic meaning because of his familiarity in arranging objects in space for artistic expression. He was soon on his way to integrating visual arts with psychoanalysis and to becoming a uniquely talented therapist, especially with children. This did not escape the Master's eyes, who said that Erik could help others "see" psychoanalysis.

As he had suspected and dreaded, Erik soon developed strong transferences with both Freuds. Day after day, he sat in the dark waiting room sandwiched between their offices, jealous of the strong bond of the daughter and the father, which he regarded as suspiciously "incestuous." He was also jealous of the "lucky" patients who were analyzed by the older Freud, a physician like his physician stepfather and thus even more clearly a father figure. At the same time, Freud's interests in the arts and culture reminded him of his mysterious absent birth father, who was supposedly an artist.

On the other side of the waiting room, Anna reminded him of the young mother of his childhood, and her smothering love from which he had struggled to escape. Many years later, when Erik reminisced on those days, he said: "Psychoanalysis was indeed a very painful process. Day after day you stared at the same ceiling, not knowing what you were saying, not knowing what you were supposed to say. Many patients become frankly psychotic while undergoing such treatments." There might indeed be a certain truth in what he said. Along with its power, psychoanalysis could be a threat to the autonomy of weaker souls. In this sense, Erik had his well-grounded wife to thank.

Joan had also started her own analysis around the same time as Erik, but she left it before it had really started. "Such an ugly old man! How could he even suggest that I was falling in love with him? He didn't know what he was doing or saying!" Joan said. However, even though she might be aversive to psychoanalysis herself, she never discouraged Erik from pursuing a career in this direction.

There might be reason to suspect that the unmarried Anna, smart and comely, could represent a psychological threat to Joan. If so, Joan never expressed any misgivings about Erik's analysis. It might not be an overstatement to say that it was because of Joan that Erik escaped from being drowned by his transferences and survived his several years of analysis, as well as his father and mother complexes.

Whichever way you see it, the Erik of 1933 was a completely different person from the Erik of 1927. Six years earlier, Erik was an aimless, rudderless vagabond. By 1933, when he and Joan were getting ready to leave Vienna, he was a proud father of two sons (the second son was born that year), a "card-carrying" member of the International Psychoanalytic Society, and a gifted therapist. It is not unreasonable to conclude that, had it not been for his time in Vienna, and had he not run into Joan and Anna, such a miraculous transformation would not have even been a remote possibility.

AFTER ALL, YOU ARE INDEED YOUR OWN FATHER

But Vienna was becoming impossible for Erik Homburger and his family. In 1933, after the Nazis' ascendance in Germany, Hitler immediately started working on taking over Austria. With anti-Semetism and anti-liberalism on the rise, Vienna was no longer a viable option for someone with Erik's background.

Since Erik had family connections in Copenhagen, Denmark would have seemed a logical choice for them to make a new home. But it turned out that, as Erik was born in Germany, he did not have Danish citizenship and therefore needed to have a work permit to be admitted to the country. He soon found out that there were two other major obstacles that were also difficult to overcome. First, even though Erik completed his psychoanalytic training, he did not have a degree from higher education. Further complicating the situation was that Wilhelm Reich (Sharaf, 1983; see also Chapter 5) had just tried to settle down in Denmark, and his radical ideas of sexual liberation had stirred up a great deal of controversy, leading the Danish licensing board to block other analysts from entering their land. Even though Erik's uncles found a high-profile lawyer to assist them with their visa applications, their attempts went nowhere.

Rejected by Denmark, Erik reluctantly decided to immigrate to the USA. During the three weeks it took to cross the Atlantic on a steamship, Erik started working on his analysis of the personality of Hitler. As luck had it, George Kennan,[6] an American diplomat with extensive connections in the American political arena, was on the same ship. With similar foreboding regarding the situation in Europe, they soon became good friends. Kennan was so impressed with Erik's article that he volunteered to translate it into English and shared it with his colleagues at the State Department. Kennan also encouraged Erik to continue his pursuits in psychohistory and actively promoted Erik's ideas to American policymakers and powerbrokers in the years to come.

Erik was warmly welcomed by American immigration officers, but finding work was a different story. A. A. Brill,[7] the first psychoanalyst to practice in the New World, wielded so much power in the field that he was nicknamed "The Tsar." Far from being cordial to him, Brill bluntly told Erik that he had no chance of making it in New York, since he spoke little English and lacked acceptable academic credentials. Instead, Brill advised him to go to one of the small towns in the Midwest to somehow eke out a living to support his family.

Instead, Erik and Joan decided to go to Boston, where Joan had relatives. After settling down, Erik started to meet with prominent leaders in the medical field. Even though his English was at that time limited, he was still the only child psychoanalyst in town, and indeed on the continent. Thus, many parents sent their children with behavioral problems to him. The children enjoyed playing with him and their parents appreciated his mild and courtly manners. Gradually he started to build up a reputation as a talented therapist and his clinic, which also served as his study in the house that he and Joan rented, became a busy place.

These initial contacts allowed Erik to gradually expand his networks within American academia. At that time, many progressive thinkers in the USA were beginning to pay attention to issues related to child development, pondering on how social and cultural forces might shape the growth of children. Freud's psychosexual development theory caught their attention,

---

[6] George Kennan was a prominent American diplomat and historian who was the main architect of the philosophy behind the Cold War and the policy of containment of the Soviet Union.

[7] Born in Austria, A. A. Brill immigrated to the USA when he was fifteen years old, and supported himself with menial jobs while attending school. He graduated from Columbia University School of Medicine at age twenty-eight, and started studying psychiatry with Adolf Meyer. He went to Zurich in 1907 to study at the Burghölzli Hospital under Eugen Bleuler and Carl Jung, who was still Freud's heir apparent at the time, and started to translate books by Freud, Jung, and Bleuler. He founded the New York Psychoanalytic Society and the American Psychoanalytic Society, and engineered to keep them at some distance from the International Psychoanalytic Society. He was also the one who was most vocal in blocking Freud's efforts to embrace non-medical analysts (including Anna Freud, Erik Erikson, and many early psychoanalytic pioneers) in the American psychoanalytic circles. His influence on the American psychoanalytic and psychiatric fields reached its zenith between 1929 and 1936.

and questions regarding its universality became a hot topic. As the only spokesperson for Freudian child psychoanalysis in America, Erik was invited to attend seminars and conferences held at major academic centers, including Harvard, Yale, and Columbia. Through these involvements he started to make friends with some of the most influential American psychologists, psychiatrists, and cultural anthropologists, including Henry Murray, the inventor of the thematic apperception test (TAT); Benjamin Spock, soon to become the guru of infant and childcare; Harry Stack Sullivan (Perry, 1982; see Chapter 11); and anthropologists such as Margaret Mead (Bateson, 1994; see Chapter 12), Gregory Bateson, Ruth Benedict, and Edward Sapir.

Mead, in particular, played a crucial role in Erik's career in the New World. One year older than Erik, Mead acted as his older sister, constantly looking out for opportunities for him. Through Mead and others, Erik became acquainted with the influential Lawrence K. Frank. Although not a researcher himself, Frank was for many years an insider at the Rockefeller Foundation, as well as other funding agencies interested in sociocultural research, and was pivotal in promoting the development of the social sciences in the USA. He had known Mead through family connections and for many years the two families lived in the same building.

Frank shared Mead's assessment of Erik's talents and engineered a scheme for Erik to join the faculty at Yale, supporting him with full salary for two years so that Erik could reduce his clinical and teaching load in order to focus on research and writing.

In 1939, the Homburgers became naturalized citizens of the USA and Erik took this opportunity to change his last name. Assuming that his birth father's first name was the same as his, Erik changed his own last name to Erikson, in line with the Scandinavian tradition of taking one's father's first name and attaching a postfix such as *sen* or *son*, turning it into one's last name (e.g., the son of Ander would become Andersen or Anderson).

Erik relegated Homburger, the last name he had inherited from his stepfather, to his middle name, which was later further abbreviated into a single letter, H. This decision was for many years an issue for scholars with Jewish backgrounds, who criticized Erikson for being ungrateful to his stepfather, intentionally and deceitfully hiding his Jewish background. Erikson argued that the change was necessary for his children's mental health. Prior to the change, they had often been teased by their playmates, being called *Hamburger* instead of *Homburger*. He also pointed out that the decision had been approved by his mother and his stepfather, who had moved to Israel prior to the onset of World War II, just in time to escape Nazi persecution.

These controversies notwithstanding, the name change signified Erikson's growing self-confidence in his life. *He had created himself.* He no long had to search for his birth father. *He became his own father.*

THE IMPORTANCE OF IDENTITY

Through his associations with "neo-Freudians" and cultural anthropologists, Erikson became interested in childhood and adolescence in various Native American cultures. This eventually led to his moving to the University of California at Berkeley, to join a research team engaged in a longitudinal study of child development.

Echoing his own struggles in his early years, his observations of youth growing up in divergent settings convinced him of the importance of adolescence as a crucial phase of human development. At this stage, questions such as "Who am I?" and "What do I want to do in my life?" come fully to the forefront, demanding serious consideration. Answers to these crucial questions, which are at the root of one's "identity," are embedded in and informed by one's culturally shaped beliefs and practices and diverge substantially and substantively across cultures and epochs. Nevertheless, the necessity and urgency for the quest of "identity" is similar, irrespective of where you are living. Thus, in growing up, we are all confronted with this monumental task, a "crisis."

Although "identity crisis" was initially used to discuss adolescents' search for themselves, it soon became clear that confusion in identity and the need to search for new directions in life resurface at other stages in one's life as well, demanding attention. This is especially so when rapid changes in a person's social environment require adjustment of his/her identity, role, self-concept, and orientation in life. Erikson was well aware of this, since he had to struggle hard to adjust himself to a totally new sociocultural environment when he moved to the New World in his mid-thirties, relearning many things that are essential for dealing with the world, making changes in order to survive and thrive.

Within a short time, the term "identity crisis" became so widely used and so deeply implanted in the daily lexicon (Gleason, 1983) that we might not realize how new the term is. The popularity of the term all over the world reflects the fact that, as our societies have become increasingly mobile and the pace of change has continued to accelerate, we are indeed facing *crises* demanding adjustment on an ongoing basis throughout our lives.

In 1950, Erikson published the book *Childhood and Society* (Erikson, 1950), which further solidified his standing as the world expert on human development. The book is a tour-de-force, whose theses were informed not only by Erikson's clinical experiences, but also supported by firsthand observations of two American Indian tribes (the Sioux in South Dakota and the Yurok in California), several multiple-year longitudinal follow-up studies, and studies on the developmental history of two historical personages: Adolf Hitler and the Russian writer Maxim Gorky.

Richness of the content aside, what made the book unique was its use of easily understood language, devoid of jargon, to describe and elaborate on thoughts that have immediate relevance to the general population. To everyone's surprise, it quickly become a best-seller and was frequently reprinted in the decades to come. It has also been included in recommended reading lists for many universities and colleges throughout the country.

The book also pushed Erikson into the limelight. Shy in temperament, he was for a while stressed out and confused by this unsolicited popularity. Fortunately, his good friend Margaret Mead came to his rescue. She provided him with much-needed encouragement, served as his coach, and drilled him on skills for media appearances.

Gradually, Erikson started to develop his own style. As reported by his biographer, Freidman, "elegantly dressed in tweed jacket and white moccasins, with a mane of white hair and rosy complexion, [Erikson] resonate charisma and charm ... [Erikson] looked deeply in the eye [of one of his young audience], and made him feel blessed by ... a strong, unwavering prophet."

ERIKSON'S EIGHT STAGES OF PSYCHOSOCIAL DEVELOPMENT

Besides "identity crisis," Erikson is best known for his "Eight Stages of Human Development." In this model, the first four stages correspond closely with Freud's psychosexual developmental model.

Predicated on the existence of the instinctual libido or sexual energy, Freud's model evolves through distinct stages, each tied to a different "erotogenic zone" in the body: oral (first year), anal (1–3 years), and phallic (3–6 years). It is believed that unresolved conflicts during these different stages are at the root of various neurotic and characterological conditions that may appear later in life. Difficulties during the oral stage may lead to passivity and dependence. Problems originating from the anal stage may result in the development of obsessive-compulsive personality disorder. Unresolved conflicts during the phallic stage may be responsible for phobia, anxiety, and narcissism.

Novel and thought-provoking at the time, Freud's psychosexual developmental model has been criticized for its heavy emphasis on biological processes, resulting in a gross neglect of sociocultural and interpersonal factors that are equally important in human development.

In contrast, Erikson's psychosocial developmental model focuses much more on the individual's sociocultural and personal backgrounds and is simultaneously interpersonal as well as intra-psychic.

For example, in the first stage of an infant's life, which was labeled by Freud as the oral stage, Erikson believed that the focus for the baby was not just the satisfaction and frustration surrounding the pleasure of sucking. Even more important was the baby's struggle in deciding how much it could trust the source of its succor and gratification. Rather than seeing this stage as dominated by the pursuit of oral gratification, Erikson thought that the real task is the establishment of "trust" (Erikson's stage of hope). Similarly, during Freud's "anal stage," the challenge for the baby is self-control and autonomy, not purely the pleasure of being able to withhold or release excreta (Erikson's stage of will). Freud's "phallic" stage was to Erikson a time for the child to develop self-initiation and a sense of efficacy (Erikson called this the stage of purpose). Following the successful resolution of the Oedipus Complex, children leave Freud's "phallic" stage and enter the relatively less conflicted "latency period," which is termed the stage of competence by Erikson, during which (roughly 6–12 years) the major challenges are industry vs. inferiority.

Through such "repackaging" and reinterpretation, psychoanalysis became connected to everyday life and is more easily understood. It is also more accepted by the general public. Erikson's contribution in this regard is indeed monumental.

Of equal importance is the fact that Erikson extended the focus of developmental studies from childhood to adolescence, as well as into middle and old ages. Rather than dwelling on the Oedipus Complex, which took place in early childhood, Erikson shifted his focus to the adolescent period. During this stage of an individual's life, the major task of a person is to break out from the familial bonds and to define his or her self-identity. The failure of such efforts might lead to role confusion. Erikson called this the stage of fidelity.

Possibly drawing from his own drifting and meandering during his prolonged adolescence, he was convinced that this process was not only strenuous, but often full of danger. Although such "soul searching" need not be prolonged indefinitely, the process requires time and could not/should not be rushed. Allowance for time and effort is not only desired, but essential. To emphasize such a need, Erikson coined the term "moratorium."

Of course, human development does not end at adolescence. For Freud, the whole of adulthood was lumped together as the "genital" stage. Erikson divided this into three stages, respectively focusing on intimacy (ages 18–40), generativity (ages 40–65), and integration (age 65+). During the first adult stage, the goal is the establishment of loving and intimate relationships; its opposite is isolation (Erikson's stage of love). During the second adult stage, the tasks are progress in one's career and caring for the young, the failure of which leads to stagnation (stage of care). The tasks for the last stage (the stage of wisdom) have to do with making sense and accepting one's life and death (ego integrity); the opposite is despair.

Erikson would readily acknowledge that these "stages" are heuristic and not to be taken concretely. They are also not meant to be taken as a linear, relentlessly forward-moving process. One does not just "complete" the tasks for one stage and leave them behind in order to move on to the next. In reality, throughout our lives we have to often revisit issues central to earlier stages. For example, although the establishment of "trust" leading to "hope" in life is central to the beginning stage of anyone's life, it does not mean that once this stage is over one has no more need to struggle with "doubts" and "distrust."

NIGHT FALLS FAST

It would be natural to think that, as the world expert on child psychoanalysis and child development, Erikson would be a model parent for everyone to emulate. However, the Erikson as seen by his children was quite different. As described in his daughter Sue Bloland's memoir, *In the Shadow of Fame*, far from being a doting father, he was often absent-minded and remote. At family parties, he often disappeared without warning, sneaking back to his study to continue revising his manuscripts. Even when the whole family went on a trip, he still spent most of his time reading and writing. Sue said: "He was an expert in child psychology, and was excellent in playing with other children, but not with us" (Bloland, 2005)

He was fortunate to have Joan, who was such a capable and caring wife and mother. Independent, self-reliant, and resourceful, she was everything to Erik, who relied on her almost completely. She never complained about this apparently one-sided dependence. She more or less single-handedly raised their three children, took care of household chores, kept in touch with relatives, organized social activities, and even had time to do landscaping. Not only that, she also found time to edit Erikson's manuscripts, often making significant suggestions and revisions. Both Erikson and Joan agreed that all of his important contributions had originated from their discussions and colla- borations. Amazingly, on top of all this, Joan still managed to find time and energy to continue pursue her own interest in the arts: dancing, weaving, and working on her jewelry-making.

Unfortunately and unexpectedly, misfortune struck just as they thought they had been doing well in their lives, professionally and personally. When Joan was pregnant with their fourth baby, they had just bought a mansion surrounded by eight acres of land and had been getting ready to move into this "paradise" of their own. They had thought that this baby would come as easily as the other three. But the labor dragged on for hours, and eventually the obstetrician put Joan under general anesthesia. The baby (later named Neal) was born with Down's syndrome.

At that time, the general consensus in the medical field was that such babies typically would not survive long, which we now know is not the case. With proper care, they not only can live into adulthood, but can live full lives. Most people with Down's syndrome have a mild temperament and cheerful outlook.

But due to the pessimistic view prevailing at the time, it was common practice to place these babies in institutions immediately after birth. What to do? As Joan was still unconscious due to the anesthesia, Erikson had to make the decision alone. Panicked, he called many of his friends, who all agreed with the obstetricians. Mead was particularly emphatic in urging quick action, believing that as separation of the baby and the mother was inevitable, it would be better if they did it before Joan regained consciousness. They thought this would make things easier for her, since she would not yet have had the time to develop an emotional bond with the baby.

Such a decision, made collectively by some of the world's top experts in child development at the time, had a damaging effect on all members of the Erikson family. Joan did not just put the whole thing behind her. She continued to miss Neal and went to see him by herself, in secret, often. Joan and Erik told their thirteen-year-old son, Kai, the truth, but kept it from their eleven-year-old son, Jon, and six-year-old daughter, Sue, instead saying that Neal died from complications in the delivery.

As is usually the case, the children knew more than what was verbally communicated. They started to sense the tension between their parents and guessed that Neal was still alive but sent away. This caused a great deal of anxiety in Jon and Sue. *If their parents could get rid of a baby just like that, the same fate could certainly fall upon them as well. So, when would it be their turns to be rejected?* Years later, Sue expressed a great deal of resentment about this family secret and its damaging effects on her. Although Jon did not say anything about it, his stuttering worsened, and he grew up to become a drifter, unable to maintain a stable adult life.

When Neal died at the age of twenty-one, Joan and Erikson refused to return from their year-long sabbatical in a hill town in Italy to organize the funeral. Instead, they asked Sue and Jon, who had never met Neal, to deal with it. Sue deeply resented this.

Were Erikson and Joan selfish? Who is to say? A more charitable explanation would be that, with their own childhood trauma, they were plagued by their own unease and were lost, not knowing how to respond to such a situation.

LUTHER HAD TO BE LUTHER

After *Childhood and Society*, Erikson published two more well-received books, both of which have since become classics: *Young Man Luther* and *Gandhi's Truth*. Both are erudite, scholarly, and yet still engaging for general readers. Their publications solidified Erikson's academic standing and at the same time made him a widely known and respected public personage, regarded as a guru and a prophet by some of the youth in the 1960s who were struggling against authority.

Martin Luther and Mahatma Gandhi were great inspirations for Erikson since his youth. They were both giants in world history, whose life courses were full of drama, laden with extremely complicated twists and turns. Of note, they both struggled during their youth and early adulthood to find their own path, defying conventional expectations and prevailing social norms.

Erikson's ancestral lands of Denmark and Germany, the nation of his childhood, were both strongholds of Lutheranism.[8] During the seven years that he had roamed the countryside, Erikson had contacts with many Lutheran ministers and he was often deeply touched by their preaching and spirituality.

So, who was Martin Luther? Luther was an Augustinian friar and a doctor of theology who, at the age of thirty, pinned his famous *Ninety-Five Theses* on the door of his own church, on the eve of Halloween, protesting against the rampant corruption and hypocrisy of the Roman Catholic Church. What triggered this action was the *en masse* offering of *indulgences* (the buying of forgiveness for sins large and small) by the Pope and the Archbishops to raise funds for the church.

When he did this, Luther had no inkling that it would trigger the Reformation Movement that came close to toppling the Catholic Church. Luther was simply desperate, tortured by self-doubt and confusion, all but convinced that he had failed his faith and his own calling. He had struggled so long and so hard, trying to stop questioning some of the Church's policies and practices. But he failed. No longer able to hold back his doubts, he fully expected to be proven wrong and crushed, if not simply neglected and brushed aside. What he did not expect was that it would usher in a new era.

It was a new era because posters were no longer just posters. Barely half a century earlier, Johannes Gutenberg "invented" movable type printing techniques,[9] enabling mass printing and wide circulation of written material. This new printing method enabled Luther's poster to be quickly reprinted and disseminated, and read all across Europe. "It went viral," as we would say in this age of social media, and his protests quickly became the rallying cry of the multitude.

But we should not blame everything on technology. So absorbed in his own inner struggles, poor Luther was not aware (nor were the Church authority or others in power) that a number of major social forces were converging, making radical change inevitable: the Renaissance had freed the minds of the intellectuals; middle-class burghers[10] had become wealthier and

---

[8] Sola fida (justification by faith alone) is a unique central thesis in Lutheranism, which emphasizes that the only salvation for humans comes from believing completely in Jesus Christ as the son of God, not by doing good deeds, following doctrines or rituals and, above all, not by the intercession of priests or saints, or even the Virgin Mary.

[9] The technique was originally invented in China around AD 1040 and brought back to Europe by Christian missionaries and traders over the next few centuries.

[10] A citizen of a town or city in medieval Europe, typically a member of the wealthy bourgeoisie.

more influential, and were unhappy with the Church's greed and corruption; and the rulers of the land, looking for ways to fund their wars and luxurious lifestyles, were covetous of the Catholic Church's vast holding of land and wealth. Driven by personal spiritual needs, Luther's act became a spark that set off unquenchable wildfires. In just a few years, most of Northern Europe was in flames, and, along with John Calvin, Luther became the de facto leader of a movement that would turn half of the continent into protestant territories (Erikson, 1958).

Why did Luther feel so compelled to question and fight against the authorities? Tracing Luther's developmental history, Erikson found out the reason. Yes, Oedipal drama is everywhere. Yes, parents are to blame. Luther's father was an exceptionally ambitious miner who had his mind made up that, as his first born, Luther should work hard at school and become a lawyer. In order to achieve such a lofty goal, the father resorted to extremely violent punishments as his tools for forcing his will on Luther. This worked. Luther entered university to study law, according to his father's wishes.

One day, as Luther braved a big storm going back to school from a short visit home, bitterly resenting his father, he was struck by thunder and fell to the ground. Regaining his consciousness, he heard the Holy Ghost directing him to study theology at the local Augustinian monastery. His father was deeply disappointed, since a career as a country vicar was much less prestigious and lucrative. But since it was God's will, the father could not do anything about it, and retreated in defeat.

However, Luther's fight against authority did not stop there. Now that the Church and its doctrines were central to his life, his battlefield shifted. He started questioning and doubting the Church doctrine and practices, which were so disturbing that he started adopting extreme measures, including prolonged starvation and constant flagellation, in the hope of shaping himself into complete submission, turning himself into a "perfect" servant of God. Yet the harder he tried to suppress these doubts, the more tenacious they became. Such struggles plunged him into bouts of extreme despondence and desperation. A modern-day psychiatrist likely would label him at that time as a severe case of obsessive-compulsive disorder with concurrent major depression.

He was lucky to have a very understanding superior who gave him all the time he needed, listening to his endless questions and self-criticisms, and never giving up on him. Impressed with how patient and supportive Luther's patron was, Erikson said that he was acting like a talented psychoanalyst. This notwithstanding, Luther continued to be tortured by his own restlessness, obsessiveness, and endless self-questioning and self-criticism. One might say that after having fought successfully against his father, Luther was expecting to find his "ideal father" in the monastery. But the Church and the monastery represented authorities too – authorities he needed to fight against as well.

Luther's fight against authority could have ended in many different ways. Many like him have been crushed in such struggles, ending in suicide or chronic incapacitating depression. Luther's fate was different. His actions heralded many generations of serious Christian thinkers searching for the meaning of the original teachings of Jesus. These religious leaders moved on to develop new ideas, leading to the establishment of new denominations, which not only stimulated the development of new and unique spiritual paths, but also triggered the transformation and revitalization of the Catholic hierarchy.

Seeing Luther's life story in this manner, one might say that the world owes much to the prolonged "identity crisis" of the young man Luther.

GANDHI COULD ONLY BE GANDHI

As depicted by Erikson, the identity crisis lasted even longer for Mahatma Gandhi than for Luther. It also was much more complicated, and more difficult to discern. This might have been one reason that Erikson hesitated for a long time before taking up the challenge and why the writing of the book took such an inordinate amount of time and effort for him. Nevertheless, he persevered and eventually completed the task.

Growing up in a rich Brahmin family, Gandhi went to London to study law when he was only nineteen years old. At that age, one could say that his identity, at least in terms of what he aspired to be, was totally Anglophile. In the following three years, he labored at morphing himself into a 100 percent English gentleman.

But identity is not a simple issue. Even though his conscious choices and intent clearly pointed in the direction of total assimilation, some of his behavior suggested otherwise. While trying hard to fit in, succeeding in gaining acceptance by British society, he was unable to stop wearing his Indian-styled turban, and was unwilling to break with his vegetarian dietary practices.

Returning home three years later, Gandhi was eager to use what he had learned to modernize, if not Anglicize, his country. But his countrymen did not share his enthusiasm. Disillusioned, and unable to financially support himself and his young family, he decided that he had had enough of his own countryfolks. He wanted to start a new life where he would not be held back by his own people, whom he perceived as backward and beyond salvation.

To search for a better place to live a life unencumbered by tradition, he moved to South Africa two years later, only to find that, no matter how hard he tried, and no matter how Anglicized he thought he was, he was still regarded as a second-class citizen of color. One particularly humiliating experience stood out in his memory. On a train to Cape Town, he was kicked out of the first-class cabin when a white passenger came on board and demanded that he yield the space. When he protested, he was thrown off the train, along with his luggage, at a tiny station with a name that no one knew. This was a wakeup call for him – he realized he would never be fully accepted by the British.

This marked the second phase of his search for his own identity, an identity involving the restoration of dignity for his fellow Indians. Participating in one after another of the protests fighting for the welfare and rights of the growing number of Indian immigrants in South Africa, he gradually became a skilled organizer in such movements and started formulating his idea of "non-violent" protests.

Nevertheless, he still did not completely give up his feelings for the British Empire. During two critical periods in British history, he openly encouraged his fellow Indians to enroll in the British army with the purpose of protecting Great Britain, his and their "mother country." This happened during the second Boer War in South Africa (1899–1902), and again toward the end of World War I (1918). These decisions led to the loss of countless Indian lives.

Often in his life, he surprised the world by leading anticolonial movements when most people thought the cause was hopeless, and yet disappearing from the scene just when he was riding high, enjoying a good reputation and wielding a strong influence. Such patterns of periodic self-negation partly reflected his Indian cultural roots along the line of the *sadhus* (wandering ascetic sages), and were readily understood, accepted, and even admired by his Indian compatriots, while at the same time they puzzled and unsettled his British opponents.

Whatever the consequences, political and personal, these pursuits of self-perfection were sincere and vigorous. He abstained from food and drink, to the point of endangering his life; he gave up sex completely; he threw away all of his fancy clothes, wearing only the coarse cloaks he wove by himself; and he gave up any forms of transportation, walking long distance with makeshift sandals. These practices vastly enhanced his moral leadership, and also served as preparation and preludes for the hunger strikes and other non-violent protests that eventually toppled British control of the Indian subcontinent.

The Salt Tax Walk served as a particularly poignant example of the potency of such protests. In 1930, Gandhi called on all Indians to protest the so-called salt law, which prohibited any form of production, transportation, or selling of salt without first paying tax to the British government. Gandhi encouraged the whole nation to use any means to openly defy the prohibition, welcoming imprisonment as a consequence. To serve as an example, he himself led a large number of followers in a walk from Delhi to the Indian Ocean – more than 400 miles – to pick up salt by the seaside in broad daylight, defiantly violating the law. He then voluntarily turned himself in, demanding that the British authorities imprison him for six whole years, the maximum punishment for such offenses as specified by the law. Following his example, hundreds of thousands of ordinary Indians made the same request, leaving no room in any of the jails for new "offenders."

Such movements led eventually to the independence of India, yet ironically Gandhi was assassinated right after independence, along with the partitioning of the former colony into Hindu India and Muslim Pakistan. This notwithstanding, his successes became models for the human rights movement in the USA and the long struggle for independence in South Africa, both decades later.

THE MANY FACES OF GANDHI

Many people believed Gandhi to be a born saint. For, otherwise, how is one to explain his remarkable power based only on moral means? This might have been what Erikson was looking for, going into the book project.

If so, he was soon disillusioned. In the middle of the book, he found himself unable to continue. Looking deeper, he saw another Gandhi who was totally different. This was a Gandhi who was not meek at all, but was intolerant, tyrannical, and even cruel, most clearly seen in his personal life. For example, although he abstained from sex early in his life, he often slept naked with two young women, supposedly not for sexual gratification. He ordered his wife, a Brahmin, to clean their untouchable guests' excreta. He told young women residing in the ashram to cut off their hair to avoid stirring male sexual urges. And he threatened to disown his oldest son for minor infractions.

Faced with this dilemma, Erikson stopped writing the biography (Erikson, 1969), and instead worked on a twenty-page letter, directly addressing the deceased Gandhi, asking him how he could be so nice and so understanding to his enemies, yet so unreasonable and ruthless to those close to him.

Naturally, Erikson did not get a direct answer from Gandhi. However, after venting his long litany of complaints, he was able to write again and soon finished the book, which became an instant best-seller despite its being close to 500 pages long. A year later, it won the Pulitzer Prize.

THE STORY CONTINUES

Erikson gradually became frail and less active after 1970. He lived another twenty-odd years, but became more and more dependent on Joan. The two of them spent a considerable amount of time and energy trying to prevent their ideas, especially the Eight Life Stages scheme, from being simplistically interpreted. To do so, they started promoting the use of *life cycle* instead of *life stages*. But no matter how hard they tried, they continued to feel unhappy with the way people concretely visualized these "stages," distorting Erikson's most important contributions.

For similar reasons, despite Erikson's emphasis on the interpersonal dimension of human development, it continues to be a struggle for the field to pay attention to the social aspect of the process, keeping it on a par with the intra-psychic aspect. Equally disturbing for them was that, precisely because Erikson's "identity crisis" became so popular, so much a part of everyday language, its original meaning and significance may have been trivialized.

Nevertheless, we should e grateful that there were people like Erikson, Luther, and Gandhi, who continued to search for their authentic selves in their lives, making it easier for us to do the same. Realizing this to be the case, a sense of gratitude might just emerge from the depths of our hearts, and silently we will then thank them for their perseverance and their contributions.

14

"My Voice Will Go With You"

How Milton H. Erickson Salvaged Hypnosis

ERICKSON IS NO ERIKSON

In the winter of 2011, my wife, a clinical psychologist, and I drove all the way from San Francisco to Phoenix, Arizona, to attend the 11th International Congress on Ericksonian Approaches to Hypnosis and Psychotherapy. For many years we had heard of the conference. Associated with it were tales of mythical proportions, of lives changed after encountering Milton Erickson or one of his disciples. We were fascinated by the possibility of change, but also fearful (at least for me) of being changed. Trepidation notwithstanding, we finally decided to jump in. It was a pilgrimage of sort for both of us.

The conference was in honor of Milton H. Erickson, a name I mixed up with Erik H. Erikson for many years. When I finally figured it out, I was surprised how different their backgrounds were. Erik Erikson was born and raised in Europe and immigrated to the USA in his early adulthood. In contrast, Milton Erickson was a homegrown American, with Scandinavian and Native American ancestry. He was born in a mining town in Eastern Nevada (soon to become a ghost town), in a makeshift log cabin with a dirt floor. The "house" was attached to a cliff, requiring only three walls.

When he was five, his father finally gave up the dream of making it big in silver mining and moved the family back to Wisconsin to take up small-scale farming in the remote countryside. Without adequate funding to attract qualified teachers or even to acquire essential books, Erickson's elementary and middle schools were, at best, of mediocre quality.

On top of that, Erickson suffered from color blindness and reading difficulties, was tone-deaf, and had no sense of rhythm. All of these things made him believe he was not college material. Thus, his original career plan was to work for his father on the farm after graduating from high school. It was an illness coming close to killing him at the age of seventeen that changed his life's trajectory (Rosen, 1991).

He suffered a severe case of poliomyelitis, an illness that used to sweep through the country annually. Before the polio vaccine became available, hundreds of thousands of children died from the epidemics, and even more were left disabled by the virus. In adolescents and adults the consequence of the infection are even more severe, and many develop paralysis and muscular atrophy if they are lucky enough to escape death. Erickson was one of the "lucky" ones.

At the height of his affliction, he was only able to move his eyeballs. One night, three out-of-town physicians converged to see Erickson and unanimously agreed that he was unlikely to live another day. They delivered this bad news to his parents in front of him, assuming he was unconscious.

Erickson was furious. After the doctors were gone, he somehow managed to make it clear to his parents to move a dresser away from his bed. At that time his parents had no idea why he would make such a request, assuming he was delirious and that the request came from a deranged mind. They did not know that he had made up his mind to live for at least one more day, to watch the sunrise one last time, and the dresser had been in the way.

Since the poliomyelitis made him completely immobile, depriving him at the time of any form of communication, either verbal or through bodily expressions, he was forced to spend all of his time passively watching and listening to everything happening around him. This turned out to be a great learning experience. He soon became an expert on the behaviors, intentions, and communication patterns of those around him. He found out that people were remarkably inconsistent between what they said and what they really meant to say or do. This did not mean they purposefully wanted to deceive others. Much more often it was just because they did not even know what they wanted to communicate or what they had in their mind. In other words, more often than not, we are not particularly *conscious*, or *cognizant*, or *aware*, of our own motivations and actions.

The recovery process was slow and torturous, during which he relearned how to make each of his muscles work and how to use them in such a way that he was able to accomplish "simple" tasks. Prior to his illness, he had not needed to think about how any of his movements was executed, and how many steps it would take for something to happen. They just came naturally and effortlessly. Now he realized that this was not the case. Far from it. His relearning involved conscious efforts to execute the many steps that he had to take in order to make anything happen. These steps had previously been performed "unconsciously." In fact, the mind was on "autopilot," taking care of almost all of these "routines," without the need to pay particular attention to them. This led him to realizing that hidden behind our conscious mind is a huge territory, where our knowledge, skills, inclinations, and emotional responses are stored. We neglect them at our peril.

He eventually regained most of his mobility, and in doing so became much more appreciative of the preciousness of life and the importance of living it to its fullest. Right after he got off the bed and was still wobbly in his gait, he used all his savings to buy a canoe, and went for a long river trip alone. Canoeing was a deliberate choice, as his legs were still weak but the strength had returned to his arms. The trip lasted several months, during which he traveled more than 1,000 miles. Remarkably, he managed to not only support himself with odd jobs along the way, but also set aside some savings.

Where to go from there? Although he eventually was able to move around with a cane, he realized that becoming a farmer was no longer an option. What career choices were still available to him? He thought that, since he had to live with his polio and its long-term consequences all his life, he might as well become a doctor. He applied for the medical school at the University of Wisconsin. Surprising himself and others, he was accepted.

HOW DID DOCTOR ERICKSON BECOME THE MAESTRO OF HYPNOSIS?

Erickson liked to mention that this life-threatening illness, as well as other "misfortunes" in his life, including his color blindness, were "blessings in disguise." It does not matter whether this was a manifestation of the psychological defense mechanism called *reaction formation* (Haley, 1993); as described above, these setbacks and defects did contribute to his interest in human behavior, motivation, and interpersonal communications and interactions.

In order to deepen his understanding of these issues, he took a course in psychology soon after entering college. At the time, Clark Hull, the preeminent American psychologist and an accomplished researcher on hypnosis, was a professor at Wisconsin. Fascinated, Erickson studied hard and soon became an expert in conducting hypnosis. As a student of Hull, he was not content with only the technical aspect of the practice, but was also devoted to objectively studying and understanding the phenomenon of the hypnotic state.

After graduation from medical school in 1927, he worked for over twenty years at a number of state hospitals in New England and the Midwest. In 1948, he moved with his family to Phoenix, Arizona, for the better weather; there, he started his private practice. During those first twenty years, he grasped at any chance to practice hypnosis on patients and friends. As a result, his skills continued to improve and mature, evolving into new forms that were adapted to different situations. However, he purposefully kept a low profile, staying away from the limelight, because hypnosis as a therapeutic method was still regarded by most physicians and academicians as a questionable practice, often associated with quackery.

This relative obscurity started to change when Erickson found an ardent supporter in the famed anthropologist Margaret Mead. She heard that Erickson was good with hypnosis and started communicating with him. Years earlier, in 1939, Mead and her husband Gregory Bateson brought back from Bali a large number of films on Balinese who were in various states of trance and possession. Far from fearful of such states of the mind, the Balinese accepted them as part of their daily lives, particularly important for religious and healing purposes (see Chapter 12).

Although their plans for collaboration were interrupted by the Pearl Harbor attack and World War II, Erickson got to know Mead's husband, Gregory Bateson, since both were involved in the screening of new recruits for military services. After the war, a divorced Bateson moved to Stanford, California and started his new career studying interpersonal and familial relationships of psychiatric patients. Bateson soon became widely known for his "double bind" theory and his concept of the "schizophrenogenic mother."[1]

In the course of his research, he also became interested in identifying factors responsible for the efficacy of psychotherapy. For this project, Bateson recruited a group of bright and ambitious research assistants and assigned them to observe some of the most effective therapists in order to tease out what they did that made them particularly effective in helping their patients (see Chapter 12). Erickson was one of the "master" therapists Bateson selected for the study.

WIZARD OF THE DESERT

These young researchers were immediately attracted to Erickson. In contrast to traditional psychotherapists, Erickson was humorous and often unpredictable. He was also fascinating for them because he was able to remain energetic and joyous despite his constant bodily aches and pains and the worsening of his post-polio syndrome, requiring him to rely on crutches for walking. Year-round, they drove back and forth between coastal California and Phoenix, the man-made oasis in the middle of the desert, even though each trip would take them several days.

Instead of figuring out answers to Bateson's research questions, they became Erickson's eager disciples. For them, Erickson was the wizard of the desert (Vesely, 2014).

Inspired by Erickson, these talented young disciples continued to promote his therapeutic approaches and speculate on theories behind the efficacy of his methods. After Erickson's passing, these efforts continued. What they

---

[1] This theory was later debunked. We now know that most patients' mothers developed maladaptive behavior toward their schizophrenic children as a consequence of their being burdened by the task of caring for their offspring, not the other way around.

developed was at times contradictory, which led to continued debate and dialogue. Over the next thirty years, they worked tirelessly, systematizing and codifying Erickson's thoughts and methods, sometimes adding mystical or spiritual layers to his original teaching and practices. Such dialogues led to the establishment of the regularly held *Congresses on Hypnosis* and *Psychotherapy* and *Evolution of Psychotherapy Conferences*, and stimulated the development of numerous training programs. Together, these institutions led to the ever-widening dissemination of Ericksonian hypnotherapy, with enduring world-wide reputation and influences.

THE HYPNOTIC STATE AND THE ORIGIN OF MODERN PSYCHIATRY

Still, overall, Erickson's influences remain peripheral to the mainstream of academic psychiatry and psychology. While there are many reasons for this relative neglect, the most deep-rooted one is the complicated history between hypnosis and psychiatry (Ellenberger, 1970).

Although hypnosis played a key role in the initial development of clinical psychiatry and psychology, it was pushed aside as these academic fields matured and needed to prove that they were strictly "scientific." They wanted little to do with the "murky" phenomena associated with hypnosis, which was often performed in circus sideshows.

Hypnosis was first introduced to Western medicine by the German doctor Franz Mesmer, at a time when intellectual leaders including Benjamin Franklin were becoming obsessed with the phenomena of electricity and magnetism. In such a context, it is not difficult to understand why Mesmer's theory of *animal magnetism* became so powerful and influential. Mesmer proposed that constantly circulating electromagnetic currents existed in all animals, including human beings, and played a crucial role for the maintenance of their health. When such circulations were blocked, illnesses set in. Following this line of thought, Mesmer experimented with the use of magnets, which he found effective in healing all kinds of diseases, including cancer and psychiatric disorders.

Somewhere along the way, by accident, Mesmer realized he did not even need to use the magnets. By staring and touching, he was able to achieve similar effects. He consequently decided that he possessed the healing power himself! His reputation and popularity led to a high-profile investigation by academic leaders, including Franklin, who concluded that his therapeutic results came from patients' imaginations and he was nothing but a charlatan. Expelled from France and Austria, Mesmer was disgraced and bankrupt. Yet his theory of *animal magnetism* remained influential, and *mesmerized* and *mesmerism* have become common words that are still widely used in everyday conversations.

More than a century later, Jean-Martin Charcot, the "father" of modern neurology, found himself besieged by hysterical patients at the Hôpital Universitaire Pitié-Salpêtrière in Paris. These patients' conversion and dissociative symptoms were so unpredictable and recalcitrant that he was driven close to despair. In desperation he reluctantly decided to give Mesmer's method a try, initially with much skepticism. To his surprise, he found that most of his patients responded dramatically. He not only was able to render them symptom-free, but, even more amazingly, he could just as easily bring their symptoms back again. Under his ministration, they fainted, became paralyzed, blind or deaf, and developed weird patterns of anesthesia or paresthesia. He was able to call these symptoms in and out of existence at will.

Performed on a weekly basis at his teaching rounds, these demonstrations soon drew wider attention and attracted scholarly visitors from all over the world. Most of these patients were young women who had arrived recently from the countryside, and were clearly naive, impressionable, and suggestible. They also had reasons, consciously or unconsciously, to want to please the great Charcot. These were the dynamics that catapulted Charcot to the forefront of research on hysteria and other kinds of neuroses.

As a neurologist, Charcot's interest was not in the development of effective treatment methods for these patients, but to demonstrate that hysteria did not result from structural damage to the neurological system. For Freud, who was in Paris at the time on a scholarship studying under Charcot, it was a different story. Watching these young women coming in and out of trance states, with heightened suggestibility, manifesting dramatic, often grotesque symptoms, Freud started to ponder psychological mechanisms that might be responsible for hysteria.

Over the next few years, Freud gradually built up his reputation as an international expert in using hypnosis to treat hysteria. However, unlike Charcot, his patients were young middle-class women whose lives, especially their sex lives, were severely confined and truncated by the stifling social norms of the Victorian era (see Chapter 1).

He soon found out that, in hypnotic states, most, if not all, of his patients "recovered" their memories of being sexually abused in childhood – often by their own fathers. This was the famous (or infamous) "Seduction Theory" that Freud retreated from several years later when he realized that in many of these cases the "seduction" scenes were the product of false memories induced by hypnotic suggestions. Horrified, Freud abandoned hypnosis completely.

Therefore, from the beginning, hypnosis had a tainted reputation in association with the genesis of psychoanalysis. In subsequent decades, most mental health professionals distanced themselves from the phenomenon of hypnosis, seeing it as an ill-understood "dark force" to be avoided at all costs. Concurrently, there continued to be a tendency for them to see the "unconscious" as a vast "dark continent," where unruly drives and impulses threatened to break through to play havoc, leading to behavioral disturbances, if not worse.

In contrast, Milton Erickson's views on hypnosis and the unconscious mind were positive. Heralding the Human Potential Movement in the 1960s, Erickson firmly believed that we should not regard our unconscious mind as something dangerous and capricious. On the contrary, it is a great reservoir of strength and resources. Just as the *hypnotic state* as a gateway to the unconscious mind has its inherent value, *suggestion* is a powerful therapeutic tool, not only for psychotherapists, but also for healthcare clinicians in general.

Contrary to popular belief, Erickson also emphasized that hypnosis worked only when patients were receptive and were open to change. Therefore, it cannot be used for mind control and manipulation, as commonly feared.

How did he come up with these positive and trusting views on hypnosis? A large part of it came from his own life experiences. He never hid the fact that, since childhood, he often found himself entering spontaneous hypnotic or trance states, during which he "saw" his insights on problems confronting him. This happened in his clinical work as well. While seeing patients, he often entered a trance state in which he was able to see his patients' issues more clearly and was also able to empathize with them and thus work with them more effectively.

Erickson was not the only hypnotist or psychotherapist of his era, so why did he become particularly influential in the last several decades? One possible answer is that he was an American through and through, and his approaches and styles reflected the American ethos and value systems. Unlike most European hypnosis experts and psychotherapists, he focused primarily on the positive side of hypnosis and suggestion as part of his psychotherapeutic endeavors. Boundlessly optimistic, he never gave up on the belief that his patients had the power and potential to cure themselves. Reflecting the American traditions of democracy and respect for the individual, his suggestions to patients, in and out of hypnotic sessions, were "indirect," incipient, and subtle. Traditional hypnotists were authoritarian in their styles, directly ordering patients to go into a trance, saying things like "Your eyelids are becoming heavier and heavier. Now I am going to count from ten to one, when you will go into trance." In contrast, Erickson would say something like: "If you want, you may close your eyes, and sit comfortably in your chair. You could then relax and go into a trance state."

But being indirect and subtle does not mean that there was less power in his ability to influence and persuade. In fact, indirect suggestions are often even more effective. They seep through the skin, often without the subject's awareness. This was why Jay Haley (1993), one of his most success-ful students, said that, luckily, Erickson was totally devoid of malevolence, otherwise he could have been even more frightful and destructive than Grigori Rasputin.

Erickson's American origins were also reflected in his sense of humor, his predilection for pranks, and his preference for storytelling over theorizing in his therapy and teaching. For these reasons he was often said to be the Mark Twain of mental health. He was also remarkable in his attentiveness to patients' behaviors and his ability to use their words to achieve therapeutic goals. Often, he would say or do things that were unexpected or puzzling, for the purpose of capturing patients' attention and lowering their defenses so he could reach their unconscious mind and enable them to explore new direc-tions. These characteristics helped to make Ericksonian psychotherapy unique among the plethora of contemporary psychotherapies.

THE UNIVERSAL NATURE OF THE "HYPNOTIC PHENOMENON"

Erickson believed that the hypnotic state was universal, hardwired in the brain and deep-rooted in human nature. Was he right? Reviewing the voluminous literature available from the fields of anthropology and cultural psychiatry, the answer to this question has to be an unqualified "yes."

To begin with, the term "hypnosis" is a misnomer; the hypnotized sub-jects do not go to sleep. Hypnosis has nothing to do with sleep and should be classified as a form of altered state of consciousness (ASC). *Battle for the Mind*, a memoir written by William Sargant, a pioneer in biological psychiatry, eloquently demonstrates the universality of such ability to enter this ASC (Sargant, 1957). In one of the chapters of the book, Sargant describes his own experiences in Africa while watching an ecstatic festival of a "native" tribe. Witnessing participants falling into a trance state, "mesmerized" by the repetitive, monotonous drumbeats, he was barely able to keep himself from jumping into the middle of the dancing circle and going into a trance himself. This experience was reminiscent of what he frequently witnessed during his childhood of the regular "revivalist" events, during which Methodist ministers – Sargant's father was one of them – worked on "converting" participants into becoming true believers. Thinking back, he realized that what happened in his father's church was not that different from what he was witnessing in Africa – both were manifestations of ASC.

In *Persuasion and Healing* (Frank & Frank, 1993), Jerome Frank delineated in detail the commonality psychotherapy shares with "non-Western" shamanistic practices, Western faith healing, and Christian "conversion" experiences. Going one step further, he argued that what made these "helping practices" effective also serves as the basis for techniques used by experts in totalitarian regimes to "brainwash" political prisoners.

If we agree that ASC is part and parcel of being human, we might then wonder what it does for us, and from where it might have initially come. The answer to these questions may lie in the human evolution that led to the emergence of the concept of the "self," unique to our ancestors, *Homo sapiens sapiens*. ASC may be regarded as the most direct and most effective route for us to transcend the burden of "self-consciousness."

Self-consciousness enabled our ancestors to learn from past experiences and to imagine and plan for the future. Such capacity to place oneself in the past and the future gave them a huge advantage in competing with other kinds of hominids as they emerged in East Africa some 100,000 years ago (see Chapter 4).

However, we also pay a huge price for having this precious "endowment" bestowed on us. Being able to imagine the future, we cannot escape from the worries and dread over the unpredictability and uncertainty that lie ahead in our lives. Disasters, both natural and man-made, can descend upon us at any time, with death as our ultimate destiny. Thinking about this, our fears become endless and boundless. This was why the ancient Taoist philosopher Zhuangzi said: "There is . . . no place he can escape to between heaven and earth" (Eno, 2019; Legge, 1891).

The sense of a unique self also engenders a profound awareness of separateness and isolation. We feel estranged from the universe, and from one another. We can't know for sure what is going on around us, what is in the minds of others, even with those who are closest to us. In gaining awareness of our existence, we lost our innocence. This must be what John Milton's story, *Paradise Lost*, tried to portray (Milton, 2012).

To return to "paradise" we need to escape from our "selves," to throw away our attachment to the idea of our separate existence. Although there are numerous ways to achieve such a goal, both adaptive (work, love, and merging with "larger forces") and maladaptive (addictions, the pursuit of power and control), the most direct and effective tool available for our ancestors (and for us) to escape the confines of our "selves" is to enter the world of ASC, where individuals merge with deities, the universe, or even just someone they can trust, whether a hypnotist, a therapist, or a guru.

We may still know little about how ASC emerged in the process of evolution, and even less about its neurobiological substrates, but of the universality and importance of ASC, there is little doubt.

THE MAGIC OF SQUAW PEAK

As Erickson's popularity and visibility skyrocketed in the last years of his life, he was increasingly inundated with demands on his time from students and visitors. Unfortunately, his post-polio syndrome, with muscle weakness, pain, and fatigue, worsened progressively with age, to the point that he was eventually incapacitated and confined to a wheelchair. As much as he loved teaching and therapy, there must have come a time when he felt overwhelmed and exhausted. This might be why he started to tell his students and patients to go climb Squaw Peak[2] when they came to seek help.

Surprisingly, the climb often turned out to be tremendously helpful. While ascending the hills, many of them were suddenly "enlightened" and "cured." Where did the power of such healing come from? Was Squaw Peak infused with spiritual power? Was it comparable to the teaching of Zen Buddhism? The answer to such questions may remain elusive, but for many, including my wife and myself, Squaw Peak has acquired mystical meaning and has become a destination of pilgrimage.

---

[2] At 2,610 feet (796 m), Squaw Peak is one of the highest points in the city of Phoenix, Arizona. As the term "squaw" is an ethnic and sexual slur, historically used for indigenous North American women, the name was changed to Piestewa Peak in honor of Army Spc. Lori Ann Piestewa, the first known Native American woman to die in combat in the US military, and the first female soldier to be killed in action in the 2003 Iraq War.

15

Consciousness, Emotion, and Free Will

William James, Father of American Psychology

In 1974, more than forty-five years ago, I first encountered William James. It happened just a few months after my arrival in Seattle to start my psychiatric residency at the University of Washington. Homesick and lonely, I spent a great deal of time "treasure hunting" at a used bookstore off University Way. One day, I happened upon a book titled *The Varieties of Religious Experience* (James, 1902). It put me off at first because the cover was gaudy, with drawings of angels and whatnot flying in the air, in shiny colors. *This must be yet another of those concoctions by New Age gurus*, I thought. However, before putting it down, I glanced at the author's short biography on the back cover. William James, the author, turned out to be the first psychology professor at Harvard, regarded as the "Father of American psychology." He was also prominent among thinkers promoting "pragmatism" and "radical empiricism," and a teacher and a good friend of John Dewey (Rogers, 2008). I knew nothing about the meaning of these "isms" at the time, but I had heard of Dewey, and knew vaguely of his influences on early twentieth-century leading Chinese intellectuals, including Hu Shih (Grieder, 1970) and Monlin Chiang (Chiang, 1945), who played pivotal roles in modernizing China.

So I bought the book, but did not get around to reading it. The volume stayed with me for more than thirty years, traveling from Seattle to Los Angeles, Taiwan, and, finally, northern California. Yet, after settling down in San Francisco, when I finally decided to give it a read, it was nowhere to be found.

By chance, I noticed that the book had just been translated into Chinese and published in Taiwan (after a whole century!). Ordered via the Internet, it flew over the Pacific Ocean and reached me in good time. After reading this tome I became engrossed by William James' writing and thoughts, and started looking further into his life history (Richardson, 2006). That was the first time I realized William James was none other than the older brother of the famous American writer Henry James, Jr. (Edel, 1985). Books on the famous brothers led to equally fascinating biographies of their father, Henry James,

Sr. (Habegger, 1994), and sister, Alice James (Strouse, 1980). Together, they enhanced my understanding of James the person, his achievements, and his time. Intrigued, I started jotting down the highlights of their personal and family sagas, summarized below.

THREE GENERATIONS OF ENTANGLEMENTS

To have an understanding of William James the person, we first need to look into his family of origin. The story started with his grandfather, "William of Albany," who left his hometown at the southern tip of Ulster County, Northern Ireland, at the age of eighteen, arriving in New York with no cash and few possessions. In a few years' time, he emerged as a mover and shaker in upper New York State, with businesses ranging from salt production to banking, and many other profitable enterprises in between. At the time of his death he was regarded as one of the richest people in the USA, leaving behind a vast holding with a net worth estimated at three million dollars – close to eighty million in today's prices.

As a devoted Presbyterian, he was exceedingly hardworking and frugal, and busy every second of his waking hours, allowing no time for rest or leisure. He was a harsh and strict disciplinarian, and applied the same standard to all of his offspring.

James' father, Henry Sr., was the fifth of the eleven surviving children of grandfather William of Albany. Unlike the rest of the brood, Henry Sr. stood out early in childhood as a troublemaker who needed close attention and supervision. As far back as he could remember, Henry Sr. felt he was forever under the constant gaze of his father. This was made even worse for him because of the belief that, lurking behind his father was the all-seeing and all-knowing Heavenly Father, from whose gaze he could never escape.

Entering adolescence, Henry Sr. rebelled. He started stealing and indulging in alcohol. Such indiscretions invited ever closer monitoring and censure, which in turn made him even more rebellious. The situation became a vicious cycle. Then came a grievous accident when Henry Sr. was thirteen years old, taken by him as heavenly retribution. One day he was with a group of boys trying to set off a hot-air balloon – a popular pastime for adolescents in the countryside at the time. Unfortunately, the blazing tar can, part of the balloon, fell off and landed on top of the haystacks in the stable. Unaware that his trouser leg was already sprinkled with tar, he rushed forward to try to stomp out the fire. As a result, his right leg was burned to the bone and he was confined to bed for almost four years, with repeated amputations eventually leaving him with only a stump.

When the wound finally healed, he was able to walk with the use of an artificial limb, but the event had been deeply traumatizing. He could not understand why he deserved such severe "punishment," and felt extremely angry at the unfairness of it. At the same time, his anger at the "Almighty God" who put him through such an ordeal served to further deepen his sense of guilt and self-blame.

However, the ordeal was not without some positive consequences. Prolonged confinement in a sickbed provided him with time to read widely and think deeply about the meaning of life. Because of his illness, he also discovered the tender and loving side of his otherwise remote and severe father. Sadly, as soon as Henry Sr. became mobile again, this tender and loving father disappeared. He found himself back where he had been before, under the thumb of his "fathers": the father of this real world and the unseen but ever-present Father of the world above.

Following his father's direction, he entered Union Seminary to become a minister. Yet, as soon as he was away from the watchful eyes of his father, he indulged in a lifestyle that was the opposite of what his father expected of him – drinking, smoking, gambling, partying, and charging all the expenses to his father's account. When questioned, he simply decamped from New York and moved to Boston, where he somehow managed to eke out a living.

Although they eventually reestablished contact, he never regained the trust of his father, who believed Henry Sr. was on his way to prison and seriously considered disowning him. When William of Albany died a few years later, Henry Sr. was stunned by the specific instruction providing him with only a small monthly allowance that was contingent upon the approval of several appointed guardians. Henry Sr. contested the will and eventually prevailed, receiving his full share of the inheritance, meaning he never needed to worry about working again for the rest of his life.

The inheritance issue settled, Henry Sr. continued to indulge himself in debauchery, but nothing could take away his deep-rooted sense of anger and sadness. He remained haunted by the loss of his leg and plagued by questions on the nature of "evil" – evil in the world and evil in himself. Hoping to find answers to these profound questions, he went back to the seminary. However, instead of finding answers to his questions, he felt only the oppression of those in positions of authority. Searching high and low but finding no answers in New England, he finally decided to cross the Atlantic Ocean, drifting around England, Ireland, and Continental Europe.

For a while, he thought he had found what he was looking for in the teachings of Robert Sandeman (Cantor, 1991) and John Walker,[1] who emphasized the personal nature of faith and questioned the need for clerical guidance in religious pursuits. But Henry Sr. could not tolerate even this level of "organized" religion and drifted away from these reformers as well.

---

[1] John Walker was a clergyman of the established church of Ireland who entirely rejected the idea of a clerical order and advocated for a return to apostolic practices. He was subsequently expelled from the church.

Persisting in his restless search, he widened his reading and gradually gained a reputation as a sharp if eccentric thinker, as well as a smart and entertaining conversationalist. His letters and essays began to appear in major newspapers and magazines, attracting the attention of the public. In this way, without ever having been engaged in any profession or holding any position, he emerged as a public figure of his time.

In 1842, Henry Sr. met Ralph Waldo Emerson[2] (Richardson, 1995) in New York and was immediately drawn to him. As the guru of transcendentalism, Emerson argued that individuals have the innate power to communicate directly with God and to realize the sacred and the ideal. In order to achieve such goals, one has to rid oneself of the restricting and confusing influences of social institutions, especially those imposed by traditional churches, in order to rediscover and return to one's "real self" and become one's own master. Furthermore, once there is a critical mass of such "emancipated" individuals, they would be able to band together to build a more natural, just, and humane world.

Emerson was such an eloquent and persuasive speaker that transcendentalism soon became a major trend. Deeply moved by Emerson's lecture, Henry Sr. immediately wrote a letter inviting him to come to visit. However, he could not even wait for Emerson's response. The next morning, unable to contain his excitement, he went straight to Emerson's hotel and sought him out. They soon became best friends, visiting and writing to each other constantly. It was thus that Emerson became William's godfather when he was born not long after Henry Sr. and Emerson met.

Henry Sr.'s boundless energy, passion, and obsessions eventually wore Emerson out. At the same time, Henry Sr. became increasingly frustrated by Emerson. He loved his ideas, but he was not convinced that his "truth" came straight from intuition and not deductive reasoning. He kept pestering Emerson to reveal to him the logics leading to these "truths." Becoming increasingly frustrated at not having been able to work out these puzzles by himself, and being unable to get a satisfactory answer from Emerson, he started to suspect that his friend was hiding important secrets from him, unwilling to share.

In order to get as close to Emerson as possible, Henry Sr. wrote to his friend saying that, instead of taking his family to Europe as he had originally planned, he would like to move from Boston to rural Concord, where Emerson lived, to be his neighbor. Emerson did not respond for two whole

---

[2] Emerson was the most influential American thinker and poet in the nineteenth century. He was originally trained as a pastor, but left the Church because he believed that individuals could achieve transcendence and peace more directly by being in touch with the natural world. He was a passionate and effective public speaker and essayist. He lectured widely in America and Europe and was widely admired for his spiritual insights. As a result, his house in Concord has become a mecca for those seeking personal growth and spiritual awakening.

months. When he eventually did so, he wrote as if he had not heard about Henry Sr.'s plan to become his neighbor, but instead lamented on missing his company, since they would soon be separated by the vast Atlantic Ocean. Accompanying the missive were a number of letters of introduction, to enable Henry Sr. to meet some of the most famous scholars in Europe. Deeply hurt, Henry Sr. cut off correspondence with Emerson and their paths did not cross again until many years later.

With his household in tow, Henry Sr. bounced all over France and England, relentlessly continuing his search for the secret of the universe. In the spring of 1844, the family settled down in a large mansion next to Windsor Castle, encircled by royal palaces and parks. Henry Sr. fell in love with the place, yet at the same time he felt uneasy living there, which reactivated memories of his childhood home where he was bedridden for many years, hampered by a putrid and festering leg and constantly threatened by the shadow of death.

One evening toward the end of May, sitting alone in the darkening dining room, idly watching the sparks crackling in the fireplace, he suddenly sensed an invisible shadow, emitting lethal, fetid smells. Although the apparition disappeared in under ten seconds, it was long enough to mortify him to the extent that he collapsed, incapacitated by extreme dread and horrors. He was diagnosed as suffering from a severe case of "brain exertion." At the time, the most advanced treatment method for such a condition was hydrotherapy.

It was Henry Sr.'s luck that Joseph Weiss, a world-renowned expert on hydrotherapy, had just moved from Austria to England and established a state-of-the-art hydrotherapy center in a mansion surrounded by several hundred acres of meadows and woods, only a few miles west of London. Like the other patients, Henry Sr. was wrapped tightly with layers of warm, wet linens, for several hours a day. Then he was either thrown into an icy cold pool or given a cold shower. Although this was the best the medical system could offer Henry Sr. at the time, it did not help alleviate his symptoms. Instead, he became increasingly irritated by his fellow patients, who talked only about nutrition or weather, paying no attention to his fear of evil forces and eternal damnation.

Fortunately, the "hospital" was next to a large, beautiful park where he could take walks. This may have been how he ran into Sophia Chichester, a well-educated aristocratic widow who told him that his symptoms were what the Swedish philosopher Emanuel Swedenborg[3] had talked about in his theory of "vastation."

---

[3] Swedenborg was originally a successful engineer, but at the age of fifty-three he started to experience dreams and visions that he believed to be messages from God, and came to see himself as Christ's new prophet. In the following twenty-eight years, he wrote prodigiously, with detailed and convincing descriptions of his experiences communicating with spiritual beings and his interstellar travels. His publications and thoughts profoundly influenced many major scholars and writers, including

Excited, Henry Sr. rushed to bookstores in town and bought all the books he could find by Swedenborg. After devouring the writings, he became a firm believer of Swedenborg's teachings. With this "conversion," all of his symptoms abated. In the fall, he was well enough to take his family on a return journey, safely crossing the Atlantic, making their way back to New England.

GROWING UP IS HARD TO DO

Years later, thinking back, James identified the year 1858, when they were at Newport, Rhode Island, as the happiest time in his life. Famed for its mild weather and beautiful scenery, with miles of white sandy beaches and a fine harbor ideal for sailing and other water sports, Newport had long been the playground for the rich and famous.

For a whole year, James and his four younger siblings were free to roam around during the day and to take part in family gatherings at night, suffused with lively discussions and debates, as well as light-hearted teasing and banter.

Newport was also a well-known artists' colony, attracting many famous painters recently returned from Europe. With his artistic talent, James was excited by the opportunity to work with these virtuosos and decided to become a career painter. Unexpectedly, his father intervened. Claiming corrupting influences of American culture on children and teenagers, he abruptly moved the whole family back to Europe, settling in Geneva.

Henry Sr. never explained what he meant by corrupting influences. One might speculate that he was referring to the artists. He did not want James to follow their footsteps. His wish was for James to become a career scientist, acquiring the most advanced, "objective" methods to help him prove that his special brand of religious beliefs spoke the truth.

James became extremely depressed and angry during the year they stayed in Geneva, constantly fighting with his father. His paintings at the time reflected his mood, filled with bloody, violent scenes. Eventually, Henry Sr. gave in and moved the family back to Newport. Many years later, commenting on this, James' brother Henry Jr. wondered why James needed to return to Newport to pursue his education in the arts. He once asked whether it would not make more sense to do so in Geneva or Paris.

To James' surprise, after winning his battle with his father and getting permission to pursue a career as an artist, he promptly lost his passion for painting. With no other alternatives, James reluctantly agreed to enter the Harvard-affiliated Lawrence Scientific School. Eager to support this decision, Henry Sr. sold their house in Newport and moved the whole family to Boston.

Emerson, William Blake, Jung, and William Butler Yeats. The Church he founded is still alive and well, with chapels and churches active and thriving in many major cities around the world.

It was indeed an exciting time for advances in science, especially the biological sciences. Just around this time, Charles Darwin published his *On the Origin of Species*. Entranced by the book, which he read in detail, James decided to study comparative anatomy and pursue a career as a biologist. However, since he was not sure if working in such an area was enough to feed and clothe himself, he decided to enter medical school first.

This was how he ran into Louis Agassiz, a world-famous biologist and geologist, who was at Harvard when James started studying there. Although an enemy of Darwin, Agassiz was a careful and serious researcher, a meticulous scholar with a long track record in collecting and classifying freshwater fish. With substantive support from private foundations, he organized an ambitious expedition in 1864 to Brazil to systematically study the anatomy and physiology of fish populating the numerous tributaries of the Amazon River, aiming to use the data collected to prove that Darwin's theories were wrong.

With high expectations and excitement, James joined the expedition. Unfortunately, he became violently seasick as soon as the journey started, throwing up all the way from New York to Rio de Janeiro. He then succumbed to variola minor, a milder form of smallpox, immediately after disembarking and was carted directly to a hospital.

Recovering from his ailment, he was finally able to participate in the research project, expecting high adventure. Instead, the daily work consisted of painstakingly sorting, preserving, and storing specimens. It showed him how serious, careful, and diligent Agassiz was as a scientist, but it also convinced him that he did not have the patience to methodically carry out projects according to Agassiz's standards. Stuck with these repetitive and tedious procedures, he realized he was not meant to be a hands-on researcher.

The trip was not a total waste for him though. Criss-crossing the immense Amazon and several thousand miles of its tributaries, James' physical health improved vastly, but he was still at a loss in terms of what to do with his life.

Reluctantly returning to medical school, he remained adrift and rudderless and started to suffer from myriad symptoms, including insomnia, blurry vision, dyspepsia, and severe backache. He was also dangerously depressed.

Family events became another source of distress. Two of his younger brothers had just returned from the Civil War, both physically and mentally traumatized. Unable to escape from the horrors of the war, one of them became an alcoholic. The other brother escaped to Nevada, where he speculated in real estate and repeatedly ended up bankrupt. James had always been emotionally close to Alice, his only sister, the youngest of the siblings. Unfortunately, shortly after she turned eighteen, Alice collapsed with depression and was hospitalized for more than six months at a psychiatric institution. Alice's breakdown was the last straw for James. He dropped out of medical school, escaped to Europe, and roamed around purposelessly for a year and a half, during which time he often felt so desperate that he was on the verge of taking his own life.

In 1868, James finally went back to Boston, forcing himself to resume his study of medicine. Although he managed to graduate the following year and passed his physician license examination, he was unable to see it through to become a practicing doctor.

Rudderless again, he slumped into another protracted period of depression that lasted almost five years. Looked at from the outside, this might be particularly puzzling. He seemed to have everything going for him. He was talented, highly educated, wealthy, and well connected. However, depression is the "Darkness Visible" (Styron, 1990). It is a "Savage God" (Alvarez, 1974), not particularly finicky in choosing victims, ravaging 15 percent of most populations at any given time (Lim et al., 2018). Genetic predisposition and intergenerational transmission of trauma effects (Yehuda & Lehrner, 2018) likely further increased James' vulnerability to such a ubiquitous affliction.

As counterintuitive as the idea might be, one might wonder if this prolonged period of suffering also served some positive function. Being "sick," he was excused from rushing prematurely along a set career path and so had plenty of time to read widely, to think deeply, and to slowly discover who he wanted himself to be and what he really wanted to do with his life. This is exactly why, decades later, Erik Erikson proposed that a "moratorium" period (Friedman, 1999) is often important and unavoidable in most people's lives, usually during late adolescence and early adulthood, in order to search for and consolidate their identity and plot out their lives' trajectories. We might take pity on the fact that James' "moratorium" lasted so long and was so painful, but without it he might not have emerged to become the William James that has given the world so much.

This "moratorium" also enabled him to come to terms with his father. Finally, he had the time, the intellectual resources, and the emotional distance to tease out what Henry Sr.'s struggles were all about. He had long thought that there was something wrong with Henry Sr.'s philosophical ideas and orientations, but could not pinpoint what it was. Reading his father's writings closely, he finally came to the conclusion that, by focusing his attention relentlessly and exclusively on the soul, Henry Sr. completely forgot the concrete side of human existence. Without taking the body and the brain into account, Henry Sr.'s theories on the psyche and the soul were disembodied, "incorporeal," often distant from real life. This led to his insight that psychology had to be based on physiology and the mind had to be "embodied." In such a manner, Henry Sr. played a crucial role in James' search for direction in life, in a way unexpected by, and contrary to, the expectation of Henry Sr.

FREE WILL AND DETERMINISM

Another issue James struggled with all his life was the question of free will, which is an issue that has plagued me for many years. When I was a freshman in college, I took an elective course in moral philosophy, hoping to find wisdom, if not answers, to puzzling questions that had plagued me for years. However, after one lesson I dropped out of the class. The professor, a kind and dignified Jesuit father, spent a whole hour explaining the meaning of the "First Cause." The argument seems to be that since everything is caused by something, there has to be an ultimate original cause of the universe and this a-priori existence of the "First Cause" proves the existence of "God," who makes it possible for us to know what is right and what is wrong. Being only eighteen, I was put off by the seemingly dogmatic tone of the argument and I was also troubled by the obscurity of "free will" in such a scheme. Ever since then, the necessity of "determinism" (the foundation of modern sciences) and "free will," both at the same time, has continued to confound and disturb me.

It seems to me that this was also what James was struggling with for a long time. Like his father, he had been craving rational and definitive answers for the nature of the universe and the human condition. Such a deterministic approach threatens to remove the room for "free will." Without free will, the "self" is but an illusion, and individuals are machines. Furthermore, if all human actions are predetermined, individuals cannot be held responsible for their decisions and actions. This, of course, is not an acceptable position.

Fortunately, Henry Sr.'s Swedenborgian connection led James to the French philosopher Charles Renouvier,[4] who provided a way out for him, rescuing him from his dilemma. Renouvier said the answer was inherent in our perception of our minds being free: "Such perception itself is determined by our action[5] which is based on our 'free will.' And the fact that we are able to take such an action already confirms the existence of freedom."

Impressed with this argument, James wrote in his diary:

I finish the first part of Renouvier's 2nd essay and saw no reason why his definition of free will – the sustaining of a thought because I choose to when I might have other

---

[4] Charles B. Renouvier was born in Montpellier and educated in Paris at the École Polytechnique. He considered himself a "Swedenborg of history" and was regarded as a "neo-Kantian." He rejected the "unknowable" (including "infinity") in all its forms and advocated for a reliance on the validity of personal experience. He identified human individuality with self-determination and free will, necessary postulates for morality and certitude in knowing.

[5] There appear to be parallels or similarities between this and the central teaching of Wang Yangming (Wang, 1916), a great fifteenth-century Chinese neo-Confucian philosopher who famously asserted that "knowing" is only possible through "action," that they are inseparable. The following passage has been quoted often to demonstrate this idea: *A friend pointed to a flowering tree hanging on a cliff and asked, "The tree blossoms and sheds its flowers all by itself, how could it be part of my psyche?" Wang replied: "Before you notice a flower, it didn't exist. Then you see the flower, suddenly the flower reveals all its brilliant color. This is how you know that the flower only exists in your psyche."*

thoughts – needs to be the definition of an illusion. At any rate, I will assume for the present – until next year – that it is no illusion. My first act of free will shall be to believe in free will. (Richardson, 2006)

This led to a mantra that James kept on telling himself: "Not in maxims, not in accumulated contemplations, but in accumulated acts of thought lies salvation."

In the following two years, while still struggling with his psychosomatic and depressive symptoms, James came up with a clear goal for himself in life: He would devote himself to the field of physiology. How did he make up his mind? James said later:

It is a pleasing confidence that ... by working our stint day by day on the one line we have chosen, without looking ahead or thinking much of the final result, we are sure of waking some fine morning, experts in our particular branch, with a tact, so to speak for truth therein: a judgment, and ideas and institutions of our own – all there without our knowing exactly how they came. (James, 1890)

With such confidence, he settled down in Boston and began to actively participate in academic activities. He soon became a key member of the Metaphysical Club, making friends with top leaders in American academia, including Oliver Wendell Holmes, Jr., Chauncey Wright, and Charles Peirce, who further enhanced his progress in scholarly pursuits.

A CAREER IS BUILT ONE BLOCK AT A TIME

Thanks to Charles W. Eliot, James' chemistry professor who became president of the Harvard University in 1869, he soon found a platform to pursue his newfound passion in physiology. Eliot was a visionary administrator who was talented at obtaining funding and recruiting teaching faculty members. Under his leadership, Harvard was transformed from an obscure local academy into an internationally renowned elite university.

One of his strategies for stretching the resources to support rapid expansion of teaching programs was to focus on hiring part-time, temporary teachers. It so happened that soon after Eliot took over at the university, the professor for comparative anatomy and physiology retired. With the recommendation from his friend Oliver Wendell Holmes, Jr., James was hired on a trial basis.

James was very surprised by how much he enjoyed teaching. His students admired him for his breadth of knowledge and were moved by his passion for the subject matter. Being busy with his job made him into a new person, no longer tied down by whatever bodily discomforts had accompanied him for so many years.

Impressed by his talent for teaching, Eliot invited James to become a full-time faculty member. Surprisingly, James hesitated, still not used to the idea of responsibilities. He asked for a year's leave without pay, during which he went back to Europe to study with prominent scholars. Eventually running out of excuses, he returned to Boston and settled down at Harvard, no longer questioning his own qualifications and abilities.

Over the years, his lectures gradually shifted from physiology and anatomy to psychology and philosophy. Teaching deepened his understanding and insights in these fields and provided impetus for him to write comments and journal articles. Based on his lecture notes, he started to systematically work on specific topics, including perception, intention, will, habits, consciousness, and emotion. These eventually became the basis for his book, *The Principles of Psychology.* Published in 1890, the book was divided into two volumes, each more than 1,000 pages long. Two years later, a "concise" version of the book, titled *Psychology: The Briefer Course,* was published, which still ran over 500 pages.

Both books were extremely well received and widely circulated, and have since been revised and reprinted numerous times. Amazingly, even today, more than a century after their first appearance, they are still widely quoted and discussed, because many of the questions raised remain relevant to contemporary scholars, and some of his major hypotheses and speculations still stir up intense debates and inform research programs.

What was even more amazing was that, while busy building up his academic career, he did not hide himself away inside an ivory tower, but often provided lectures to the general public. His deftness in using common language devoid of jargon to explain obscure philosophical and psychological issues made him an effective and popular public speaker. Much of what he said was so succinct and to the point that he became widely quoted. Many of these quotes have since become common aphorisms.

HAPPINESS IS HAVING ONE'S OWN FAMILY

James has his father to thank for finally ending his status as a "perpetual bachelor." One day in the spring of 1876, Henry Sr. casually mentioned to James that he had just met a lovely young lady at the Radical Club who might be an ideal match for James. She was an elementary school teacher by the name of Alice Gibbens. Like James, she was the first born among her siblings. Her father had been a physician with a weakness for alcohol, unable to either have a successful practice or to hold on to a stable job. To make a fresh start, he took the whole family to California to set up a farm when Alice was still a child, but he soon ran into financial and legal troubles and was forced to close the business. Drifting from place to place all over the country, the family struggled to stay afloat. Eventually, in 1965, the father snapped and committed suicide when they were on the way back to Boston from New Orleans. The sixteen-year-old Alice shouldered the responsibility of holding the family together, surviving one crisis after another.

Hearing the whole story, Henry Sr. was so impressed with her dependability, resilience, and resourcefulness that he decided she would be good for James. As predicted by Henry Sr., James found himself "madly" in love with Alice as soon as they met. But he was mortally frightened by what this might mean for his life and at a loss as to how to proceed. Alternating between ecstasy and despair, he became sick again. All of his previous psychosomatic symptoms, including nausea, dyspepsia, and backaches, returned with a vengeance. These symptoms in turn made him question if, with his poor physical health, he could make Alice happy.

Following seven long weeks of torturous insomnia, he finally overcame his doubts and gathered up enough courage to express his love in a letter. Unfortunately, the letter was extremely long and indirect, filled with explanations on why he believed he had fallen in love and whether he was really in love. It read more like a philosophical thesis than a love letter.

It was Alice who came up with a plan for him to solve the dilemma. She started by saying that since she caused him so much misery it would be logical for him to just leave her. However, as he apparently could not bring himself to do so, she would make it easier for him by going away to Canada to distance herself from him. As a farewell gift, she gave him a compass, telling him to use it to find his way.

It took a whole year for James to find his way back to her, but eventually he was able to put aside his doubts and convinced her that he was ready. The marriage turned out to be a lifesaver for him, and reaffirmed his faith in life. He said: "Before marriage, I was utterly sick. Now I regained my health because of you."

COLLATERAL DAMAGE

Unexpectedly, someone else paid a heavy price for his happiness. James' little sister, also named Alice, fell ill as soon as James became engaged to Alice, his future wife. Little Alice had always been close to William, and felt sidelined by his relationship with his wife. She remained so depressed that she was constantly on the verge of suicide and was unable to attend James' wedding.

Fortunately, at this critical juncture, her childhood friend Katherine Peabody Loring came to the rescue. Under Loring's care, young Alice gradually recovered. The two of them bought a house by the sea and started living together. Later they moved to England and spent the rest of their lives living with Henry Jr.

Ten years later, after the death of little Alice from breast cancer, Loring surprised everyone by publishing Alice's diaries (James & Edel, 1999). These detailed how Alice struggled with psychological problems all her life, as well as the fact that Alice and Loring had loved each other as husband and wife.

HENRY SENIOR REFUSED TO FADE AWAY

For a few years, it seemed like everything was going well for James. He was happily married and progressing well in his teaching career. But then came 1882. At the beginning of the year, his mother suddenly died. This was followed by the death of his hero Charles Darwin and his godfather Ralph Waldo Emerson. James did not take these losses well. Becoming ill again, he needed time to be by himself. He sent his wife and two of their children, including a newborn, to be with his in-laws and again set off to Europe alone.

Unfortunately, a few months after James' departure, Henry Sr. fell ill and his condition deteriorated precipitously. Alice, James' wife, who had been taking care of Henry Sr., realized that there was not much time left. She immediately informed both James and Henry Jr. of the situation, but clearly indicated that she needed only one of them to rush back from Europe. She insisted that she would prefer this person to be Henry Jr. rather than James, as she knew James would not be able to deal with the loss of his father and she sought to protect him.

Henry Jr. arrived just before Henry Sr. passed away. In addition to arranging for the funeral, his presence made the dispersal of the inheritance easier, including setting aside funds to provide for the comfort and support of their sister, Alice. James stayed away in Europe throughout the process, returning to Boston in March the following year, after everything had been settled. He agreed with his wife this was for the best as he was ill-equipped to deal with his father's death face to face. Instead, he mourned in his own way.

Once home, he went into a frenzy, working on compiling and editing Henry Sr.'s writings, complete with an introduction running over 100 pages. In this long introduction, he lauded his father as a misunderstood "prophet" who spent his lifetime trying to express his insight on what really mattered in life. But Henry Sr.'s project was too big, too ambitious, impossible to accomplish. Consequently, most of Henry Sr.'s writings were opaque, loosely organized, and difficult to decipher. Yet, despite the almost insurmountable obstacles, Henry Sr. never gave up. He kept on redoubling his efforts, writing one book after another, desperately trying to convince people of his brand of the "truth." No matter how frustrated he had been, he kept at it until the last days of his life.

James said that his father's efforts did not go to waste; Henry Sr.'s messages did get through to him. All his life, Henry Sr. was deeply troubled by the fact that the world was full of disappointments, imperfections, and injustice, which he refused to accept. He continued to search for ways to eliminate the suffering and imperfections. Moved by his father's life-long struggles, James said that people like his father did not have easy lives because they either were ignored or were prematurely put on a pedestal to be worshipped as saints and prophets. This made them into idols, to be kept at a distance from those of us who continue to face the same kind of suffering and imperfections, and keep on craving salvation.

The memorial volume James compiled served a most important purpose. It so moved his siblings that they forgave him completely for not coming back from Europe for their father's funeral. Beyond that, the book may be regarded as a failure, as altogether it only sold five copies to those outside of the family. However, despite its commercial failure, its meaning and impact were substantial, for himself and for those close to him.

THE MIRACLE OF OUR "STREAM OF CONSCIOUSNESS"

James may be regarded as a late bloomer when it comes to his academic career. He spent close to four decades of his life searching for his own destiny while struggling with depression and myriad health problems, real or imagined. Once he found his niche and was clear about his direction, he went full force and became amazingly productive. In the second half of his life, lasting for less than three decades, he kept on writing and lecturing, formulating ideas that were often uniquely influential but also controversial. In the following sections, I will focus only on the three contributions for which he is most famous. These have been chosen also because they address questions that have puzzled me for most of my adult life.

I will start with James' ideas about the phenomenon that is commonly called "consciousness." Consciousness is so much of our existence that we typically take it for granted, assuming that we know what it is. But what is it really? Where does it reside? How does it work?

One typical answer to this age-old question is tied to René Descartes' *Cogito ergo sum* (I think, therefore I am). Departing from Descartes, James regarded "the thinker" and "thoughts" as one, inseparable. Since there is no "thinker" behind the person, consciousness could not be attached to anything concrete, but is best regarded as a "function" of the brain.

So, what is this "function" that is our consciousness? Why do we need such a function? James said that, no matter what we think about the nature of the "consciousness," we all need it in order to survive. Without it, we would not be able to decide what to think, and on what to direct our attention. At any given time in our lives, we, or our brains, are bombarded by numerous "external" messages from the natural world and from other people, as well as myriad "internal" messages coming from bodily sensations, inducing pleasure, pain, or discomfort. Without a filtering mechanism we would be totally and constantly confused and lost, not knowing what is going on and how to respond. This filtering is the job of the consciousness (James, 1904).

As a firm believer in Darwinism, James proposed that our ability to pay discriminating attention to selective messages came from evolution over the eons. Since evolution depends on individual and group variations, the way "consciousness" operates is also highly unique, varying from individual to individual.

A central character of consciousness is continuity. It is like a river, flowing constantly. Despite the appearance of the discreteness of thoughts, they are all connected and inseparable. He thus came up with the term "stream of consciousness."

The term not only became an important concept in the field of psychology, but also changed the landscape of literature and arts. It might not be an overstatement to say that the concept fundamentally reshaped civilization throughout the twentieth century. Indeed, his works paved the way for the arrival of "phenomenology" and existential philosophy, which in turn revolutionized our understanding of human nature.

"EMOTION" IS "EMBODIED"

Another of James' theories that has remained controversial has to do with the relationship between emotions and their physiological correlates (James, 1902). Contrary to common sense, James proposed that physical and physiological changes precede the experiencing of emotions. His most famous example is that, when someone encounters a bear, his first response is trembling, which then causes him to become aware of his fear, motivating him to run. For the same reason, one notices sadness after becoming aware of being weepy or feeling heavy in one's body. It is because of this that people are often surprised by themselves suddenly bursting into tears, long before they are even aware of their sadness.

This is also true in terms of anxiety. In most cases, we are not aware of our fear, anxiety, or even panic attacks until we start palpitating, sweating, and having trouble breathing. Far too many of us continue to suffer from severe and persistent headaches or back pain, not knowing, at least initially, that they are caused by muscle tension secondary to ongoing tension and worries in our lives. James quipped: "We don't laugh because we are happy, we realize that we are happy when we find ourselves smiling or laughing."

For those of us who have been living in a modern world valuing "psychological mindedness," such exposition might sound exotic or abstruse. But when we try to describe how we feel, the language that we rely on is typically metaphorical and the terms we use are suffused with references to bodily sensations. For example, we commonly use expressions such as "being punched in the guts," "feeling empty in the chest" and "getting out on the wrong side of bed" to describe how we feel. This may also be why Winston

Churchill described his depression as "a black dog on my back" and Nathaniel Hawthorne referred to it as "a black veil."

We often are not aware of how much we have been affected by stress unless we listen to our bodies. In research, anxious patients are often surprised by measurements of the tension in their muscles, and the level of serum cortisol might be a more reliable indicator of their distress than their own self-awareness. This is exactly why, in behavioral therapy for anxiety and phobic disorders, the main tool is the practice of progressive muscle relaxation.

But many leaders in the field continue to question the validity of the so-called James–Lange Theory.[6] A prominent example is Walter Bradford Cannon, a world-famous physician and physiologist who coined the term "fight-or-flight." He pointed out that even patients whose brains have been disconnected from their spinal cords and the autonomic nervous system are still able to have emotional responses. He also indicated that physiological responses are non-specific, and if we were only able to discern our emotional states through perceptions of bodily changes, we would often be misled. For example, palpitation could be due to fear, anger, happiness, or fever.

In any case, what is remarkable is James' willingness and courage to stick his neck out to propose a hypothesis that went against mainstream thought, raising questions that are still being debated more than a century later.

RELIGION AND MYSTICISM

As mentioned above, it was Henry Sr.'s death that pushed James into seriously pondering the nature of religious experiences. These efforts eventually led to the writing and publication of yet another of his masterpieces, *The Varieties of Religious Experience: A Study in Human Nature*.

Running over 500 pages, it includes numerous lively case studies through which various religious experiences are vividly described and discussed in great detail. It is a tribute to his genius and writing skills that he managed to accomplish this monumental work with both objectivity and compassion.

In the book, James divided people with religious experiences into two major categories: the *once-born* and the *twice-born*. The once-borns were the lucky ones who naturally perceive the order and beauty of the universe and, along with it, a sense of being part of the universe and being sustained by the universe. The *twice-borns* were those who needed to go through a prolonged and torturous process of struggling with doubt, dread, and despair, until one day, through mystical or trance experiences, they were graced with "epiphanies" and were able to finally feel at peace with themselves. As important as these experiences were, he believed that they were primal, intuitive, and beyond logic. No matter how illogical, how bizarre such

---

[6] Carl Lange was a Danish physician who proposed a similar theory around the same time.

"awakenings" appeared, they were real to them because they were felt in the gut. They had to be real because they were at the foundation of the meaning of life.

WILLIAM JAMES AND THE "GHOSTHUNTERS"

This brings us to the question regarding James' view on psychic and "paranormal" phenomena. From the point of view of pragmatism, James never excluded the possibility of psychic energy and mediumship (Blum, 2006). Growing up under the wings of Henry Sr. and Emerson, James was intimately familiar with séances and related activities from his childhood, and he never stopped being fascinated by these phenomena. Such fascinations led to his becoming one of the founding members of the Society for Psychic Research in 1882, serving as the president of its American branch for many years.

However, until the summer of 1885, he had maintained his role strictly as an observer and researcher. Sadly, this changed when his third son died of diphtheria at the age of one. He and his wife were unable to accept the fact that the baby had really disappeared from the world and their grief was beyond description. Two months later, his mother-in-law and sister-in-law told James and Alice about the remarkable supernatural power of a famous medium by the name of Leonora Piper. Having worked with many mediums in his role as a psychic researcher, James had encountered many charlatans before. He thus went with Alice to visit Piper with deep skepticism and was completely surprised when he heard his son talking with him through the medium. They started going to see Piper on a regular basis, which eventually led to Alice acquiring the ability to communicate directly with the deceased as well.

With the endorsement of James, Piper became a popular subject and informant for many other psychic researchers. Throughout his life, James published more than fifty research papers on psychic phenomena. In 1909, just one year before his death, he even published an article in the popular *American Magazine*, describing his experiences frankly and in detail.

Did James believe in the existence of spirits and the ability of some psychics to communicate with the deceased? He would be the first to admit that he did. He remained a believer even though time and again he was disappointed by many of the psychics who turned out to be nothing other than con artists. Because of Piper, he could say that there were at least some exceptions.

THE AMERICAN CENTURY OF WILLIAM AND HENRY JAMES

At the beginning of the twentieth century, James and Henry Jr. were two of the most active, well-known, and influential scholars and writers. Since this article's focus is on William James, Henry James Jr. (Bradley, 2000) is mentioned only peripherally. In reality, Henry Jr. is the more commonly known of the two of them. In his life he published twenty-three best-selling novels and numerous short stories, essays, travelogues, and commentaries. Many of his writings remain on the reading lists for college students, even a century later. At least ten of the novels he wrote have been adapted into movies.

Even more remarkable than their achievements is the fact that, throughout their lives, the two brothers remained close, encouraging and influencing each other. This might be why Henry Jr.'s novels are so good at describing the workings of the human mind and William James' scientific publications could be so well crafted, to the point that they often read like masterpieces of literature.

Conclusion

In a sense, the seeds of this book started germinating somewhere around 1951, when I was six years old. A nerdy child narrowly escaping the wrath of polio, with a slight limp, I was an easy target for school bullies (Lin, 2018). Books (extracurricular ones especially) provided solace and safe harbor. However, upon entering adolescence, disturbing questions suddenly erupted. Questions such as "Who am I?" and "What's the meaning of life?" and "How do I quiet my mind and tame my body?" and "What is happiness?" refused to fade, compelling me to look for answers in religion, mythology, ancient wisdom, philosophy, and, eventually, psychology, though at the same time remaining deeply suspicious of any easy answers.

This was the path that eventually led me to the people included in this book. For years, I was attracted to and puzzled by their ideas and life stories, intuitively seeing them as my people – thinkers, doers, and seekers. They seemed to have lived lives worth living, difficult or not. The fact that they were all so different from one another, and that they fought like cats and dogs, made them even more fascinating and puzzling.

My attempts at understanding who they were and what their theories meant were, of course, complicated, and hopefully also enriched, by my personal and cultural background. Born and raised in Taiwan, my upbringing and education were necessarily steeped in Chinese languages and cultural traditions, and my early exposure to modern psychology and psychiatry was filtered through such lenses, which continued to exist in subtler manners after my move to the USA in 1974. It is so that, naturally, I tend to see ideas and theories in terms of their cross-cultural relevance, and to use this as a yardstick to gauge the extent of their "universality," and, in turn, hopefully, greater truth. Or, at least, their greater relevance and utility. This is how it came to be that this book was written in both Chinese and English. The favorable reception of the Chinese versions, published separately in Taiwan (2014) and China (2016), supports the idea that thoughts that originated in Central Europe and were elaborated upon in the Americas are resonant with modern Chinese-language readers. In this English-language volume, I have further elaborated on and embellished my original theories with comments and references from English and Chinese sources (as well as my own personal experiences), hoping that these additions can further enrich our understanding of these pioneers' thinking.

ENCOUNTERING OEDIPUS REX

I first read about psychoanalysis and psychotherapy in the late 1960s, when I was still a high-school student in Taiwan. I remember neither the title nor the author's name. What stays fresh in my mind is how excited I was to read about Sigmund Freud's ideas, and how fascinated I was with what he had to say on *sexuality* and *the unconscious mind*. Being a sex-obsessed teenager desperately trying to understand myself and others, the book opened up a brave new world for me, mystifying and mind-bending, and at the same time, eerily familiar. However, as I ran into terms such as *transference* and *countertransference*, I was baffled. Not having anyone to ask for clarification, I felt defeated and retreated to the safer grounds of history, biology, and even probability theory.

Several years later, while I was in medical school in Taiwan, Freud was brought back to me by Yun-fan Liaw,[1] a charismatic young doctor who had just translated Freud's *An Autobiographical Study* (Freud, 1963) from English to Chinese. At the same time, he also organized a group of doctors in training to translate the two-volume, 2,000-plus page *Harrison's Principles of Internal Medicine* (Wintrobe et al., 1970; its 2018 edition, the twentieth, is more than 4,000 pages long). Our success in this task encouraged the group to inaugurate a medical journal for continuing education, named *Medicine Today*, and a magazine for the general public, named *Healthy World*. These two publications have played a crucial role in medical education and health promotion in Taiwan for the ensuing forty years.

Another of the group's ambitions was to translate the complete works of Freud. It was thus that I translated *The Psychopathology of Everyday Life* (Freud, 1914). It was a thoroughly delightful experience enhanced by modest financial rewards, allowing me to buy a new bike and some presentable clothing for dating.

The translation of *Three Essays on the Theory of Sexuality* (Freud, 1920) was a totally different matter. While astounded by the seemingly infinite variations of human sexual behavior and the complexity of the drives hidden in the deeper layers of the human mind, I was at the same time exhausted by the mental acrobatics needed to follow the themes and

---

[1] Dr. Yun-fan Liao subsequently completed his training in internal medicine and gastroenterology and became a world-renowned expert in hepatitis, and hepatology in general.

logic of the book. In this I was lucky to have Wen-Shing Tseng[2] as a mentor. Recently returned from his three-year training in psychoanalytically oriented psychotherapy at the esteemed Massachusetts Mental Health Center of Harvard Medical School, he generously offered his time and expertise to explore these ideas with me and review the manuscript, ensuring its accuracy and readability.[3]

While working with the publisher of these translations, I was recruited into its editorial team, participating in their efforts toward introducing major books in depth psychology to Chinese readers. The work exposed me to classics including Alfred Adler's *What Life Should Mean to You* (Adler, 1931) and Carl Jung's *Modern Man in Search of a Soul* (Jung, 1933), as well as those written by other luminaries including Viktor Frankl, Erich Fromm, Karen Horney, and Rollo May. Together their theoretical constructs enriched my understanding of human nature, but they also puzzled me in their divergences. Even more disturbing were the disputes among these great thinkers, often devolving into animosity that was clearly reflected in their writings. Admiration of their ingenuity, audacity, and creativity aside, I was mystified by the deep gulfs and mistrust that existed among them, and dismayed that, even to this day, such divisions persist between many of their followers.

What fascinated me most was the question of the origin of their inspiration and the source of their passion. *Who were they? What made them decide to look into the mystery that is the human mind? How did their theories originate?*

The few biographical books I managed to lay my hands on at the time, including *Sigmund Freud: Man and Father* by his son Martin Freud (1958), *The Passions of the Mind* by the novelist Irving Stone (1971), and the monumental *Freud: A Life for Our Time* by the eminent historian Peter Gay (2006), focused on Freud's courage, tenacity, and ingenuity. Certainly, Freud deserves praise and even worship, but a Freud on a pedestal is hard to imagine in flesh and blood. Similarly, while Jung's *Memories, Dreams, Reflections* (Jung & Jaffe, 1962) awed me, his actual personage remained shrouded in layers of fog too dense for me to penetrate.

---

[2] Dr. Wen-Shing Tseng later moved to the University of Hawaii at Manoa and served as director of its psychiatric training program, became one of the most renowned world leaders in cultural psychiatry, and was founding president of the World Association of Cultural Psychiatry. He was a prolific writer who published several dozens of influential professional books, in both English and Chinese.

[3] Dr. Tseng and my other mentors in Taiwan also supervised my translation of Karl Menninger's *Theory of Psychoanalytic Technique* (Menninger, 1958), Don D. Jackson and William J. Lederer's *The Mirage of Marriage* (1968), and part of Freud's *Totem and Taboo* (Freud, 1918). They were published in Taiwan between 1972 and 1975. During this time I also co-authored a book titled *Sleep and Its Disorders*.

RETURN TO THE BEDSIDE

I put these questions aside a few years later when I began my psychiatric residency training at the National Taiwan University Hospital. Dealing with the severely mentally ill, psychopharmacology and psychopathology (e.g., is the patient bipolar or schizophrenic?) became priorities. Although concepts derived from depth psychology were sometimes helpful to my understanding of the symbolic meaning of patients' thoughts and behaviors, "practical" matters took precedence. Some of the most powerful, and often dangerous, medications, including antipsychotics, antidepressants, and lithium, had been newly introduced to Taiwan, and we young clinicians were kept busy guessing when we might witness "miracles," while at the same time desperately hoping that we would not inadvertently compound patients' miseries with troubling side effects.

CULTURE SHOCK AND AFTER-SHOCKS

In 1974, I moved to Seattle to continue my professional training at the University of Washington. The profound culture shock, which I had not anticipated, reshaped my life as well as my career trajectory (Lin, 2018). For years after the move, my primary focus was on survival, from the most mundane logistics (e.g., negotiating the awe-inspiring, but also insane, free-way systems; ordering food without knowing what it was) to things that were much harder to define: Who am I really? How do I embrace or resist changes in my identity; and do I even have a say in the process?

Fortunately, with support from mentors including Arthur Kleinman[4] and Minoru Masuda[5] in Seattle and Milton Miller[6] in Los Angeles, I was able to complete my residency and research training and pursue a gratifying academic career. Continuing to struggle with culture shock, I became fascinated with the intersections between culture, ethnicity, and psychiatric care. Over the following years, these interests led to the development of a multi-year follow-up study on the health and adjustment of Vietnamese

[4] Dr. Arthur Kleinman has been a professor of medical anthropology and social medicine at the Harvard Medical School since 1978. He has trained a large number of prominent medical anthropologists and cultural psychiatrists who are leaders in these fields worldwide, and has numerous influential publications in these fields as well as in global health, social medicine, and medical humanities.

[5] Dr. Minoru Masuda was a nisei (second-generation) Japanese-American who as a relocation camp internee joined the legendary 442 battalion during World War II. As professor of psychiatry at the University of Washington, he made substantial contributions to studies on stress and health. He supervised my multi-year follow-up study on the health and adjustment of Vietnamese refugees.

[6] Dr. Milton Miller was a professor of psychiatry at UCLA and chair of the Department of Psychiatry at the Harbor-UCLA Medical Center (1978–2004). He was an existential philosopher, public mental health leader, and a WHO expert consultant. My entire academic career at UCLA was made possible because of his unyielding support.

refugees (Lin, Tazuma, & Masuda, 1979; Lin, Masuda, & Tazuma, 1982), the establishment of two community mental health centers providing care for the rapidly expanding Asian-Pacific populations in the Greater Los Angeles area (Lin, 2019), and a series of pioneering studies demonstrating the importance of culture and ethnicity in patients' responses to medications, as well as mechanisms behind such influences (Lin, 2009; Lin & Lin, 2013; Lin, Poland, & Nakasaki, 1993).

THE EMERGENCE OF THE THEME OF WOUNDED HEALERS

While my career focus shifted, my curiosity about the life and work of the pioneering explorers of the mind persisted. Over the years, I continued to keep a keen eye on emerging literature that shed new light on the personal backgrounds of depth psychology's founding mothers and fathers, the socio-political milieu and intellectual traditions they were immersed in, and the paths leading to the development of their theories. In the process, I also stumbled upon other innovative and profound thinkers who have made key contributions to the field of psychiatry. These included William James, Otto Rank, Wilhelm Reich, Melanie Klein, Frieda Fromm-Reichmann, Harry Stack Sullivan, and Erik Erikson, among many others.

In 2008, I had the great honor of spending a year at the Center for Advanced Study in the Behavioral Sciences (CASBS) at Stanford, where I finally had the time and freedom to systematically survey the vast fields of psychobiography and psychohistory and to contemplate the lives of these remarkable pathfinders. A main theme emerging from such reflections was that they were not only exceptional thinkers and healers, but were also all, each in their own way, deeply familiar with suffering (Ellenberger, 1970; Goldwert, 1992). Their personal struggles lay at the core of their discoveries. They struggled with major traumatic events at different stages of their lives and suffered from significant emotional and behavioral difficulties for pro-longed periods. Their suffering compelled them to search for answers. Struggling to resolve their own conflicts, within themselves and with their worlds, made them into perceptive and empathic clinicians and informed their approaches to mental illnesses. Their insights grew from a desperate need to understand their own afflictions, to overcome obstacles, to save themselves. Their discoveries did not stem from abstract thought; they repre-sented crucial matters of life and death to themselves. In this sense, one could describe them as "wounded healers."

Hetu-Pratyaya

As mundane as it might seem in hindsight, this new perspective represented a milestone in my understanding of the genesis of a great number of the foundational concepts in depth psychology. Such new insights paved the way for the writing of this book.

According to *Hetu-Pratyaya* (Skorupski, 2016), the Buddhist concept of causality, "*Hetu*" (*yin* in Chinese; the primary cause or motivation) itself is not enough to achieve *Phala*, the desired results (*guo* in Chinese). Embedded in the process is another element called *Pratyaya* (*yuan* in Chinese; imperfectly translated in English as "contributory cause"). A common analogy for this view on causality is that, in order to grow a fruit-bearing plant (*Phala* literally means fruit in Sanskrit), you not only need to have the seed (*hetu*), but also earth, sunlight, and water (*Pratyaya*).

In the case of this book, the *Pratyaya* is *Medicine Today*, the journal that my friends and I founded more than thirty years earlier. With the platform and audience provided by the journal, I was able to work on these biographies on a monthly basis and to receive valuable feedback, resulting in the finalization of the pieces that were eventually compiled into a book in Chinese (released in 2014 and 2016), and in English, as presented here.

OUR HETU-PRATYAYA, OR SEEDS SEEKING GOOD SOIL

As long as we live, we continue to ask questions. Questions like, "Who am I?" and "How do I live a good life?" and "How do I help others live good lives?" are some of the things that make us *Homo sapiens sapiens*. These questions are like seeds scattered by sowers aiming at good soil, but often they land on rocks or among thorns. Though their seeds did not always end up with good soil, this has not prevented them from persevering. It is because of these sowers before us that we have this beautiful, raucous variety of flowers and plants in our gardens and in our fields. In our turn, we have our own seeds (*Hetu*) to scatter. Hopefully we have learned from our predecessors to better aim at rich soil (*Pratyaya*) and to grow the very fruits (*Phala*) that we have all been longing for.

REFERENCES

Adler, A. (1931). *What life should mean to you.* London: George Allen & Unwin, Ltd.

Aeschylus (2009). *Prometheus bound and other plays.* (Philip Vellacott, Trans.). New York, NY: Oxford University Press.

Altman, L. K. (1987). *Who goes first? The story of self-experimentation in medicine.* Berkeley, CA: University of California Press.

Alvarez, A. (1974). *The savage god: A study of suicide.* Markham, ON: Penguin Books Canada Ltd.

Andreasen, N. C., (1987). Creativity and mental illness: Prevalence rates in writers and their first-degree relatives. *American Journal of Psychiatry, 144,* 1288–1292.

Bair, D. (2003). *Jung: A biography.* Boston, MA: Little, Brown.

Bateson, G. (1936). *Naven: A survey of the problems suggested by a composite picture of the culture of a New Guinea tribe drawn from three points of view.* Cambridge: Cambridge University Press.

Bateson, M. C. (1994). *With a daughter's eye: A memoir of Margaret Mead and Gregory Bateson.* New York, NY: Harper Perennial.

Bauby, J.-D. (1997) *The diving bell and the butterfly.* New York, NY: Alfred A. Knopf.

Becker, E. (1997). *The denial of death.* New York, NY: Simon and Schuster, reprinted.

Behling, K. (2005). *Martha Freud: A biography.* (R. D. V. Glasgow, Trans.). Cambridge: Polity Press. (Original work published 2002.)

Bloland, S. E. (2005). *In the shadow of fame: A memoir by the daughter of Erik H. Erikson.* New York, NY: Viking.

Blum, D. (2006). *Ghost hunters: William James and the search for scientific proof of life after death.* New York, NY: Penguin Press.

Boehlich, W. (Ed.) (1992). *The letters of Sigmund Freud to Eduard Silberstein, 1871–1881.* (A. J. Pomerans, Trans.). Cambridge, MA: Belknap Press. (Original work published 1989.)

Borch-Jacobsen, M., & Shamdasani, S. (2012). *The Freud files: An inquiry into the history of psychoanalysis.* Cambridge: Cambridge University Press.

Bottome, P. (1957). *Alfred Adler: A portrait from life.* New York, NY: Vanguard.

Bradley, J. R. (2000). *Henry James's permanent adolescence.* New York, NY: Palgrave Macmillan.

Brady, M. E. (1948). The strange case of Wilhelm Reich. *Bulletin of the Menninger Clinic, 12*(2). Reprinted from *The Republic,* May 26, 1947. Retrieved from https://pdfs.semanticscholar.org/f521/f8bd472947ca783e34d5576df651b83d3e3b.pdf.

Breger, L. (2000). *Freud: Darkness in the midst of vision*. Hoboken, NJ: Wiley.

Breger, L. (2009). *A dream of undying fame: How Freud betrayed his mentor and invented psychoanalysis*. New York, NY: Basic Books.

Breuer, J., & Freud, S. (1955). *Studies on hysteria*. (James Strachey, Trans. and Ed.) London: Hogarth Press.

Brothers, L. (1997). *Friday's footprint: How society shapes the human mind*. New York, NY: Oxford University Press.

Brown, R. (1991). *Ganesh: Studies of an Asian god*. Albany, NY: State University of New York Press.

Buber, M. (1947). *Tales of the Hasidim: The early masters*. New York, NY: Schocken Books.

Burlingham, M. J. (2002). *Behind glass: A biography of Dorothy Tiffany Burlingham*. New York, NY: Other Press. Originally published as *The last Tiffany: A biography of Dorothy Tiffany Burlingham*. New York, NY: Atheneum, 1989.

Bush, K. (2010). Cloudbusting. Retrieved from www.youtube.com/watch? v=pllRW9wETzw.

Campbell, J., Moyers, B. D., & Flowers, B. S. (1991). *The power of myth*. New York, NY: Anchor Books.

Camus, A. (1955). *The myth of Sisyphus*. London: Hamish Hamilton Limited.

Cantor, G. (1991). *Michael Faraday: Sandemanian and scientist: A study of science and religion in the nineteenth century*. New York, NY: Macmillan.

Carotenuto, Aldo. (1982). *A secret symmetry: Sabina Spielrein between Jung and Freud*. New York, NY: Pantheon Books.

Chiang, M. (1945). *Tides from the West: A Chinese autobiography*. New Haven, CT: Yale University Press.

Clark, J. (2017). How much nicotine is in a cigar? Retrieved from https://healthfully .com/much-nicotine-cigar-5485715.html.

Clay, C. (2016). *Labyrinths: Emma Jung, her Marriage to Carl and the early years of psychoanalysis*. London: William Collins.

Cleary, T. (Trans.). (2003). *The Taoist classics, volume one: The collected translations of Thomas Cleary*. Boulder, CO: Shambhala.

Copeland, W. E., Shanahan, L., Hinesley, J., Chan, R. F., Aberg, K. A., Fairbank, J. A., ..., Costello, E. J. (2018). Association of childhood trauma exposure with adult psychiatric disorders and functional outcomes *JAMA Network Open*, 1 (7), e184493.

Cornett, C. (2008). Of molehills and mountains: Harry Stack Sullivan and the malevolent transformation of personality. *American Imago*, 65(2), 261–289.

Crews, F. (2017). *Freud: The making of an illusion*. New York, NY: Henry Holt and Co.

Cronenberg, D. (director) (2011). A dangerous method. London: Recorded Picture Company.

Crosby, J. F., & Crosby, M. E. (1970). Primal birth trauma: Rank, Janov and Leboyer, *Birth and the Family Journal*, 3(4), 171–177.

Dai, B. (1984). Psychoanalysis in China before the revolution: A letter from Bingham Dai. *Transcultural Psychiatry*, 21, 280–283.

Daneault, S. (2008). The wounded healer: Can this idea be of use to family physicians? *Canadian Family Physician 54*, 1218–1219.

Davis, D. (1999). Lost girl. Retrieved from www.haverford.edu/psych/ddavis/anna freud.losing.html.

Davidson, H. R. E. (1964). *Gods and myths of Northern Europe*. Baltimore, MD: Penguin Books.

Dobrin, L. M., & Bashkow, I. (2010). The truth in anthropology does not travel first class: Reo Fortune's fateful encounter with Margaret Mead. In R. Darnell and F. W. Gleach (Eds.), *Histories of anthropology annual.* vol. 6, (pp. 66–128). Lincoln, NE: University of Nebraska Press. Retrieved from http://muse.jhu.edu /article/398061.

Dow, J. (1986). Universal aspects of symbolic healing: Theoretical synthesis. *American Anthropologist, 88,* 56–69.

Dube, S. R., Felitti, V. J., Dong, M., Chapman, D. P., Giles, W. H., & Anda, R. F. (2003). Childhood abuse, neglect, and household dysfunction and the risk of illicit drug use: The adverse childhood experiences study. *Pediatrics 111,* 564–572.

Dunne, C. (2000). *Carl Jung: Wounded healer of the soul – an illustrated biography.* New York, NY: Parabola Books.

Edel, L. (1985). *Henry James: A life.* New York, NY: Harper & Row.

Ellenberger, H. F. (1968). The concept of creative illness. *Psychoanalytic Review, 55*(3): 442–456.

Ellenberger, H. F. (1970). *The discovery of the unconscious: The history and evolution of dynamic psychiatry.* New York, NY: Basic Books.

Eno, R. (2019). Zhuangzi: The inner chapters. Retrieved from https://terebess.hu/ english/Zhuangzi-Eno.pdf.

Erikson, E. H. (1950). *Childhood and society.* New York, NY: W.W. Norton.

Erikson, E. H. (1958). *Young man Luther: A study in psychoanalysis and history.* New York, NY: W.W. Norton.

Erikson, E. H. (1969). *Gandhi's truth: On the origins of militant nonviolence.* New York, NY: W.W. Norton.

Ersche, K. D., Turton, A. J., Chamberlain, S. R., Müller, U., Bullmore, E. T., & Robbins, T. W. (2012). Cognitive dysfunction and anxious-impulsive personality traits are endophenotypes for drug dependence. *American Journal of Psychiatry, 169* (9), 926–936

Fabrega, H., Jr. (1997). Earliest phases in the evolution of sickness and healing. *Medical Anthropology Quarterly, 11*(1), 26–55.

Feng, G. F. (Trans.). (1972). Lao Tsu: The Tao Te Ching. Retrieved from https:// terebess.hu/english/tao/gia.html#Kap02.

Frank, J. D., & Frank, J. B. (1993). *Persuasion and healing: A comparative study of psychotherapy,* 3rd ed. Baltimore, MD: Johns Hopkins University Press.

Frankl, V. (1959). *Man's search for meaning.* Boston, MA: Beacon Press,

Frankl, V. (1996). *Viktor Frankl: Recollections – an autobiography.* (J. Fabray & J. Fabray, Trans.) New York, NY: Plenum Publishing.

Freeman, D. (1983): *Margaret Mead and Samoa: The making and unmaking of an anthropological myth.* Cambridge, MA: Harvard University Press.

Freeman, L. (1990). *The story of Anna O.* St. Paul, MN: Paragon House Publishers.

Freud Museum London. (2013). About us. Retrieved from www.freud.org.uk/about/ faq.

Freud, M. (1958). *Sigmund Freud: Man and father.* New York, NY: Vanguard Press.

Freud, S. (1884). Uber Coca. *Zbl. ges. Ther.,* 2, 289–314.

Freud, S. (1909). Analysis of a phobia in a five-year-old boy. In *The standard edition of the complete psychological works of Sigmund Freud, volume X: Two case histories ('Little Hans' and the 'Rat Man').* New York, NY: W.W. Norton.

Freud, S. (1911). *The interpretation of dreams,* 3rd ed. (A. A. Brill trans.). Retrieved from: www.psywww.com/books/interp/index.html.

Freud, S. (1914). *Psychopathology of everyday life*. (A. A, Brill, Trans). New York, NY: Macmillan. Published in Chinese as Lin, K. M. (Trans.). *Hsin-Ch'ao Series No. 39*. Taipei: Chih-Wen Publishing Co., 1970.

Freud, S. (1918). *Totem and taboo: Resemblances between the psychic lives of savages and neurotics* (A. A. Brill, Trans.). New York, NY: Moffat, Yard & Co. Retrieved from https://en.wikisource.org/wiki/Totem/and/Taboo. (Original work published 1913). Published in Chinese as Yang, Y. Y., & Lin, K. M. (Trans.). *Hsin-Ch'ao Series No. 114*. Taipei: Chih-Wen Publishing Co., 1975.

Freud, S. (1920). *Three Contributions to the Sexual theory*. (A. A. Brill. Trans.). New York, NY: Nervous and Mental Disease Publishing Co. Published in Chinese as Lin, K. M. (Trans.). *Hsin-Ch'ao Series No. 48*. Taipei: Chih-Wen Publishing Co., 1971.

Freud, S. (1963). *An autobiographical study* (J. Strachey, Ed.). New York, NY: W.W. Norton.

Freud, S., & Jones, E. (1993). *The complete correspondence of Sigmund Freud and Ernest Jones, 1908-1939*. (R. A. Paskauskas, Ed.). Cambridge, MA: Belknap Press/Harvard University Press.

Freud, S., & Jung, C. G. (1994). *The Sigmund Freud Carl Gustav Jung letters*. Abridged ed. Princeton, NJ: Princeton University Press.

Friedman, L. J. (1999). *Identity's architect: A biography of Erik H. Erikson*. New York, NY: Scribner.

Fromm, E. (1960). *Zen Buddhism and psychoanalysis*. New York, NY: Harper & Brothers.

Fromm-Reichmann, F. (1960). *Principles of intensive psychotherapy*. Chicago, IL: University of Chicago Press.

Fu, C. W.-H. (1983). Viktor Frankl and logotherapy. *China Times*, May 12, 1983. Retrieved from http://charlesweihsunfu.org/.

Gay, P. (2006). *Freud: A life for our time*. New York, NY: W.W. Norton.

Ghaemi, S. N. (2007): Adolf Meyer: Psychiatric anarchist. *Philosophy, Psychiatry, & Psychology*, 14(4): 341-345.

Gleason,. P. (1983). Identifying identity: A semantic history. *Journal of American History*, 69(4): 910-931.

Goldwert, M. (1992). *The wounded healers: Creative illness in the pioneers of depth psychology*. Lanham, MD: University Press of America.

Goleman, D. (1985). New insights into Freud. *New York Times*, March 17, 1985. Retrieved from www.nytimes.com/1985/03/17/magazine/new-insights-into-freud.html.

Green, M. B. (1974). *The Von Richthofen sisters, the triumphant and the tragic modes of love: Else and Frieda Von Richthofen, Otto Gross, Max Weber, and D. H. Lawrence, in the years 1870-1970*. New York, NY: Basic Books.

Greenberg, J. (1964). *I never promised you a rose garden: A novel*. New York, NY: Holt, Rinehart and Winston. (Originally published under the pen name Hannah Green.)

Grieder,J. B. (1970).*Hu Shih and the Chinese renaissance: Liberalism in the Chinese revolution, 1917-1937*. Cambridge, MA: Harvard University Press.

Grosskurth, P. (1986). *Melanie Klein: Her world and her work*. New York, NY: Alfred A. Knopf.

Grosskurth, P. (1991). *The secret ring: Freud's inner circle and the politics of psycho-analysis*. Reading, MA: Addison-Wesley.

Habegger, A. (1994). *The father: A life of Henry James, Sr*. New York, NY: Farrar, Straus and Giroux.

Haley, J. (1993). *Jay Haley on Milton H. Erickson*. New York, NY: Brunner/Mazel.

Hamblin, J. (2013). Why we took cocaine out of soda. *The Atlantic*, January 31. Retrieved from www.theatlantic.com/health/archive/2013/01/why-we-took-cocaine-out-of-soda/272694

Hanh, T. N. (1974). *Zen keys: A guide to Zen practice.* Garden City, NY: Anchor Press/Doubleday.

Hanh, T. N. (1987). *Old path white clouds: Walking in the footsteps of the Buddha.* Berkeley, CA: Parallax Press.

Heuer, G. (2016). *Freud's "outstanding" colleague/Jung's "twin brother": The suppressed psychoanalytic and political significance of Otto Gross.* New York, NY: Routledge.

Hidaka, B. H. (2012). Depression as a disease of modernity: Explanations for increasing prevalence. *Journal of Affective Disorders, 140*(3), 205–214.

Hornstein, G. A. (2005). *To redeem one person is to redeem the world: The life of Frieda Fromm-Reichmann.* New York, NY: Other Press.

Hsu, F. L. K. (1983). *Rugged individualism reconsidered: Essays in psychological anthropology.* Knoxville, TN: University of Tennessee Press.

Imber, G. (2010). *Genius on the edge: The bizarre story of William Stewart Halsted, the father of modern surgery.* New York, NY: Kaplan Publishing.

Incayawar, M., Wintrob, R., & Bouchar, L. (Eds.). (2009). *Psychiatrists and traditional healers: Unwitting partners in global mental health.* Hoboken, NJ: Wiley-Blackwell.

Ivey, G., & Partington, T. (2014). Psychological woundedness and its evaluation in applications for clinical psychology training. *Clinical Psychology and Psychotherapy, 21,* 166–177.

Izenberg, G. (1991). Seduced and abandoned: The rise and fall of Freud's seduction theory. In J. Neu (Ed.), *The Cambridge companion to Freud* (pp. 25–43). Cambridge: Cambridge University Press.

Jackson, D. D., & Lederer, W. J. (1968). *The mirage of marriage.* New York, NY: W.W. Norton. Published in Chinese as Lin, K. M. (Trans.). *Hsin-Ch'ao Series No. 77.* Taipei: Chih-Wen Publishing Co., 1972.

Jackson, S. W. (1999). *Care of the psyche: A history of psychological healing.* New Haven. CT: Yale University Press.

Jackson, S. W. (2001). The wounded healer. *Bulletin of the History of Medicine, 75*(1), 1–36.

James, A., & Edel, L. (1999). *The diary of Alice James.* Boston, MA: Northeastern University Press.

James, W. (1890). *The principles of psychology.* New York, NY: Henry Holt.

James, W. (1902). *The varieties of religious experience: A study in human nature.* Mineola, NY: Dover Publications. Retrieved from https://www.gutenberg.org/files/621/621-pdf.pdf.

James, W. (1904). Does consciousness exist?. *Journal of Philosophy, Psychology and Scientific Methods, 1*(18), 477–491.

Jamison, K. R. (1993). *Touched with Fire: Manic-depressive illness and the artistic temperament.* New York, NY: Free Press.

Jamison, K. R. (1995). *An unquiet mind.* New York, NY: Vintage Books.

Jones, A. E. (1953). *Sigmund Freud: Life and work,* volume 1. London: Hogarth Press.

Jones, A. E. (1955). *Sigmund Freud: Life and work,* volume 2. London: Hogarth Press.

Jones, A. E. (1957). *Sigmund Freud: Life and work,* volume 3. London: Hogarth Press.

Jung, C. G. (1912). *Psychology of the unconscious: A study of the transformations and symbolisms of the libido, a contribution to the history of the evolution of thought.* (B. M. Hinkle, Trans., 1916). London: Kegan Paul, Trench, Trübner and Co.

(Revised in 1952 as *Collected works volume. 5: Symbols of Transformation*, Princeton, NJ: Princeton University Press.

Jung, C. G. (1916). The seven sermons to the dead. Retrieved from http://gnosis.org /library/7Sermons.htm.

Jung, C. G. (1933). *Modern man in search of a soul.* (C. F. Baynes with W. S. Dell, Trans.). London: Kegan Paul, Trench, Trübner and Co.

Jung, C. G. (2009). *The red book: Liber novus.*(S. Shamdasani, Ed.; M. Kyburz, J. Peck, & S. Shamdasani, Trans.). New York, NY: W.W. Norton.

Jung, C. G., & Jaffe, A. (1962). *Memories, dreams, reflections.* London: Collins.

Kaplan, R. (2004). O Anna: Being Bertha Pappenheim – historiography and biography. *Australas Psychiatry*, 12 (1), 62–68. Retrieved from https://www.researchgate.net/pub lication/8016927_O_Anna_Being_Bertha_Pappenheim_-_Historiography_and_Bio graphy.

Kawai, H. (1996). *Buddhism and the art of psychotherapy.* College Station, TX: Texas A&M University Press.

Kerr, J. (1993). *A most dangerous method: The story of Jung, Freud and Sabina Spielrein.* New York, NY: Knopf.

Kierkegaard, S. (1971). *Either/or, volume I.* (V. Eremita, Ed.; D. F. Swenson & L. Marvin Swenson, Trans.). Princeton, NJ: Princeton University Press.

Kierkegaard, S. (1986). *Fear and trembling.* London: Penguin Classics.

King, L. (2014). *Euphoria.* New York, NY: Atlantic Monthly Press.

Kirmayer, L. J. (2003). Asklepian dreams: The ethos of the wounded-healer in the clinical encounter. *Transcultural Psychiatry*, 40(2), 248–277.

Kleinman, A. (1980). *Patients and healers in the context of culture: An exploration of the borderland between anthropology, medicine, and psychiatry.* Berkeley, CA: University of California Press.

Kleinman, A. (1988). *The illness narratives: Suffering, healing, and the human condition.* New York, NY: Basic Books.

Kleinman, A. (1991). *Rethinking psychiatry: From cultural category to personal experience.* New York, NY: Free Press.

Krüll, M. (1986). *Freud and his father* (A. J. Pomerans, Trans.). New York, NY: W.W. Norton.

Kuhn, T. S. (1962). *The structure of scientific revolutions.* Chicago, IL: University of Chicago Press.

Lachman, G. (2010). *Jung the mystic: The esoteric dimensions of Carl Jung's life and teachings – a new biography.* New York, NY: Jeremy P. Tarcher/Penguin.

Lamb, S. D. (2014). *Pathologist of the mind: Adolf Meyer and the origins of American psychiatry.* Baltimore, MD: Johns Hopkins University Press.

Launer, J. (2005). Anna O and the "talking cure." *QJM: An International Journal of Medicine*, 98(6), 465–466.

Launer, J. (2014). *Sex vs. survival: The life and ideas of Sabina Spielrein.* London: Overlook Duckworth.

Launer, J. (2016). The career of William Osler. *Postgraduate Medical Journal*, 92, 751–752.

Legge, J. (1891). *The writings of Chuang Tzu.* Oxford: Oxford University Press. Retrieved from https://ctext.org/zhuangzi.

Lieberman, E. J. (2010). *Acts of Will: The life and work of Otto Rank.* New York: The Free Press.

Lim, G. Y., Tam, W. W., Lu, Y., et al. (2018). Prevalence of depression in the community from 30 countries between 1994 and 2014. *Scientific Reports*, 8, 2861.

Lin, K. M. (2009). Progress in the pharmacogenomics of antidepressant response. *Pharmacogenomics, 10*(10), 1165–1168.

Lin, K. M. (2018). My identity. In S. Seigel (Ed.). *Endangered species, enduring values: An anthology of San Francisco Area writers and artists of color.* San Francisco, CA: Pease Press.

Lin, K. M. (2019). Do Asian-Americans need psychiatry? In S. Seigel (Ed.). *Civil liberties united: Diverse voices from the San Francisco Bay Area.* San Francisco, CA: Pease Press.

Lin, K. M., & Lin, W. L. (2013). Culture, ethnicity and psychopharmacology. In E. Sorel (Ed.), *21st century global mental health* (pp. 95–118). Burlington, MA: Jones & Barlett Learning.

Lin, K. M., Tazuma, L., & Masuda, M. (1979). Adaptational problems of Vietnamese refugees. Part I: Health and mental health status, *Archives of General Psychiatry, 36,* 955–961.

Lin, K. M., Masuda, M., & Tazuma, L. (1982). Adaptational problems of Vietnamese refugees. Part III. Case studies in clinic and field – adaptive and maladaptive. *Psychiatric Journal of the University of Ottawa, 7,* 173–183.

Lin, K.M., Poland, R.E., & Nakasaki, G. (Eds.). (1993). *Psychopharmacology and psychobiology of ethnicity.* Washington, DC: American Psychiatric Press.

Lindorff, D. (2004). *Pauli and Jung: The meeting of two great minds.* Wheaton, IL: Quest Books.

López-Muñoz, F., Pérez-Fernández, F., Álamo, C., & García-García, P. (2017). Cervantes read by Freud: A perspective. *Athens Journal of History 3*(4): 275–296.

Maddox, B. (2006). *Freud's Wizard: Ernest Jones and the transformation of psycho-analysis.* Cambridge, MA: Da Capo Press.

Maines, R. (1999). *The technology of orgasm: "Hysteria," the vibrator, and women's sexual satisfaction.* Baltimore, MA: Johns Hopkins University Press.

Mahony, P. J. (1986). *Freud and the rat man.* New Haven, CT: Yale University Press.

Malinoski, B. (1922) *Argonauts of the western Pacific.* London: G. Routledge & Sons.

Markel, H. (2011). *An anatomy of addiction: Sigmund Freud, William Halsted and the miracle drug, cocaine.* New York, NY: Pantheon Books.

Masson, J. M. (1984). *The assault on truth: Freud's suppression of the seduction theory.* New York, NY: Farrar, Straus and Giroux.

Masson, J. M. (Ed.). (1985). *The complete letters of Sigmund Freud to Wilhelm Fliess, 1887–1904.* Cambridge, MA: Harvard University Press.

Mata, D. A., Ramos, M. A., Bansal, N., Khan, R., Guille, C., Di Angelantonio, E., & Sen., S. (2015). Prevalence of depression and depressive symptoms among resident physicians: A systematic review and meta-analysis. *JAMA, 314*(22), 2373–2383.

McCabe, I. (2018). *Carl Jung and Alcoholics Anonymous: The twelve steps as a spiritual journey of individuation.* London: Karnac.

McGlashan, T. H. (1986). The prediction of outcome in chronic schizophrenia. IV. The Chestnut Lodge follow-up study, *Archives of General Psychiatry, 43*(2), 167–176.

McRae, J. (2000). *The Platform Sutra of the Sixth Patriarch: Translated from the Chinese of Zongbao.* Berkeley, CA: Numata Center for Buddhist Translation and Research. Retrieved from http://promienie.net/images/dharma/books/sutras_plat form-sutra_mc-rae.pdf.

Mead, M. (1928). *Coming of age in Samoa: A psychological study of primitive youth for western civilisation.* New York, NY: William Morrow and Company.

Mead, M. (1935). *Sex and temperament in three primitive societies.* Oxford: William Morrow.

Mead, M. (1972). *Blackberry winter: My earlier years.* New York, NY: William Morrow and Company.

Mencius (372–289 BC). *Mengzi.* (J. Legge, Trans.) Retrieved from https://ctext.org /mengzi.

Mercer, J. (2016). Zusha comes home. Retrieved from https://haam.org/2016/03/28/ zusha-comes-home.

Merchant, J. (2012). *Shamans and analysts: New insights on the wounded healer.* New York, NY: Routledge.

Milton, J. (2012). *Paradise Lost.* Retrieved from www.samizdat.qc.ca/arts/lit/paradise lost.pdf. (Originally published in 1664.)

Moerman, D. E. (1979). Anthropology of symbolic healing. *Current Anthropology. 20,* 59–80.

Noll, R. (1997). *The Aryan Christ: The secret life of Carl Jung.* New York, NY: Random House.

Nouwen, H. (1972). *The wounded healer: Ministry in contemporary society.* Garden City, NY: Doubleday.

Nuland, S. B. (2007). *The art of aging: A doctor's prescription for well-being.* New York, NY: Random House.

Ollendorff, I. (1969). *Wilhelm Reich: A personal biography.* New York, NY: St. Martin's Press.

Ottoboni, M. A., & Frank, P. (1985). *The dose makes the poison: A plain-language guide to toxicology,* 3rd ed. New York, NY: Wiley.

Ozarin, L. D. (1999). William A. White, M.D.: A distinguished achiever. *Psychiatric News,* January 1999. Retrieved from http://www.psychiatricnews.org/pnews/99-01-01/ hx.html.

Pagnin, D., de Queiroz, V., De Oliveira Filho, M. A., Gonzalez, N. V., Salgado, A. E., Cordeiro e Oliveira, B., . . . Melo, R. M. (2013). Burnout and career choice motivation in medical students. *Medical Teacher, 35,* 388–394. Retrieved from https://www.research gate.net/publication/235785604_Burnout_and_career_choice_motivation_in_ medical_students.

Pasulka, D. W. (2019). *American cosmic: UFOs, religion, technology.* New York, NY: Oxford University Press.

Pearlman, L. A., & Saakvitne, K. W. (1995). *Trauma and the therapist: Countertransference and vicarious traumatization in psychotherapy with incest survivors.* New York, NY: W.W. Norton.

Perry, H. S. (1982). *Psychiatrist of America, the life of Harry Stack Sullivan.* Cambridge, MA: Belknap Press.

Phillips, A. (2014). *Becoming Freud: The making of a psychoanalyst.* New Haven, CT: Yale University Press.

Quote Investigator. (2011). Sometimes a cigar is just a cigar. Retrieved from http:// quoteinvestigator.com/2011/08/12/just-a-cigar.

Rank, O. (1929). *The trauma of birth.* Oxford: Harcourt, Brace.

Red Pine (2000). *The collected songs of Cold Mountain.* Port Townsend, WA: Copper Canyon Press. Retrieved from https://www.semanticscholar.org/paper/The-col lected-songs-of-Cold-Mountain-%E5%AF%92%E5%B1%B1-Pine/83c650b3a2fcffe0 c8508cba6bac8c5aa5988be9.

Reich, P. P. (1973). *A book of dreams.* New York, NY: Harper & Row.

Reich, W. (1988). *Passion of youth: An autobiography, 1897–1922.* New York, NY: Farrar, Straus and Giroux.

Reik, T. (1944). *A psychologist looks at love.* New York, NY: Farrar and Rhinehart.

Rice, C. A. (2011). The psychotherapist as "wounded healer": A modern expression of an ancient tradition. In R. H. Klein, H.S. Bernard, & V. L. Schermer (Eds.), *On becoming a psychotherapist: The personal and professional journey* (pp. 165–189). Oxford: Oxford University Press.

Richardson, R. D. (1995). *Emerson: The mind on fire*. Berkeley, CA: University of California Press.

Richardson, R. D. (2006). *William James: In the maelstrom of American modernism – a biography*. Boston, MA: Houghton Mifflin.

Rieff, P. (1979). *Freud, the mind of the moralist*. Chicago IL: University of Chicago Press.

Rippere, V., & Williams, R. (1985). *Wounded healers: Mental health workers' experiences of depression*. New York, NY: Wiley.

Roazon, P. (1969) *Brother animal: The story of Freud and Tausk*. New York, NY: Knopf.

Robinson, P. (1993). *Freud and his critics*. Berkeley, CA: University of California Press.

Rodman, F. R. (2004). *Winnicott: Life and work*. New York, NY: Perseus Books Group.

Rogers, M. (2008). *The undiscovered Dewey: Religion, morality, and the ethos of democracy*. New York, NY: Columbia University Press.

Rosen, S. (1991). *My voice will go with you: The teaching tales of Milton H. Erickson*. New York, NY: W.W. Norton.

Sagan, C. (1995). *The demon-haunted world: Science as a candle in the dark*. New York, NY: Random House.

Sargant, W. (1957). *Battle for the mind: A physiology of conversion and brainwashing*. London: Heinemann.

Sartre, J.-P. (1956). *No exit, and three other plays*. New York, NY: Vintage Books.

Sayers, J. (1993). *Mothers of psychoanalysis: Helen Deutsch, Karen Horney, Anna Freud, and Melanie Klein*. New York, NY: W.W. Norton.

Scasta, D. L. (2003). John E. Fryer, MD, and the Dr. H. Anonymous episode. *Journal of Gay & Lesbian Psychotherapy*, 6(4), 73–84.

Schneiderman, S. (1991). One for all and all for Freud. *New York Times*, November 17. Retrieved from www.nytimes.com/1991/11/17/books/one-for-all-and-all-for-freud.html.

Schwartz, J. (1999). *Cassandra's daughter: A history of psychoanalysis*. New York, NY: Viking.

Sedgwick, D. (1994). *The wounded healer: Countertransference from a Jungian perspective*. New York, NY: Routledge.

Segal, J. (1992). *Melanie Klein*. London: Sage.

Sharaf, M. R. (1983). *Fury on Earth: A biography of Wilhelm Reich*. New York, NY: St Martin's Press/Marek.

Sheehan, E. (1981). Victorian clitoridectomy: Isaac Baker Brown and his harmless operative procedure. *Medical Anthropological Newsletter*, 12(4), 9–15.

Showalter, E. (1987). *The female malady: Women, madness and English culture, 1830–1980*. London: Virago.

Silver, A. S. (2002). Psychoanalysis and psychosis: Players and history in the United States. *Psychoanalysis and History*, 4(1), 45–66.

Silver, H. (2009). Reflections on Alfred Adler: A social exclusion perspective. *Journal of Individual Psychology*, 65(4). Retrieved from http://connection.ebscohost.com/c/articles/49022343/reflections-alfred-adler-social-exclusion-perspective.

Skorupski, T. (2016). *Buddhist theories of causality (karma, pratītyasamutpāda, hetu, pratyaya)*. Oxford: Oxford University Press.

Smith, R. C. (1996). *The wounded Jung: Effects of Jung's relationships on his life and work*. Evanston, IL: Northwestern University Press.

Spanos, N. P., Burgess, C. A., & Burgess, M. F. (1994). Past-life identities, UFO abductions, and satanic ritual abuse: The social construction of memories. *International Journal of Clinical and Experimental Hypnosis. 42* (4): 433–446.

Stepansky, P. (1983). *In Freud's shadow: Adler in context*. Mahwah, NJ: Lawrence Erlbaum.

Stone, I. (1971). *The passions of the mind*. New York, NY: Doubleday.

Strachey, J. (Ed. & Trans.). (1953). *The standard edition of the complete psychological works of Sigmund Freud*. London: Hogarth Press.

Straussner, S. L. A., Senreich, E., & Steen, J. T. (2018). Wounded healers: A multistate study of licensed social workers' behavioral health problems. *Social Work, 63*(2), 125–133.

Strouse, J. (1980). *Alice James: A biography*. Boston, MA: Houghton Mifflin.

Styron, W. (1979). *Sophie's choice*. New York, NY: Random House.

Styron, W. (1990). *Darkness visible: A memoir of madness*. New York, NY: Random House.

Sullivan, H. S. (1954). *The psychiatric interview*. Oxford: W.W. Norton.

Sulloway, F. (1992). *Freud, biologist of the mind: Beyond the psychoanalytic legend*. Boston, MA: Harvard University Press.

Sussman, M. B. (2007). *A curious calling: Unconscious motivations for practicing psychotherapy*, 2nd ed. Lanham, MD: Jason Aronson.

Sutherland, J. D. (1989). *Fairbairn's journey into the interior*. London: Free Association Books.

Suzuki,. D. T. (1932). *Lankavatara Sutra*. Abingdon: Routledge Kegan Paul. Translated into English from the Sanskrit. Retrieved from https://daitangkinh.net/Books/T16n0670/The%20Lankavatara%20Sutra%20(Suzuki)/.

Taft, J. (1958). *Otto Rank: A biographical study based on notebooks, letters, collected writings, therapeutic achievements and personal associations*. New York, NY: Julian Press Inc.

Tauber, A. I. (2010). *Freud: The reluctant philosopher*. Princeton, NJ: Princeton University Press.

The Śūraṅgama Sūtra Translation Committee of the Buddhist Text Translation Society. (2009). *The Śūraṅgama Sūtra: With Excerpts from the commentary by the venerable master Hsüan Hua – a new translation*. Ukiah, CA: Buddhist Text Translation Society.

Torres-Roman, J. S., Cruz-Avila, Y., Suarez-Osorio, K., Arce-Huamani, M. A., Menez-Sanchez, A., Aveiro-Robalo, T. R., . . ., Ruiz,. E. F. (2018) Motivation towards medical career choice and academic performance in Latin American medical students: A cross-sectional study. *PLoS ONE, 13*(10): e0205674. Retrieved from https://doi.org/10.1371/journal.pone.0205674.

Torrey, E. F. (1986). *Witchdoctors and psychiatrists: The common roots of psychotherapy and its future*. New York, NY: Harper & Row.

Turner, C. (2011). *Adventures in the orgasmatron: How the sexual revolution came to America*. New York, NY: Farrar, Straus and Giroux.

Verghese, A. (2009). *Cutting for stone*. New York, NY: Alfred A. Knopf.

Vesely, A. (2014). *Wizard of the desert*. Beverly Hills, CA: Noetic Films.

Wake, N. (2006). "The full story by no means all told:" Harry Stack Sullivan at Sheppard-Pratt, 1922–1930, *History of Psychology*, 9, 325–358.

Wang, Y. (1916). *The philosophy of Wang Yang-Ming* (F. Henke, Trans.). London: Open Court. (Original work published 1517.) Retrieved from https://openlibrary.org/works/OL124665W/The_philosophy_of_Wang_Yang-ming.

Watson, B. (1989). *The Tso Chuan: Selections from China's oldest narrative history.* New York, NY: Columbia University Press.

Wintrobe, M. M., Thorn, G. W., Adams, R. D., Bennett, I. L. Jr., Braunwald, E., Isselbacher, K. J., & Petersdorf, R. G. (Eds.). (1970). *Harrison's principles of internal medicine, volume one and volume two,* 6th ed. New York, NY: McGraw-Hill.

Wong, P. T. P. (Ed.) (2012). *The human quest for meaning: Theories, research, and applications,* 2nd ed. New York, NY: Routledge.

Wu, J. C. H. (2004). *The golden age of Zen: Zen Masters of the T'ang dynasty.* Bloomington, IN: World Wisdom Books.

Yalom, I. D. (2017). *Becoming myself: A psychiatrist's memoir.* New York, NY: Basic Books.

Yang, L. (2008). *Handbook of Chinese mythology.* Oxford: Oxford University Press.

Yehuda, R., & Lehrner, A. (2018). Intergenerational transmission of trauma effects: Putative role of epigenetic mechanisms. *World Psychiatry, 17,* 243–257.

Yep, L. (2008). *Auntie tiger.* New York, NY: HarperCollins.

Young-Bruehl, E. (1988). *Anna Freud: A biography.* New York, NY: Summit Books.

Zerubavel, N., & Wright, M. O. (2012). The dilemma of the wounded healer. *Psychotherapy, 49*(4), 482–491.

INDEX